THE WORLD'S CLASSICS

THE SATIRES

JUVENAL (Decimus Iunius Iuuenalis), born about AD 60 in the reign of Nero, spent his teens under Vespasian, and his early manhood under the terrible Domitian. He began to publish about AD 112 in the reign of Trajan, and finished about 130 under Hadrian. Over the centuries many readers have seen him as a stern moralist, others, more recently, as an extravagant wit. No one has doubted his status as a master of language. His powerful attacks on the vices of imperial Rome have been admired and exploited by several English writers, including Dr Johnson, who described his style as 'a mixture of gaiety and stateliness, of pointed sentences and declamatory grandeur.'

NIALL RUDD, a graduate of Trinity College Dublin, lectured at Hull and Manchester in the 1950s, and at Toronto in the 1960s. After five years at Liverpool he became Professor of Latin at Bristol, where he taught until 1989. He has also held a number of visiting posts in Canada and the United States. His books include *The Satires of Horace* (Cambridge, 1966); *Lines of Enquiry* (Cambridge, 1976); *Themes in Roman Satire* (Duckworth, 1986), and an edition of Horace *Epistles II* and *Ars Poetica* (Cambridge, 1989).

WILLIAM BARR was Senior Lecturer in the Department of Latin, Liverpool University.

THE WORLD'S CLASSICS

JUVENAL

The Satires

Translated by
NIALL RUDD

Introduction and Notes by
WILLIAM BARR

Oxford   New York
OXFORD UNIVERSITY PRESS
1992

Oxford University Press, Walton Street, Oxford OX2 6DP

Oxford New York Toronto
Delhi Bombay Calcutta Madras Karachi
Petaling Jaya Singapore Hong Kong Tokyo
Nairobi Dar es Salaam Cape Town
Melbourne Auckland

and associated companies in
Berlin Ibadan

Oxford is a trade mark of Oxford University Press

Translation © Niall Rudd 1991
Introduction and Notes © William Barr 1991

First published as a World's Classics paperback 1992

British Library Cataloguing in Publication Data
Data available

Library of Congress Cataloging in Publication Data
Juvenal.
[Works. English. 1992]
The satires / Juvenal; translated by Niall Rudd; introduction
and notes by William Barr.
p. cm.—(The World's Classics)
Includes bibliographical references and index.
1. Juvenal—Translations into English. 2. Verse satire. Latin—
—Translations into English. I. Rudd, Niall. II. Barr, William,
1922– . III. Title. IV. Series.
PA6447.E5R8 1992 871'.01—dc20 91–3978
ISBN 0–19–281762–0

Printed in Great Britain by
BPCC Hazell Books
Aylesbury, Bucks.

To E.C.

ACKNOWLEDGEMENT

Thanks are due for permission to base this translation on the text of Juvenal edited by Professor E. Courtney and published in Rome in 1984 by Edizioni dell'Ateneo. The lines which Courtney has bracketed as spurious are translated in the notes; and where he has marked a word as unintelligible a conjecture has been translated. On the few occasions when the translation diverges from Courtney's text, this has been indicated in the notes. Professor Courtney's text is distributed in the United Kingdom by the Bristol Classical Press.

CONTENTS

THE SATIRES

INTRODUCTION

As well as being the author of two of the best known Latin tags, *panem et circenses* ('bread and races', 10. 81) and *mens sana in corpore sano* ('a healthy mind in a healthy body', 10. 356), Juvenal has two other, more important, claims on our attention. In the first place, there is no surviving Roman satirist whose approach more nearly matches most modern readers' expectations of the genre. In the second place, he is the last Roman poet of any great significance. After his death, some time after AD 130, Latin poetry went into decline and its revival in the fourth century produced no one of comparable stature.

The verse form of satire practised by Juvenal had been evolved, after some experimentation, by Lucilius, an outspoken gentleman-poet of the second century BC, whom Horace in the next century, then Persius (first century AD), and Juvenal, at the beginning of the second century, all acknowledge as their model and inspiration. Lucilius' satires now exist only as a collection of fragments, preserved by later writers in the form of quotations or, more often, cited for their interest to the grammarian and the lexicographer. Such as they are, however, these fragments and the comments of his followers and critics leave us in no doubt about Lucilius' satirical method in two important respects. Firstly, he assailed his victims fearlessly, and, in defiance of Roman feeling on this point, did not scruple to use their names, a feature heavily underlined in ancient assessments of his work. Secondly, he made of his poems a record of his life, a habit that deeply impressed Horace, in stylistic matters one of his sternest critics, as something he could usefully imitate (*Satires* 2. 1. 30 ff.). His outspokenness he admired (*Satires* 1. 4. 1 ff., 1. 10. 3 f.), but, whether from inclination or prudence, he did not try to copy it.

Juvenal, in marked contrast, while claiming both of these poets as his models, shows the aggressive spirit of Lucilius (though reluctant to attack living targets) but not the personal or autobiographical element. Lucilius, Horace, and, to a more limited extent, Persius use

their satire as a repository of personal confidences, presenting them-
selves to their readers on a level of carefully controlled intimacy.
(Significantly, each of the three is at some pains to specify his
preferred readership.) Juvenal, however, lurks in the shadows of his
own satire. There are no anecdotes of childhood or family and,
throughout his work, he remains as evasive and as difficult to
identify as the few individuals he addresses in the later poems.
Moreover, the declamatory tone he favoured makes intimacy im-
possible, and in consequence the only indications in the satires that
have a bearing on his life add up to little more than the claim to have
received a rhetorical training, his connection with Aquinum, his
place at Tivoli, and a few dates as often as not of doubtful value.

External evidence is equally lacking. Publication of the five books
of satires produced no immediate reaction that we know of. The
reading public's awareness of Juvenal came much later. The only one
of his contemporaries to name him is Martial, the writer of epigrams,
who addresses him more as a friend than as a fellow poet. His name
does not appear among the host of famous people of the day
mentioned in the extensive correspondence of Martial's friend Pliny
the younger, a wealthy patron of learning and literature, but whether
because of Juvenal's obscurity or Pliny's hostility is not clear. An
inscription from Aquinum, now lost, commemorates an offering to
Ceres by one (Iu)nius Iuvenalis, a local magistrate, the tribune of a
cohort of Dalmatian auxiliaries and a priest of the deified emperor
Vespasian, but though Juvenal speaks of Aquinum and its shrine of
Ceres as a place of retreat, there are no grounds for assuming that this
man (possibly no more than a relative or a namesake) and the poet
were one and the same.

By the time Juvenal's popularity was established with the reading
public in the fourth century (Ammianus 28. 14. 4), notes (*scholia*) had
to be supplied to assist their understanding and some biographical
details to satisfy their curiosity. The few pieces of information put
forward by the scholiast, based generally on what were felt to be
clues given by the poet himself, were later worked up into a number
of 'Lives'. These are found in an inferior class of manuscripts
presenting a text of Juvenal characterized by spurious insertions.

The most plausible of these Lives (Clausen, edn., 179; Courtney,
comm., p. 6) describes Juvenal as the son or foster-son of a freedman,
who until middle life practised declamation, though not in a pro-

fessional way. The freedman father may be a borrowing from the well-established details of Horace's life (*Satires* 1. 6. 6 etc.); the references to declamation and middle life probably derive from Juvenal himself (1. 15 ff., 1. 25). On a more sensational level we are informed that he wrote some verses attacking a favourite of the emperor Domitian, a dancer called Paris executed in AD 83, and his librettist, for trafficking in military commissions, and that he then took up this kind of writing with enthusiasm but without seeking publicity. Later, we are told, a warm reception of his verses broke down that reserve and he inserted the lines on Paris into his seventh satire as verses 90–2. They seemed to fit another court favourite of the time, offence was taken, and Juvenal, then in his eighties, was given command of a cohort then being posted to Egypt, where he soon died of distress and boredom.

Other versions differed in detail, but the story of Juvenal's exile kept cropping up with such persistence that in the past many scholars felt obliged to accept it, using it as the basis of elaborate theories about his life and temperament, and modifying or disregarding its inherent improbabilities as they felt inclined. The story is open to many objections. Why, for example, should Juvenal in his eighties, after a lifetime of cautious reticence and having lived through Domitian's reign of terror, so far forget himself as to risk imperial vengeance by reviving his remarks about a long dead favourite in Satire 7, which is now widely assumed to have been written in the early days of Hadrian's beneficent rule? Why again should Hadrian, who never spent much time in Rome after his accession, have taken notice of anything said by a writer so apparently obscure as Juvenal? Or why was an offence described in the Life as slight and amusing punished in this way or punished at all?

Some get over these difficulties by accepting the Scholiast's assertions (1. 1, 4. 37, 7. 90) that he was banished by Domitian (on the evidence of Martial 7. 24 and 91 this could only have been after AD 92) and, returning to Rome after Domitian's death in 96 an embittered man, turned his hand to writing satire. Some modern critics like Highet (*Juvenal the Satirist*, 40 f.) and, after him, Green (1974, 21 f.) have managed to create attractive and by no means implausible reconstructions of the poet's life, largely on the basis of the inscription and these stories of exile, while fully aware of the pitfalls. (Highet, in a later work, *Poets in a Landscape* (1957), 193 ff., goes even further along these lines, adding many details that could only have originated in his own imagination.) The consensus of opinion among scholars of the present day is that the story of Juvenal's exile, like many other details in the Lives, was a late fabrication, needed to supply a biographical background to a virtually unknown author and to account for the bitterness of his tone.

As to the life and circumstances of Juvenal, there is little to guide us except the evidence of Martial and some scattered shreds of evidence supplied by the poems themselves. Indications of date are slight enough in all conscience, but enough to suggest that the five books came out in chronological order:

Book 1 (Satires 1–5), with its reference to the trial of Marius Priscus (1. 49–50), must have been published some time after AD 100 but before 112 or thereabouts.

Book 2 (Satire 6) has a reference (407 ff.) to a comet visible in November of AD 115, therefore *c*.117.

Book 3 (Satires 7–9), if the Caesar of 7. 1 is rightly taken to be Hadrian, was probably published after his accession in 117 and before his departure from Rome in 121: say 121.

Book 4 (Satires 10–12) has no clear indications of date except that it is obviously after Trajan (12. 80): say 125.

Book 5 (Satires 13–16), where Satire 13. 17 refers to one born in AD 67 (probably) as having turned 60, has a date later than 127: say 130.

The reference to his youth as something in the past (*Sat.* 1. 24–5) would have meant to a Roman that he had passed the age of 45, giving a birth-date of about AD 60. In Satire 11 he represents himself as old (201–3), leaving us to infer that the Satires were the work of his middle and later years.

Martial addressed Juvenal in three epigrams, 7. 24, 91, and 12. 18. (Juvenal never returned the compliment, though he was obviously well acquainted with Martial's work.) The first two can be dated to AD 92 and must imply that Martial and Juvenal knew each other in Rome. Martial (7. 91) calls him *facundus* ('eloquent'), an epithet equally applicable to poets and orators. The third epigram (12. 18), with a date of AD 101–2, is much more interesting. It is written from Bilbilis in Spain, the place of Martial's retirement, and draws a picture of Juvenal plodding wearily through the noisy Subura (see on

3. 5) or paying his respects at the houses of the upper classes, sweating under the uncomfortable toga worn by clients in the performance of this duty. We have insufficient evidence to enable us to pinpoint with anything like accuracy Juvenal's position in the echelons of the Roman class system, but his own descriptions in the earlier satires of the condition of the respectable poor at Rome seem to imply that he was no stranger to the hardships and humiliations imposed on those at the lower end of the social scale.

Aquinum, where possibly he had some family connection (though the name Iuvenalis suggests that he came of a stock originally Spanish), offered an occasional escape from the discomforts of the capital (3. 319 ff.). In a later satire (11. 65 ff.) he speaks of his own farm at Tivoli with its steward and his wife as the source of the simple country fare he proposes to offer at his dinner-party. Tivoli was one of the most delectable spots within easy reach of Rome, favoured by the rich and noble, and, at this period, the place chosen by Hadrian for the construction of a more than ordinarily splendid villa. The possession of a place here, however modest, raises the possibility that Juvenal's circumstances had improved materially. Some such improvement in fortune has often been taken as the reason for the noticeable decrease in Juvenal's obsession with the poor and oppressed between his earlier work and his later, as well as accounting for a general mellowing of temper, notwithstanding a return to something like his old fire in the fifth book. But certainty is not to be had.

The literary output of Juvenal begins at a time when the bad years of Domitian were giving way to the humane and tolerant rule of Nerva (96–8) and Trajan (98–117), the start of the period of which Gibbon wrote that

if a man were called to fix the period in the history of the world, during which the condition of the human race was most happy and prosperous, he would, without hesitation, name that which elapsed from the death of Domitian to the accession of Commodus (Bk. 1, ch. 3).

Human satisfaction is never, of course, unalloyed, and Gibbon went on to surmise that this happiness must have been tempered by the reflection that its stability depended always on the character of a single man, the emperor. His optimism was obviously based with hindsight on a global view of those years, taking little account of individual lives.

For many undoubtedly it was the best of times. There was still plenty of 'old money' to be found in the hands of men like the younger Pliny, who lived in a style that could reasonably be called princely, though he himself did not consider it remarkable. The large landed estates in Italy and abroad were, in the right hands, constantly being increased by inheritance, marriage, prudent management and reinvestment. The extent of these holdings can be judged from the statement of Pliny the elder that at one time half of the province of Africa was owned by six men (*Natural History* 18. 35). Not everyone, however, had the good luck to keep their fortunes intact. Imperial disfavour was easily incurred under a Nero or a Domitian, and disgrace was usually accompanied by the confiscation of the family estates, as in the case of Rubellius Plautus (Tacitus, *Annals* 14. 60). In Juvenal, a wealthy freedman sneers at the idea of a descendant of the once great house of Messala Corvinus, now reduced to tending sheep that were not even his own (1. 107 f.). Many were brought to similar straits by the all too prevalent Roman tendency to luxury and display.

The temper of the times helped others on the way up. The rise of the ex-slave (see on 1. 109) was by Juvenal's day a well-established phenomenon, though not perhaps so common in real life as its prominence in literature might suggest. There are no good grounds, moreover, for accepting Juvenal's impression of Crispinus or the pushy freedman of 1. 102 ff. as entirely true to real life. These are probably caricatures of the type made famous by Petronius' Trimalchio. Still, the rich freedmen did exist, and, often backed or even partnered by their former owners, they applied themselves successfully to making money, unhampered by any class taboos about what was or was not a fitting occupation for a gentleman.

In this respect they had a distinct advantage over those shabby-genteel individuals described by Umbricius in Satire 3. (At an earlier date one might have said 'like Juvenal himself', but sheer lack of information on this head and the concept of the *persona* nowadays rightly forbid these rigid assumptions.) The existence of slave-labour on a large scale placed many kinds of work below the level of free-born men and, in regard to what profession or occupation a man might follow without compromising his own respectability or the pretensions of his class, Roman society had traditionally been as sensitive as our own. Philosophy too had something to say on the subject. In his treatise *On Duties* 1. 150 f., a work which draws heavily on the Stoic Panaetius, one of whose guiding principles was 'the fitting' (Greek, *tò prépon*; Latin, *decorum*), Cicero declares that medicine, architecture, and teaching are well enough for those whose rank does not rule out that sort of thing. One could get away with trade, but only if it was conducted on a large enough scale (retail trade was vulgar); and successful traders had been known to retire from business, buy an estate and become country squires. Farming as a means of making money was above reproach. Principles like these, by which educated Romans of good standing tended to regulate their conduct, help to explain why such umbrage is taken at the entrepreneurial activities of the people described in Satire 3. 21 ff. Theirs were not 'respectable skills' (the expression recalls Cicero's own words); but, respectable or not, those who chose to live by them could stand on their own feet. Those who, like Umbricius, felt superior to them had few other ways of making ends meet than by attaching themselves to a patron, from whom, if nothing else came of the connection, they were at least sure of a hand-out (1. 95 and note), sufficient to keep body and soul together, or an occasional dinner. Patronage, of course, was never disinterested, and Juvenal in Satires 5 and 9 fuels the reflection that Trebius and, even more so, Naevolus are paying too heavily in humiliation and degradation for anything they receive or are likely to receive from their despicable patrons. The beggar's mat is mentioned in both satires as the final stage of destitution, but the advice tendered by Juvenal is remarkable for the ironic delicacy with which he steers clear of suggesting better ways of avoiding it than scrounging or sodomy, just as the reader's attention is focused on the moral aspects of Naevolus' chosen mode of life more effectively by Juvenal's affectation of bland acceptance than by any overtly expressed condemnation.

However, in many ways less concerned with the actual problems of day-to-day living, life was improving. Martial, perhaps detecting a change in the temper of the times under Nerva and Trajan, had decided that there was little more to be gained by his particular talent for obsequiousness and obscenity (not that he had done especially well out of it before), and retired back to Spain. To Juvenal, on the other hand, the more relaxed and more tolerant atmosphere seems to have given the idea of devoting himself to a branch of literature to which he was well suited by temperament and training, and one that provided the opportunity for unburdening himself of certain things that badly wanted saying. His highly individual conception of satire gave him ample scope for exploiting the techniques developed by his rhetorical training and the practice of declamation. In one important respect he differs from his predecessors. Whereas they have much to say about the kind of readership they prefer, and sometimes, as in the case of Horace, couple this with a disclaimer of any malicious intention in writing satire, Juvenal addresses himself to the task of writing satire in a torrent of rhetorical energy without the slightest attempt to limit or define his audience. Speaking for the most part in monologue, rarely introducing an interlocutor or adversary figure, the satirist makes his point less by the arts of conversation than by overpowering rhetoric. But the rhetoric of the Silver Age was very much a thing of the schools, and the opportunities for using it to gain some point in the real world against real opponents were more limited than they had ever been. Reflecting this, Juvenal's arguments often lose in force (for example in Satire 6 and Satire 10) from his apparent refusal to countenance the possibility that any man of ordinary sense and experience could with little difficulty cite examples that tell as heavily against him. Rhetorical commonplaces, like the superiority of country to town, of past to present, take the place of reasoned argument. The great heroes of the Roman Republic, an important part of the stock-in-trade of the rhetoric schools, are set up again and again as examples of the ideals of manhood (*virtus*) from which their unworthy descendants have progressively sunk.

The rhetorical influences at work in Silver Age literature of every kind are nowhere more apparent than in the prevalence of the *sententia*. This is a short pithy saying or epigram, in which a point is made so emphatically and so neatly that the listener involuntarily accepts it as proven. Juvenal is particularly skilful at making and using *sententiae*, some so brilliant that they have virtually acquired the force of proverbs. Several of these state a truth that we accept readily, like 3. 152 f.:

> Of all that luckless poverty involves, nothing is harsher
> than the fact that it makes people funny.

or 2. 83:

> No one sinks to the bottom at once.

(In each case, Latin, as usual, contrives to put the idea in far fewer words.) Other specimens, however, for all their brilliance will not stand up to close examination, and expose the device as a poor substitute for argument, for example 10. 96:

> Even people with no desire to kill
> covet the power,

and the empty-handed traveller of 10. 22 would seem to be asking for trouble if he acted as Juvenal suggests and sang in the face of the disappointed robber.

All successful satire relies heavily on the licence to exaggerate, but Juvenal not infrequently abuses this licence, both in the grossly overdrawn caricatures he presents of individuals like his particular bugbear Crispinus, and in unabashed mispresentation. Bad as Rome may have been, it is absurdly overstating the case to allege that its streets were swarming with murderesses to the extent that (6. 655 f.)

> Every morning you meet Eriphýles in dozens, and also
> daughters of Danaus; every street has a Clytemnestra.

It is equally absurd to describe the father of Demosthenes, a wealthy armourer, as a grimy blacksmith with bloodshot eyes (10. 130 ff.). But it is all magnificent stuff provided it is not accepted as gospel.

Whatever the defects in his manner of conducting an argument, Juvenal emerges as a brilliantly effective and forceful stylist, particularly in the earlier and more declamatory sections of his work. The rhetorical question is constantly used, sometimes to suggest an identity of interest or a measure of agreement between the satirist and his reader; or sometimes, as at 1. 1 ff., a run of such questions is used to convey exasperation. Points are underlined by the repetition of leading words (anaphora), and arguments are balanced and values highlighted by a skilful use of antithesis. He can rise seemingly at will from a fairly pedestrian level into the grand style; lines 81 ff. of the first satire give a good example of this.

The formal structure of verse satire was not something that came within the scope of rhetorical theory, and Juvenal had an entirely free hand in determining the manner of introducing his satires and thereafter of directing the argument to his desired conclusion. Sometimes he uses an outline borrowed from another genre. Satire

3, for example, is loosely a *syntacticon*, or speech of a departing
traveller, and Satire 13 is, equally loosely, a 'consolation'. Elsewhere, as
in 7, 8, 10, 14, his satire takes the form of a *thesis*, a proposition
discussed in the manner of the schools, or, as in 5 and 6, of a harangue
designed to turn the recipient away from a particular course of action
or style of life. Disproportion in the scale of treatment accorded the
different sections of a satire has frequently left Juvenal open to
criticism. Duff, for example, speaks of a tendency to sacrifice the
whole to the parts (p. xxxii; compare Courtney comm., p. 454), and
much modern criticism has grappled, with varying degrees of
success, with the problem of trying to impose some sort of structural
or thematic order on his material. But one of the charms of satire was
the very desultoriness of its nature; and our enjoyment of the
brilliantly delineated scenes and descriptions that follow each other
in rapid succession, the witty aphorisms and scathing comments, is
not significantly increased by searching examination or detailed
analysis.

Juvenal's satires, though numbered consecutively from one to
sixteen, were actually grouped into five separate books, published,
as explained above, at different times; and it is important not to think
of them as a single production. The first satire of the first book
(Satires 1–5), is largely programmatic in character, following lines
by now well established by the earlier satirists. Having listened with
mounting frustration to other poets giving recitations of their works,
Juvenal can remain silent no longer. He must write, not the myth-
ological claptrap favoured by these people, but satire, a condemnation
of the times. The streets of Rome will provide all the material
needed, crowded as they are with individuals stained with every
kind of vice and malpractice, perverting the whole order of things,
natural and social, and, what is worse, evidently thriving on it.
A man might fill a whole notebook just standing at the crossroads
watching them file by. It is impossible not to write satire. If his
nature should prove unequal to the task, then his verse will be born
of indignation (79–80). (This should not be taken to mean that all
Juvenal's satires were written in a white-heat of indignation. Such a
state is hardly compatible with creativity. Juvenal's indignation is in
part factitious: the mood is not consistently maintained, nor is the
persona of the angry man worn throughout. The place of *indignatio* in
rhetoric, as a means of conveying or arousing a sense of outrage,

should also be borne in mind.) His theme will be the whole range of human activities and emotions from the Flood to his own day, but it is plain from what follows that Juvenal's preoccupation is with the failings of men to the exclusion of their more innocent pleasures and joys. Greed and acquisitiveness are what he most deplores and, above all, the failure of the rich and powerful to discharge the obligations attached to their rank, particularly insofar as their dependents are concerned. The voice of an interlocutor is momentarily heard, warning Juvenal that conditions have changed since the days when Lucilius openly attacked his victims with impunity; if he must write, let him stick to the subjects of mythology. Juvenal takes the point so far as to promise to limit himself to attacks on the dead. (References to living individuals by name, disparaging or otherwise, are in fact rare, and the people named serve for the most part as examples, not targets. See note on 1. 170 f.) Juvenal's programme takes account of his stance, his material and his method. The idea of the observer of line 63, a satirist taking to the streets and recording delinquencies in a book for future use, is something new. There is always a hint of menace about such a figure, and satirists were traditionally a dreaded species. Viewed in one light, he could re- semble the informers of Juvenal's day (see on 1. 33 ff.), in another, the pair of abusive preachers with their notebooks whose practice Horace so emphatically repudiates for himself (*Satires* 1. 4. 65 ff.). Looking at him again, we are reminded more perhaps of the figure of the poet/corregidor in Browning's *How it Strikes a Contemporary*, 'not so much a spy, / as a recording chief inquisitor' who 'walked about and took account / of all thought, said and acted, then went home, / and wrote it fully to our Lord the King'.

Satire 2 is a denunciation of homosexuals, in particular those who conceal their perversion under an air of rigid Stoic morality, a kind of hypocrisy reminiscent of the emperor Domitian, who sought to promote national purity while guilty of incest himself. An interesting feature of the satire, particularly in view of Juvenal's attitude in Satire 6, is the introduction of a woman, Laronia, to uphold the conduct of women, especially when contrasted with such unworthy repre- sentatives of the male sex. Juvenal resumes with the example of a lawyer who addresses the court in a 'see-through' gown and is warned that from one such vice a man will quickly descend to worse, like Gracchus, who betrayed his class, first by going through a form of marriage with a bugler, and then capped that (the priorities are characteristically Juvenalian) by appearing in public as a gladiator.

Satire 3, which provided the inspiration for Johnson's *London*, ranks high among Juvenal's productions. Juvenal introduces a friend, Umbricius, who is proposing to shake the dust of Rome off his feet and go to live in Cumae, wisely in Juvenal's opinion. While the furniture-van is being loaded, the two go into the grove of Egeria, where Umbricius tells Juvenal his reasons for leaving, in a long monologue, to which Juvenal listens without comment or inter-ruption. The speech ends as the sun sinks, and Umbricius responds to his driver's call to be off, so that the end of the satire answers to the beginning (the so-called 'ring-composition'), making an attractive frame for the body of this finely structured satire. Umbricius complains that others less principled, especially Greeks and other foreigners, are taking the bread out of the mouth of the poor but respectable Romans like (presumably) himself. He discourses in fascinating detail on the environmental hazards and discomforts of living in Rome (fire, noise, high rents, traffic, crime), introducing the standard rhetorical town versus country topic to brilliant effect. This poem has the same highly realistic approach to the cruel City as the first, and was obviously conceived in the same spirit. It is sometimes held to be, as much as anything else, a reflection on the attitudes and conduct of Umbricius, in that, for example, he cannot stand a Rome overrun by Greeks, but takes refuge in Cumae, the oldest Greek colony in Italy. But Cumae is now almost deserted, and anyway it is Rome, not Umbricius, that is the main target of Juvenal's satire. Many of the complaints here voiced by Umbricius are borne out by other evidence. Gellius 15. 1. 3, for example, supports what is said about high rents and the risk of fire, and Tacitus, *Annals* 15. 44 and elsewhere amply confirms the impression of Rome as a positive magnet for all that was shameful and pernicious. Juvenal gives Umbricius his head, and the fact that he is at no pains to disparage his views must be taken as indicating agreement: silence may here be taken to mean consent. Nor is there much point in asking why, if Juvenal hated Rome, he did not follow his friend's example. Rome was the main centre of Hellenistic culture and the only place for an aspiring man of letters.

Satire 4 leaves the Rome of Juvenal's day and returns to the principate of Domitian, who is represented as convening a meeting of his council merely to consider what to do with a turbot of record size presented to him by the man who caught it. The poem opens with a searing condemnation of Crispinus (1. 26), awkwardly related to the second part of the poem, though Crispinus and fish figure in both parts. The enumeration of the members of a council which combined distinguished men of integrity and servile flatterers and informers is enhanced by a subtle parody (verses 94 ff.) of a poem by Statius, a poet known for his adulation of Domitian. It is the only satire in Book 1 to drop the criticism of life in contemporary Rome.

Satire 5 describes the degrading treatment of poor clients at dinner-parties, with special reference to one Trebius and his patron Virro. The practice of putting clients in their place by serving them with food and wine of an inferior order is condemned by Pliny (*Epistles* 2. 6) from the point of view of a host, and Martial, speaking as a guest (1. 20, 3. 60). The practice is symptomatic of the failure of the upper classes to discharge their responsibilities in the old-fashioned way. It must be said that there is nothing in the poem to show that Juvenal was actually on the same footing as Trebius, whom he attempts to convince that dependence such as his is not much different from slavery; yet the appeal to Virro (108 ff.) does suggest a keenly felt, almost personal, interest in the matter.

Satire 6, running to nearly 700 lines and occupying the whole of Book 2, is the longest of the satires. It purports to be an attempt to dissuade one Postumus from taking a wife, and is conceived and executed, not so much as an attack on the institution of marriage, as a condemnation of the alleged enormities of female behaviour within the context of marriage, and the discomforts and humiliations men suffer as a consequence of the modern woman's failure to live up to the obligations imposed on her by the married state. It begins with a somewhat facetious expression of nostalgia for the days when the world was new and men and women lived in caves in conjugal felicity. Now Chastity has withdrawn from the earth. Juvenal rests his case on a series of brilliantly drawn stories and descriptions of misconduct and betrayal on the part of the married woman. Towards the mid-point of the satire (286 ff.) he returns to the theme of the superior virtues of the women of an earlier age, not of the world at large, but of Rome, an age when the City was under threat from foreign invaders, when incomes were small and long hours at the distaff and the loom (wool-working was the traditional occupation of the model Roman matron) left no time for getting into mischief. With the extension of Roman dominion abroad came Luxury, deadlier than any enemy in arms. It is wealth and the adoption of foreign ways that have destroyed Roman morals in the way that Juvenal describes. The list of delinquencies culminates in the observation that the women of high tragedy, the Medeas and Clytemnestras, who murdered out of passion, in no way match the cold-blooded females of today, who perform their acts of murder, not openly with the sword, but with insidious poisons and from more mercenary motives.

This is one of Juvenal's most striking satires, though it is difficult to discern his motive in writing it. It can most obviously be criticized on the score of gross over-statement and his customary tendency to blind himself to anything that does not support his thesis. Happy marriages and good wives, even heroic wives, are not unknown in the literature of the period, but Juvenal's techniques of argumentation are not so strong that he could afford to mention them without doing irreparable damage to his case. Noteworthy too is his Stoic-like failure to differentiate between the degrees of enormity in the actions perpetrated by his women. There is a difference between, say, immorality and pretensions to scholarship, though one is made out to pose as great a threat to marital comfort and happiness as the other. The structure owes something to a tradition of attacks on women which follow a catalogue form. Semonides of Ceos (sixth–fifth century BC) uses this sort of pattern in his poem on women, who, in their worst qualities, are compared to animals (sow, vixen, bitch, etc.). His verdict on the sex is not good, though one exception is made in favour of the bee-like woman (J. M. Edmonds, *Elegy and Iambus* (1918), ii., 217 ff., H. Lloyd-Jones, *Females of the Species*, (1975)). Juvenal, however, finds nothing good in women.

It would be rash to infer that the views here expressed were based on an unhappy personal experience of marriage (Highet, *Juvenal the Satirist*, 103), or that they represented a completely thought-out position. Yet unfavourable views of women occur again in Satire 11. 186 ff. and Satire 13. 189 ff. To say that his opinion of men was not much higher leaves the problem of Satire 6 largely unsolved. Nowhere does he impute to men the same uninhibited zest for the grosser satisfactions of human nature.

Satire 7 introduces Book 3 (Satires 7–9) and begins with the assertion that nowadays only the emperor can be regarded as the source of literary patronage, and that Caesar is looking about for talent to encourage. But the emphasis of the poem falls heavily on the negative side: no help can be expected from any *other* quarter. It is fairly clear that Juvenal is about to carry his strictures on neglectful patrons into the sphere of literature. The petty meanness of the patron may not, perhaps, deter those committed to making their name as poets; but even men of the highest genius, like Horace and Virgil, could not have risen to the heights they did if they had not been free from mundane worries. Statius makes a living, not from his accomplished *Thebaid*, but by selling pieces written for the stage to the influential actor Paris. Historians, barristers, teachers of rhetoric, all fare badly, but worst off of all is the schoolmaster. Parents demand the highest standards from him, but can hardly bring themselves to part with his modest, hard-earned fee. In describing the plight of those who depend on literature or the practice of law Juvenal's sympathies are never quite fully engaged and the section on poets in particular shows distinct traces of irony.

Satire 8 offers advice to Ponticus, a man otherwise unknown, who may have had expectations of the consulship and a provincial governorship. The theme of the poem, stated at some length in the introduction (1–70), is that noble birth is nothing without virtue. It is on this, not breeding, that Ponticus must rely, especially when he goes to his province. He is to pity those he governs and spare their property: the depredations of governors have gone quite far enough. He must also take account of their temper: not all of them are decadent Greeks who could be relied on not to revolt if pressed too hard. This is sound enough advice, even though its ethical basis is distinctively negative. There follows a series of *exempla*, members of the nobility who in their conduct fell below the standards expected of them: Lateranus, the horse-mad consul; Gracchus, who fought in the arena; Nero's savage and bloody reign and, not least, his theatrical appearances; the conspirators of 63 BC, Catiline and Cethegus. As to the latter, the consul who crushed their attempt on the City was Cicero, no scion of a noble family but a mere provincial knight. Rome owed much to its men of lowly origin. The satire is remarkable as being the first to offer positive advice, albeit advice based on examples to be avoided rather than examples to be followed.

Satire 9 takes up the theme of the client–patron relationship again, this time as it subsists between Naevolus, a disgruntled male prostitute, who feels that his services to his patron, a pathic homosexual, and his patron's wife have not been adequately rewarded. On the subject of patronage, here explored at the very lowest level of degradation, this satire invites comparison with Satire 5. The only advice offered to Naevolus is that a wise client does not criticize his patron. This advice and the later assurance that he will never want for customers are coolly received. Naevolus has a very precise idea of what is due to him. It is only Fortune that stands between him and his not over-modest requirements. The satire is remarkable for the ironic restraint shown by Juvenal and his avoidance of open censure. There is, indeed, indignation; but it comes from the ridiculous and discredited Naevolus. Again, this is the only satire cast in the form of a dialogue, the form favoured by Horace in his later satires.

The Tenth Satire opens Book 4 (Satires 10–12), which shows an even greater movement away from Juvenal's earlier vehemence. The poem takes the form of a *thesis*, viz. the folly of mankind in praying for what, if granted them, could only result in their ruin. The philosopher Heraclitus wept for their folly, but Democritus laughed at their cares, their sorrows and sometimes even their tears. This Democritean laughter signals a distinct change of attitude from the indignation of the earlier books. Yet it is a harsh, sardonic laughter (*rigidi censura cachinni*), far removed from the 'chearful wisdom and instructive mirth' which we meet in Johnson's imitation (*The Vanity of Human Wishes*). The foolish objects of human prayer are taken in turn and disposed of in sections of varying length. The first is the prayer for political power, illustrated by the single example of the fallen Sejanus. Cicero and Demosthenes are cited as examples of men whose eloquence in public life proved their destruction in the end. Military glory and its ultimate futility are exemplified in three foreign generals, Hannibal, Alexander, and Xerxes. The sorrows attendant on long life are illustrated by two examples from epic (Nestor and Priam) and two from Roman history (Marius and Pompey). The prayer for good looks is dismissed by reference to the fate of Silius. The conclusion of the poem has, uncharacteristically for Juvenal, a convincingly positive ring. The things that a man may rightly pray for include a mind brave and unafraid of death, indifferent to long life, ready to suffer any hardship, a stranger to anger; and this a man may secure for himself, independently of Fortune. The goal is tranquillity of life, and the path that leads to it is through virtue.

Mood and treatment have changed drastically in this most celebrated of Juvenal's poems. The scope is wider, the tone less recriminatory than in the earliest satires. The illustrations are not now drawn from the sights and scenes of the cruel City and its inhabitants, but from literature, history and mythology; and such realism as there is is confined to the description of the physical characteristics of old age. This is one of those later satires that exhibited differences so marked as to prompt a German scholar of the last century to advance the theory that most of the satires of Book 4 and Book 5 were spurious (O. Ribbeck, *Der echte und der unechte Juvenal* (Berlin, 1865)), a view that provoked much discussion but attracted few supporters. It is enough to say that Juvenal was under no obligation to confine himself to one style of satire, and the movement away from the aggression of Lucilius is accompanied, especially in Satires 11 and 12, by a change to something more approaching the familiarity of Horace, whom he had also claimed as a model.

Satire 11 is addressed to Persicus, who has accepted an invitation to dinner. It opens with a disquisition on the imprudence of those who insist on dining in a manner beyond their means. In this, as in all else, people should take stock of themselves and their resources, and not think of ordering salmon if all they can raise is the price of a kipper. Juvenal bids Persicus come and see whether he lives up to the principle he has just stated, and describes the simple fare, the produce of Juvenal's farm at Tivoli, that he proposes for his friend's entertainment. In Rome of old the highest magistrates used to hurry home to such a dinner. The old Republican heroes gave no thought to dining-room furniture: all their silver went into their arms, and earthenware plates were considered quite good enough. Now rich men take no pleasure in food unless eaten off an elegant table. Juvenal's cutlery, on the other hand, is of the plainest. He has no trained carvers; the meal will be served by healthy young country lads. There will be no Spanish dancing-girls but readings from Homer or Virgil. Persicus is to forget his worries (even his wife's adultery!) and relax with him while younger men enjoy the excitement of the races. The poem generally has an air of easy charm, strongly reminiscent of one of Horace's epistles or odes of invitation, like that in which Maecenas is

offered a less pretentious entertainment than he is accustomed to
(*Odes* 3. 29).

Satire 12 is addressed to Corvinus. The occasion is the sacrifice
that Juvenal proposes to make as a thank-offering for the escape from
a storm at sea of his friend Catullus, an adventure described with
many lively touches of humour. But Juvenal disclaims any mercenary
motive in his attentions to Catullus. He is no legacy-hunter. (The
name Corvinus is derived from *corvus* (crow), suggestive perhaps of
a predatory instinct and an interest in the subject of legacy-hunting
here introduced.) There can be no expectations of this kind from a
man with three children, who is therefore not worth the gift of a hen
or a quail. But there are those like Novius and Pacuvius Hister who
in pursuit of a legacy, would not hesitate to vow a hundred oxen for
the recovery of someone rich and childless, and that only because
elephants are not procurable locally. (There follows a curious digres-
sion on elephants, their origin and history, very much out of place
even if it is intended as a parody of one of those learned disquisitions
found in silver-age epic and elsewhere.) Pacuvius Hister would even
offer up his own daughter, as Agamemnon offered Iphigenia, if he
thought it would make someone alter their will in his favour.

Satire 13 uses some of the topics of the *consolatio*, a formalized
expression of sympathy offered to a bereaved person. The addressee
is called Calvinus (the name suggests a well-to-do individual of good
family: compare Calvina, 3. 133), but his loss is not the loss of a
loved one. He has been cheated out of 10,000 sesterces, a sum hardly
likely to make much of a dent in his bank-balance. Such things
happen all the time. He should by now have learned that morals at
Rome have sunk so low that a man who does *not* take advantage of a
friend is now regarded as a portent. Men contemplating a crime
reassure themselves with the thought that it will be long before
divine vengeance catches up with them. Juvenal (120 ff.) then goes
on to offer Calvinus some non-technical advice. He is to think of
more serious crimes and curb his anger. Revenge is not the answer. It
is the mark of a mean and petty spirit to want revenge. And the
proof? No one gets more satisfaction from revenge than a woman.
The wrongdoer's own conscience and the fear it engenders will
ensure an end of his peace. One crime will lead to another and land
him in exile or jail. The gods are not blind.

This is not intended as a parody of the literary *consolatio*, as is sometimes claimed. The irony of the piece consists in the use of certain aspects of the *consolatio* to highlight the folly of Calvinus' immoderate anger and distress over a trivial misfortune. The sympathy offered is less than whole-hearted, and Juvenal is using the *consolatio* in an ironical and teasing sort of way. As Pliny points out (*Epistles* 5. 16. 10), even sincere consolations can produce annoyance rather than comfort, if they are not sensitively phrased.

The opening theme of Satire 14, addressed to Fuscinus, is the power of example, particularly where parents and children are concerned. Children will readily acquire from their parents the vices of gambling, gluttony, cruelty in the treatment of slaves, and adultery. A parent must have the utmost respect for his children and shield them from the very sight of sin. The ideal should be to train for the benefit of the country a son who will be a good farmer and of service in war and peace. Two further things in which the young are inclined to follow their elders spontaneously are a passion for the construction of lavish villas and a subservience to the Jewish religion. Avarice, however, is something they need to be actually taught. They have to be trained to imitate the despicable shifts of men prepared to live like beggars merely in order to die millionaires. Avarice is the mother of crime, for those who want unbounded wealth want it at once. Not for them the small holdings of land and the hard living they afforded to the sturdy Italian peasants of an older time. Now parents urge their young to prepare themselves for the practice of law or the life of a centurion or a trader, all in the pursuit of wealth. Perjury, murder, swindling, all follow from this, and even parricide. The life of the trader is more entertaining than any play. Keeping one's wealth is harder work than getting it in the first place. Juvenal's advice is that we should content ourselves with just enough to support life.

The two themes of avarice and the force of parental example are not very convincingly fused, and by the end the latter has been lost sight of altogether. As in the previous satire, Juvenal's trenchant humour, his flair for vivid illustration, and even his stock of examples are less in evidence; they are replaced by a lengthy development of hackneyed commonplaces, like the greedy and foolhardy merchant. But the highly critical stand taken against parents and misers recalls his earlier mood.

Satire 15 has for its subject an occurrence of cannibalism in Egypt.

It is an account of a battle between two Egyptian towns, in the course of which one side tore to pieces and devoured the flesh of one of the enemy who fell in flight. This was an act of sheer savagery; they were not reduced to eating human flesh like people suffering the privations of a siege. Nature has raised man above the animal creation by endowing him with the capacity to pity and to shed tears for the misfortunes of others. It was this difference that gave men the ability to create a civilized society. But now the wild animals show more mercy to one another than man shows to man. It is not enough for men to have invented the sword. Killing is not enough: they must eat their foes as well. The scorn exhibited by Juvenal in this satire is for once occasioned by something other than a manifestation of contemporary Roman wickedness, and the reflections it prompts have a universal application. The treatment again shows a recrud-escence of Juvenal's earlier intensity. The Egyptian provenance of the story, coupled with the words 'or so I have found' (15. 46), probably helped to create the story of Juvenal's exile. But these words need not imply residence in Egypt.

The incomplete Satire 16 is a tirade against the privileges enjoyed by military personnel *vis-à-vis* the civilian. It is uncertain whether the poem's incomplete state is to be attributed to the death of the poet or to the loss of the final pages of a codex (a manuscript in the form of a book) on which all subsequent copies of the text depended. This satire, like the previous one, helped to supply the compilers of his 'life' with the further detail that it was as commander of a cohort that he went to Egypt, though his antagonism to the military does not suggest that he had ever been a soldier.

W.B.

Liverpool
1989

TRANSLATOR'S PREFACE

It goes without saying that there is no such thing as a wholly satisfactory translation. A 'literal' translation, which may be the best for someone needing help with the Latin, cannot also be a 'literary' translation. But while in theory the two types, with their different objectives and criteria, stand at opposite ends of a spectrum, actual translations represent varying degrees of compromise. No one, so far as I know, not even the Revd Lewis Evans in the Bohn translation, begins the tenth satire with the words: 'In all lands which are from Gades to Aurora and the Ganges few men are able to distinguish true goods from things very different from those, the cloud of error having been removed.' That is an accurate decoding of the original, but is too crude, and indeed too false, to be acceptable as a translation. On the other hand, a version which aspires to reproduce the essence or spirit of the author also ceases to qualify as a translation if it strays too far from the letter. As Dryden indicated, this is what happens in the case of an imitation, 'where the translator (if now he has not lost that name) assumes the liberty, not only to vary from the words and sense, but to forsake them both as he sees occasion; and taking only some general hints from the original, to run division on the ground-work, as he pleases' (*Preface to the Translation of Ovid's Epistles*).

In working out his own compromise, the translator must first decide between prose and verse. If he believes (as I do) that the element of rhythmical regularity is too important to sacrifice, what sort of formal discipline should he accept? Should he, for a start, keep to the same number of lines as his author? Juvenal's first satire has 171 lines (ignoring possible lacunae). Humphries renders it in 164, Green in 200, and Creekmore in 182. Although one doesn't wish to be too mechanical in such matters, this suggests that Humphries's version may be rather thinner than the original, and that the other two may represent varying degrees of elaboration. I do not claim, of course, that by sticking to 171 lines I have got the consistency just right; only that it is prudent to use the author's total as a guide.

This argument can be opposed by any translator employing heroic couplets, on the grounds that he is working with five iambic feet as against Juvenal's six dactyls or spondees. Thus Dryden's total for Satire 1 is 258 lines and Gifford's 274. But the heroic couplet, notwithstanding (or perhaps because of) its splendid achievements in the seventeenth and eighteenth centuries, will not serve today. The Latinate syntax, the freedom of its word-order, and those minor variations of diction that were freely permitted in the past (such as 'e'en', 'ne'er', and 'oft'), now make it sound contrived. And in any case the recurrent rhymes, which are justifiable in Ovid's *Amores* and perhaps essential in Martial's *Epigrams*, interfere with the flow of Juvenal's rhetoric. Dryden's accomplished version of 3. 21–8 will give some idea of the strengths and limitations of the form:

> Then thus Umbritius (with an angry frown,
> And looking back at this degen'rate town):
> 'Since noble arts in Rome have no support,
> And ragged virtue not a friend at court,
> No profit rises from th' ungrateful stage,
> My poverty increasing with my age,
> 'Tis time to give my just disdain a vent,
> And, cursing, leave so base a government.
> Where Daedalus his borrow'd wings laid by,
> To that obscure retreat I choose to fly:
> While yet few furrows on my face are seen,
> While I walk upright, and old age is green,
> And Lachesis has somewhat left to spin.'

If, then, the couplet is discarded, and Juvenal's numerical limits are observed, one needs a line of adequate length. So why not try to reproduce the Latin hexameter? A fairly close approximation to that form may be seen in John Betjeman's *In Memory of Basil, Marquess of Dufferin and Ava*, which begins:

> On such a morning as this
>   with the birds ricocheting their music
> Out of the whelming elms
>   to a copper beech's embrace
> And a sifting sound of leaves
>   from multitudinous branches
> Running across the park
>   to a chequer of light on the lake . . .

The very first syllables, however, show that, whether from choice or necessity, Betjeman is varying the dactylic rhythm. For (and we are really talking of stress, not quantity) the beat naturally falls on 'such' rather than 'on'. Similarly, in the opening of the third line ('And a sift-'), an anapaest has been substituted for a trochee. Again, the English stress system works against spondees. In two-syllable feet, except when the poet gives special orders to the contrary, we tend to stress one syllable rather than the other. Thus there is no stress on '-ing' or '-er' (2), on '-ing' or 'of' or 'from' (3), or on 'the' (4). Finally, in lines 2 and 4 the hexameter's final syllable is missing. This may be intended to recall the rhythm of an elegiac couplet; but if so, the effect is not maintained throughout the poem. So it is clear that Betjeman does not attempt to reproduce, in a strict sense, the rhythm of the Latin hexameter. No doubt the poet was well aware that, after a few lines, such attempts invariably become monotonous; for they work solely through stress, whereas a Latin hexameter exploits a subtle counterpoint of stress and quantity. The disadvantage can be seen very clearly in A. H. Clough's *The Bothie*, of which the second part opens like this:

> Morn, in yellow and white, came broadening out from the mountains,
> Long ere music and reel were hushed in the barn of the dancers.
> Duly in matutine bathed before eight some two of the party,
> There where in mornings was custom, where over a ledge of granite
> Into a granite basin descended the amber torrent.

Consideration of this and other attempts (one recalls, for example, Longfellow's *Evangeline* and Tennyson's 'Barbarous experiment') supports the view that there is something in the actual structure of English that tells against the metre—something that appears to be less of an obstacle in the case of German.

The present translation, then, is intended to recall, but not to reproduce, the rhythms of the Latin hexameter. Every line can (I hope) be read naturally with six stresses. Green allows himself greater latitude, as he signals in his opening lines:

> Must I *always* be stuck in the audience at these poetry-readings,
>   never (seven stresses)
> Up on a platform myself, taking it out on Codrus (six stresses)
> For the times he's bored me to death with ranting speeches
>   (five stresses).

Creekmore, on the other hand, imposes a much tighter discipline on himself; for as well as observing six stresses throughout he manages (nearly always) to rhyme:

> Must I be forever only a listener—
>   never talk back,
> Though bored so often by the *Theseid*
>   of Cordus, the hack?

This represents a considerable technical feat, of which I would not have been capable. But it is not (I think) wholly a matter of sour grapes to suggest that rhymes are not wanted, and that the compulsion to produce them results at times in artificiality, as in the opening of 16:

> Who, Gallius, can count the benefits
>   of serving a term
> In the fortunate army? If I could
>   enter a camp of affirmed
> Prosperity under a lucky star, I
>   myself would enlist
> As a trembling recruit. For an hour
>   of generous fate will assist
> You more than a letter of recommendation
>   to Mars from the hands
> Of Venus, or his mother, who delights
>   in the Samian sands.

The question of form is part of the larger question of authenticity. Here again there are different views. Robinson in his introduction says: 'What good is an ambition to give the pearls of ancient culture a readership such as today's best-sellers command, if the richness and the ancientness are thereby destroyed? For invariably they are . . . To adapt an old classic for popular consumption is to injure the qualities which make a confrontation with it worth some effort . . . Preserve the art, then, and preserve the strangeness' (pp. 12–13). Green, however, after drawing an illuminating parallel between Juvenal and Dickens (p. 23), concludes his introductory essay thus: 'Yes; Juvenal is a writer for this age. He has (in spite of his personal preoccupations) the universal eye for unchanging human corruption; he would be perfectly at home in a New York dive or a rigged political conference, ready to pillory the tycoons or degenerates who were elbowing him out of an easy job in some international organisation' (p. 63).

While granting to Robinson that some effort is needed to grasp the 'ancientness' of Juvenal's Rome, I doubt if, by producing something strange, one is necessarily preserving *Juvenal*'s strangeness, still less preserving his art. Here is how Robinson begins 16:

> Who could number the prizes, Gallius, of successful
> Soldiering? If one is entering prosperous barracks
> Under their lucky star me let the gate receive,
> Timid recruit. For one hour's kindly fate works more
> Than if from Venus a letter should commend us to Mars,
> She [*sic*] and his mother who delights in the Samos sand.

Surely Juvenal must be more accessible than that.

On the question of immediacy and relevance, then, I take much the same view as Green. More than that, I am aware of the qualities which have made his translation, along with its introduction and notes, the most widely-read version in recent times. Even if one knew nothing of his other work, one could tell from his Juvenal that Green was both an accomplished scholar and a resourceful writer. If I now indicate some divergencies in my own approach, I do so in the knowledge that these are matters of policy and tactics. First, to smooth the reader's path, Green supplies what he terms 'silent glosses' and 'functional substitutes'. Thus in 1. 20 the expression *magnus Auruncae alumnus* ('the great nursling of Aurunca', Loeb) is rendered by 'great Lucilius'. But (i) the reader may still be baffled by 'great Lucilius', and indeed Green quite rightly provides a note to say who he was. (ii) Although the reader may well fail to identify 'the great nursling of Aurunca', he can still infer that he was a respected predecessor of Juvenal's. (iii) The gloss involves the loss of the honorific periphrasis. If Juvenal had wanted to call Lucilius simply by his name, he would have done so. In 1. 12–13 Juvenal writes:

> Frontonis platani conuulsaque marmora clamant
> semper et adsiduo ruptae lectore columnae.

Green renders:

> The stale themes are bellowed daily
> In rich patrons' colonnades, till their marble pillars
> Crack with a surfeit of rhetoric. The plane-trees echo . . .

Here 'rich patrons'' is a functional substitution for 'Fronto's'. But in this case again, the necessary conclusion could have been drawn from the text, and the specific reference has been lost. True, there are numerous places where guessing is no good. In such instances, the reader of the present translation will have to refer to the notes, even if he happens to know some Latin. This is regrettable. However, most of its users will probably be students, reading Juvenal as part of an academic course. In the main such readers would prefer to know what is, and what is not, in the original text, even if that involves keeping their thumb in the notes. This point also applies in the case of very free versions like that of Mazzaro:

> Must I just listen? Mustn't I strike back
> when plagued by inept critics till I'm deaf?
> Shall writers spout their metrics till they're hoarse?
> Shall huge *Telephus* turn a good day black,
> *Orestes* with its scholarship still rife,
> unfinished, yet drone on without recourse?

There remains the matter of stylistic level. In the 1950s, Rolfe Humphries decided that the best way to convey Juvenal's liveliness was to employ (not continuously, but from time to time) the colloquial, even slangy, idiom of contemporary American speech. Thus, within a brief passage of Satire 1, we have 'when a limp eunuch gets wived', 'Curly the Cur of Canopus', and 'the man . . . greased by Dearie the dwarf with a bribe, with a lay by Miss Honey'. The same policy is adopted by Green; and it is fair to suppose that this kind of raciness has contributed something to the popularity of both his version and that of Humphries. Now nobody would want to deny that Juvenal was lively. But when, for example, between 6.42 and 6. 75 we come across expressions like 'You were once the randiest / Hot-rod-about-town', 'man, . . . you're aiming over the moon', 'that fellow who scored such a hit in the late-night / Show . . . camping it up like mad', 'One has a kink for ham actors . . . What else / Do you expect them to do? Go ape on a good book?', we wonder whether this can be the poet whose distinctive quality was described by Dr Johnson as 'a mixture of gaiety and stateliness, of pointed sentences [i.e. sharp epigrams] and declamatory grandeur'. It may be useful at this point to recall the distinction between two, overlapping, senses of 'vulgarity': (i) reference to sex, excretion, and other topics ignored in polite conversation; and, more generally (ii), the employment of colloquialisms in common use but avoided in more formal and dignified speech. As for (i), although Juvenal could at times be shockingly indecent, he rarely used the more basic verbal obscenities. He was equally sparing in regard to (ii). Both categories are briefly discussed in Courtney pp. 45–6. So although, to judge from his imitations, Johnson may have exaggerated the overall dignity of Juvenal's style, he was right not to see him as a vulgar writer in sense (ii). In that respect too, then, the present version will be more conservative than those of Humphries and Green.

In preparing it I have occasionally adopted suggestions made by Duff, Courtney, and Ferguson in their commentaries. And, notwithstanding what has been said above, I owe a good deal to the work of previous translators, in particular Evans, Ramsay, Humphries, and Green. A detailed account of my procedure is probably unnecessary. It will be enough to say that I would begin each passage by jotting down various key words, suitable phrases, and metrical units. After preparing a rough draft, I would then consult the commentaries and translations. If one or two of them had already thought of the same phrase, I did not feel obliged to discard it on that account. On other occasions, there might be a point or two in my draft where I was not satisfied with any of the possibilities that had occurred to me. On turning to the translations I would pick what seemed to be the most suitable idea, but I always tried to alter it in some way so as to preserve a decent degree of independence. Once or twice such modifications appeared to be impossible. For example, at 8. 155 Juvenal used the archaic, ritualistic, phrase *lanatas robumque iuuencum*. Green ingeniously renders it by 'a dun steer and eke a shearling'. This could not be taken over as it stood; nor did it seem possible to produce an acceptable variation. So I had to be content with a different and less striking expression.

The reader now knows, at least in theory, what kind of translation to expect. The important question, however, is whether he likes it. And that is something which only he can decide.

N.R.

Berkeley, 1988
Bristol, 1989

SELECT BIBLIOGRAPHY

For periodical literature between 1968 and 1978 see W. S. Anderson, *Classical World* 75 (1982). See also J. Ferguson's edition, pp. xxxiii–ix and the bibliographical notes appended to each satire. More recent work is noted in M. Coffey's 2nd edition.

Texts

W. V. Clausen (Oxford, repr. 1980)
E. Courtney (Rome, 1984)
J. R. C. Martyn (Amsterdam, 1987)

Commentaries

J. D. Duff (repr. with new introduction by M. Coffey, London, 1970)
J. Ferguson (London, 1979)
E. Courtney (London, 1980)

Translations

J. Dryden and others (London 1693, 2nd edn., 1697)
W. Gifford (London, 1802)
L. Evans (London, 1869)
G. G. Ramsay (London, 1918, rev. and repr. 1979)
R. Humphries (Indiana, 1958, repr. 1966)
H. Creekmore (New York, 1963)
J. Mazzaro (Ann Arbor, 1965)
P. Green (Harmondsworth, 1967, 2nd edn. 1974)
C. Plumb (London, 1968)
S. Robinson (Manchester, 1983)

Imitations

N. Rudd (ed.), *Johnson's Juvenal* (Bristol, 1981)

Studies of Juvenal

G. Highet, *Juvenal the Satirist* (Oxford, 1954)

H. A. Mason, 'Is Juvenal a Classic?', in *Critical Essays in Roman Literature: Satire*, ed. J. P. Sullivan (London, 1963), 93–167

J. Bramble, 'Martial and Juvenal', in *The Cambridge History of Classical Literature*, vol. 2 (Cambridge, 1982), 597–623

R. Jenkyns, 'Juvenal the Poet', in *Three Classical Poets* (London, 1982), 151–221

J. Ferguson, *A Prosopography to the Poems of Juvenal* (Brussels, 1987)

S. Braund, *Beyond Anger* (Cambridge, 1988)

R. E. Colton, *Juvenal's Use of Martial's Epigrams* (Las Palmas, forthcoming 1992)

Books on Roman Satire

U. Knoche, *Roman Satire* (Eng. trans. Bloomington and London, 1975)

W. S. Anderson, *Essays on Roman Satire* (Princeton, 1982)

N. Rudd, *Themes in Roman Satire* (London, 1986)

M. Coffey, *Roman Satire* (2nd edn. Bristol, 1989)

Books of Related Interest

R. Syme, *Tacitus*, 2 vols. (Oxford, 1958)

H. J. Rose, *A Handbook of Greek Mythology* (repr. London, 1965)

L. Friedländer, *Roman Life and Manners under the Early Empire*, 4 vols. (Eng. trans. repr. London, 1968)

Z. Yavetz, 'The Living Conditions of the Roman Plebs', in *The Crisis of the Roman Republic*, ed. R. Seager (Cambridge, 1969), 162–79

G. Kennedy, *The Art of Rhetoric in the Roman World*, *300 BC–AD 300* (Princeton, 1972)

A. Garzetti, *From Tiberius to the Antonines* (Eng. trans. London, 1974)

S. F. Bonner, *Education in Ancient Rome* (London, 1977)

J. P. V. D. Balsdon, *Romans and Aliens* (London, 1979)

J. N. Adams, *The Latin Sexual Vocabulary* (London, 1982)

B. K. Gold (ed.), *Literary and Artistic Patronage in Ancient Rome* (Austin, 1982)

R. P. Saller, *Personal Patronage under the Early Empire* (Cambridge, 1982)

C. M. Wells, *The Roman Empire* (Fontana, 1984)

A. Wallace-Hadrill (ed.), *Patronage in Ancient Society* (London, 1989)

LIST OF DATES

THE SATIRES

SATIRE 1

Why Write Satire?

Must I be always a listener only, never hit back,
although so often assailed by the hoarse *Theséid* of Cordus?
Never obtain revenge when X has read me his comedies,
Y his elegies? No revenge when my day has been wasted
by mighty Telephus or by Orestes who, having covered
the final margin, extends to the back, and still isn't finished?
No citizen's private house is more familiar to *him*
than the grove of Mars and Vulcan's cave near Aeolus' rocks
are to *me*; what the winds are up to, what ghosts are being
    tormented
on Aeacus' rack, from what far land another has stolen   10
a bit of gold pelt, how huge are the ash-trunks Monychus
    hurls—
the unending cry goes up from Fronto's plane-trees, his marble
statues and columns, shaken and shattered by non-stop
    readings.
One gets the same from every poet, great and small.
I too have snatched my hand from under the cane; I too
have tendered advice to Sulla to retire from public life
and sleep the sleep of the just. No point, when you meet so many
bards, in sparing paper (it's already doomed to destruction).
But why, you may ask, should I decide to cover the ground
o'er which the mighty son of Aurunca drove his team?   20
If you have time and are feeling receptive, here's my answer.

When a soft eunuch marries, and Mevia takes to sticking
a Tuscan boar, with a spear beside her naked breast,
when a fellow who made my stiff young beard crunch with his
    clippers

can challenge the whole upper class with his millions, single-
    handed;
when Crispinus, a blob of Nilotic scum, bred in Canópus,
hitches a cloak of Tyrian purple onto his shoulder
and flutters a simple ring of gold on his sweaty finger
(in summer he cannot bear the weight of a heavy stone),
it's hard *not* to write satire. For who could be so inured   30
to the wicked city, so dead to feeling, as to keep his temper
when the brand-new litter of Matho the lawyer heaves in sight,
filled with himself; then one who informed on a powerful friend
and will soon be tearing what's left of the carcase of Rome's
    aristocracy,
one who makes even Massa shiver, whom Carus caresses
with bribes, and Thymele too, sent by the frightened Latinus;
when you're shouldered aside by people who earn bequests at
    night,
people who reach the top by a form of social climbing
that now ensures success—through a rich old female's funnel?
Proculéius obtains a single twelfth, but Gillo eleven: 40
each heir's reward is assessed by the size of his organ.
Very well. Let each receive the price of his life-blood, becoming
as pale as a man who has stepped on a snake in his bare feet,
or is waiting to speak in the contest at the grim altar of Lyons.
Why need I tell how my heart shrivels in the heat of its anger,
when townsfolk are jostled by the flocks attending on one who
    has cheated
his ward and left him to prostitution, or on someone condemned
by a futile verdict? For what is disgrace if he keeps the money?
The exiled Marius drinks from two, happily braving
the wrath of heaven; the province which won is awarded—
    tears.
                                                                           50
Am I not right to think this calls for Venusia's lamp?
Am I not right to attack it? Would you rather I reeled off epics—
of Heracles or Diomédes or the labyrinth's frantic bellows,
the splash of the youngster hitting the sea, and the flying joiner,
when a pimp, if his wife is barred from benefit, coolly pockets
the gifts brought by her lover, trained to stare at the ceiling,
trained to snore in his cups through a nose that's wide awake;
when this man feels entitled to covet command of a cohort,

no longer possessing a family fortune, having presented
every cent to the stables—look at Autómedon junior   60
as he flies along the Flaminia, whipping the horses and holding
the reins himself, swanking in front of his girl in her greatcoat.
There, at the intersection, wouldn't you like to fill
a large-size notebook when a figure comes by on six pairs of
    shoulders
in a litter exposed on this side and that and almost indecent,
recalling in many ways the limp and sprawling Maecenas,
a forger of wills who has turned himself into a wealthy
    gentleman
with the simple aid of a sheet of paper and a moistened signet?
Here is a high-born lady, who just before handing her husband
some mellow Calenian adds a dash of shrivelling toad.   70
Surpassing Lucusta herself, she trains untutored neighbours
to brave the scandal and walk behind their blackened lords.
If you want to be anything, dare some deed that merits
    confinement
on Gýara's narrow shore; honesty is praised, and shivers.
Crime pays—look at those grounds and mansions and tables,
the antique silver, and the goat perched on the rim of the cup.
Who can sleep when a daughter-in-law is seduced for money,
when brides-to-be are corrupt, and schoolboys practise
    adultery?
If nature fails, then indignation generates verse,
doing the best it can, like mine or like Cluvienus'.   80

Once, when torrents of rain were raising the ocean's level,
Deucalion sailed to the top of a hill and sought for guidance.
Little by little the stones grew warm and soft with life,
and Pyrrha displayed her naked girls to the gaze of men.
What folks have done ever since—their hopes and fears and
    anger,
their pleasures, joys, and toing and froing—is my volume's
    hotch-potch.
Was there, at any time, a richer harvest of evil?
When did the pocket of greed gape wider? When was our dicing
ever so reckless? Your gambler leaves his wallet behind

as he goes to the table of chance; he plays with his *safe* at his
    elbow!   90
There what battles are to be seen, with the banker supplying
the weaponry! Is it just simple madness to lose a hundred
thousand, and then refuse a shirt to a shivering slave?
Which of our grandfathers built so many villas, or dined off
seven courses, alone? Today a little 'basket'
waits in the porch, to be snatched away by the toga'd rabble.
First, however, the steward anxiously peers at your face
for fear you may be an impostor using another's name.
No dole until you are checked. The crier is ordered to call
even the Trojan families; they too besiege the portals   100
along with us: 'See to the praetor, then to the tribune'.
A freedman's in front: '*I* was here first,' he says, 'why shouldn't I
stand my ground, without any fear or uneasiness? Granted,
I was born beside the Euphrates (the fancy holes in my ear-lobes
would prove it, whatever I said); but the five boutiques that I
    own
bring in four hundred thousand. What use is the broader purple,
if while Corvinus is tending the flocks which someone has leased
    him
out in the Laurentine country, I have a bigger fortune
than Pallas or Lícinus?' So, just let the tribunes wait;
let wealth prevail; no deference is due to their sacred office   110
from one who recently came to the city with whitened feet.
In our society nothing is held in such veneration
as the grandeur of riches, although as yet there stands no temple
for accursed Money to dwell in, no altar erected to Cash,
in the way we honour Peace, Good Faith, Victory, Valour,
and Concord, who when her nest is hailed replies with a clatter.

When the highest magistrate reckons up, at the end of the year,
what the 'basket' is worth, how much it adds to his assets,
what of his clients, who count on that for their clothes and
    footwear,
bread and fuel for their houses? The litters are jammed together   120
as they come for their hundred pieces. A sick or pregnant wife
follows behind her husband, and is carted round the circuit.
This man claims, with a well-known ruse, for an absent spouse.

Indicating an empty chair with its curtains drawn,
'That's my Galla,' he says. 'Don't keep her too long. Are you
    worried?
Galla, put out your head.'
                  'Leave her, she must be sleeping.'
The day itself is arranged in a splendid series of highlights:
'The basket', then the city square, with Apollo the lawyer
and the generals' statues—one, which some Egyptian wallah
has had the nerve to set up, listing all his achievements;   130
pissing (and worse) against his image is wholly in order.
. . . .
Weary old clients trudge away from the porches, resigning
what they had yearned for, though nothing stays with a man so
    long
as the hope of a dinner. Cabbage and kindling have to be
    purchased.
Meanwhile the magnate will lounge alone among empty
    couches,
chewing his way through the finest produce of sea and
    woodland.
(Yes, off all those antique tables, so wide and so stylish,
they gobble up their ancestors' wealth at a single sitting.)
Soon there'll be no parasites left. But who could abide
that blend of luxury and meanness? What size of gullet could
    order   140
a whole boar for itself, an animal born for parties?
But a reckoning is nigh. When you strip and, within that bloated
    body,
carry an undigested peacock into the bath-house,
death steps in, too quick for a will; old age is cancelled.
At once the joyful news goes dancing around the dinners.
The funeral cortège departs to the cheers of indignant friends.

There'll be no scope for new generations to add to our record
of rottenness; they will be just the same in their deeds and
    desires.
Every evil has reached a precipice. Up with the sail, then;
crowd on every stitch of canvas. Perhaps you may say 'But,   150
where is the talent fit for the theme? Where is the frankness

of earlier days which allowed men to write whatever they
    pleased
with burning passion ("Whose name do I not dare mention?
What does it matter if Mucius forgives what I say or not?")?
Portray Tigellínus; soon you will blaze as a living torch,
standing with others, smoking and burning, pinned by the
    throat,
driving a vivid pathway of light across the arena.'
So take this man who administered poison to three of his
    uncles—
is he to go by, looking down on us all from his aery cushions?
'Yes, when he comes to *you*, seal your lips with your finger.   160
Simply to utter the words "That's him!" will count as
    informing.
Without a qualm you can pit Aeneas against the ferocious
Rutulian; no one is placed at risk by the wounded Achilles,
or Hylas, so long sought when he'd gone the way of his bucket.
Whenever, as though with sword in hand, the hot Lucilius
roars in wrath, the listener flushes; his mind is affrighted
with a sense of sin, and his conscience sweats with secret guilt.
That's what causes anger and tears. So turn it over
in your mind before the bugle. Too late, when you've donned
    your helmet,
for second thoughts about combat.'   170
                    'I'll try what I may against those
whose ashes are buried beneath the Flaminia and the Latina.'

SATIRE 2

Hypocritical Perverts

One longs to escape from here beyond Sarmatia and the frozen
sea, when some people dare to pronounce on morality—those
    who
affect the Curii's style while living a Bacchic orgy.
First, they are ignorant, in spite of the plaster casts of
    Chrysippus
that fill their houses. The nearest any of them comes to culture
is to buy a copy of Aristotle's head or Píttacus' image,
or to have an original bust of Cleanthes placed on their
    sideboard.
Faces are not to be trusted. Why, every street is just full
of stern-faced sodomites. How can you lash corruption when
    you
are the most notorious furrow among our Socratic fairies?   10
Hirsute limbs, it is true, and arms that are stiff with bristles,
bespeak 'a soul of adamant'; but your anus is smooth, as the
    surgeon
notes with a grin when he takes a knife to your swollen piles.
Such fellows rarely talk. They've a mighty passion for silence;
and they keep their hair as short as their eyebrows. Peribomius,
    therefore,
provides a more honest and genuine case. *That* I put down to
the workings of fate. His walk and expression proclaim his
    disorder.
Such folk, by their candour, call for pity; their very obsession
secures indulgence. Far worse are those who condemn
    perversion
in Hercules' style, and having held forth about manly virtue,   20
wriggle their rumps. As the vile Varillus retorted to Sextus:
'Am I to respect a spaniel like you? You're no better than I am!'

Let the straight-limbed laugh at the cripple, the white at the
    negro;
but who could endure the Gracchi inveighing against sedition?
Would you not think the sky had fallen and the seas run dry,
if Verres expressed an abhorrence of thieves, and Milo of
    murderers?
if Clodius railed at seducers of wives, Catiline at Cethégus;
if Sulla's trio of pupils thundered against proscriptions?
Lately we saw such a man—an adulterer stained by a union
worthy of the tragic stage—reviving harsh legislation   30
which brought alarm to all, even to Mars and Venus,
at the very time when Julia was relieving her fertile womb
of so many a foetus, with every lump the image of Uncle.
So isn't it fair and just that the most depraved should be scornful
of bogus Scauri, and, when chastised, should snap in reprisal?

When one of those grim-faced ascetics was crying 'O Julian law,
where are you now? Wake up!' Laronia could not endure it,
and answered thus with a smile: 'It's a happy age that has you,
    sir,
to reform its morals; Rome had better clean itself up;
a third Cato has dropped from the sky! But seriously, tell me,   40
where did you get that lovely scent that is wafted in waves
from your hairy neck? You mustn't be shy about naming the
    shop.
If laws and statutes have to be wakened, you'd better begin,
    then,
by calling the Scantinian. Turn your attention first to the
    menfolk,
and scrutinize *them*. What they do is worse, yet they are
    defended
by their sheer numbers—serried ranks with shields
    interlocking.
Great unanimity reigns amongst effeminates; women
provide not a single case of such disgusting behaviour.
Tedia doesn't lick Cluvia's body, nor Flora Catulla's.
Hispo accommodates men, and is addicted to both perversions.   50
Do any of *us* plead at the bar, or set up to be experts
in civil law, or disturb your courts by causing an uproar?

Few of us wrestle; few of us feed on fighters' meat.
You card wool; and when you have finished, you carry the
    fleeces
back in baskets; you twirl the big-bellied spindle, and finger
the fine-spun thread, Penelope's peer, more deft than Arachne,
much like that slighted woman who sits, unkempt, on a tree-
    stump.
Everyone knows why Hister bequeathed his all to a freedman,
and why, when he lived, he showered gifts on his girlish wife.
The woman who sleeps third in a bed is bound to be wealthy.   60
Marry and shut your mouth; the price of silence is rubies.
In view of all this, does our sex deserve the verdict of guilty?
Our censor's rule condemns the doves while acquitting the
    ravens.'

On hearing such evident truths our Stoic brethren decamped
in disorder; for who could deny what Laronia said? But what
will the others stop at when Creticus wears a dress of chiffon,
and, as the audience stares at his clothes, inveighs against wives
like Prócula, say, or Pollitta? Fabulla dishonours her husband.
Condemn Carfinia too, if you wish. But however guilty,
she'll never be seen in a gown like that.   70
                              'But this is July, dear;
I'm hot!'
        Then plead in your loincloth; lunacy's less degrading.
What a garb for presenting new laws and enactments
before a community fresh from its triumphs, with wounds still
    open—
mountain folk who have left their ploughs to come and hear
    you!
Think of what you would say if you saw such clothes being
    worn
by a judge. I question if even a witness should appear in chiffon.
Creticus, fiery and headstrong, master of fearless expression,
you're shining through! This plague of yours has been caught
    through contact,
and will spread to others, as in the country a single pig
with scab or mange can cause the collapse of the total herd,   80
and as one grape can develop mould at the sight of another.

Soon you will venture something worse than a matter of
    clothing.
No one sinks to the bottom at once. Little by little
you will come to be welcomed within the houses of characters
    wearing
bonnets with flowing ribbons, and chokers around their necks.
These placate the Bona Dea with a young sow's belly
and a generous bowl of wine. But inverting the normal custom,
they drive all *women* away, and forbid them to enter the
    doorway.
The goddess's altar is only for men. 'Away with you, women,
outsiders all! No girl plays here on a groaning oboe!'   90
Such were the secret torchlight orgies in which the Dippers
used to disgust the goddess Cotyto in Cecrops' city.
One, with a slanting pencil, lengthens his eyebrows, touching
them up with moistened soot; raising his fluttering lids,
he blackens the rims. Another drinks from a phallic wine-glass,
the billowing mass of his hair confined in a golden hairnet.
He wears a blue checked robe, or a garment of greenish satin;
and his servant swears by his master's 'Juno'—a sign of his
    gender.
A third is clutching a mirror—the gear of Otho the pathic,
taken off the Auruncan Actor. He saw himself in it,   100
clad in full armour just as he ordered the troops to advance.
(A kit in a civil war containing a mirror—now *there*'s
a thing which rated a mention in the recent annals and history.
It was surely the mark of a supreme commander to eliminate
    Galba
and to take care of his skin, to aspire to the throne of the emperor   105
and to put bread on his face, spreading it out with his fingers.   107
The quivered Semíramis never did *that* in the realm of Assyria,
nor did the fierce Cleopatra on board her Actian warship.)
No restraint in language here or respect for the table;   110
here is Cybele's crew, with their uninhibited babel
of squeaky voices. A crazy old man with snow-white hair
presides at the rites, a rare and truly remarkable case
of voracious greed. He ought to be paid to give master classes.
But why hold back? It's time to follow the Phrygian mode:
just take a knife, and sever the lump of useless meat.

Four hundred thousand is the size of the dowry given by
    Gracchus
to a cornet player (or perhaps his horn was the straight variety).
The contract is signed, the blessing pronounced, a numerous
    party
is waiting; the newly-wed 'bride' reclines in the lap of her   120
    husband.
Shades of our forefathers! Is it a censor we need, or an augur?
Would you feel more horror, or think it more appalling a
    portent,
if a woman dropped a calf, or a cow gave birth to a lamb?
A long dress with veil and flounces is worn by a man
who carried a sacred shield of Mars by its mystic thong,
sweating beneath the swaying burden. Father of our city,
from where did such evil come to your Latin shepherds? From
    where
did this itch arise, o Lord of War, to plague your descendants?
Look—a man of family and fortune—being wed to a man!
Do you not shake your helmet or bang the ground with your
    spear,   130
or complain to your father? Away, then; quit the strenuous acres
of that great Park which you have forgotten.
                          'At dawn tomorrow
I have to keep an appointment, down in Quirinus' valley.'
'What's the occasion?'
                    'What do you think? A friend's being
married—
a small affair.' Such things, before we're very much older,
will be done in public—in *public*, and will want to appear in the
    papers!
These brides, however, are racked by one intractable problem:
they cannot conceive, and hold their husbands by having a baby.
It is well that Nature has given no power to their twisted
    emotions
over their bodies. They die without issue. For them no
    assistance   140
can be had from the bloated Lyde with her box of fertility drugs,
nor does it help to proffer their hands to the running Luperci.
(Gracchus surpassed even this enormity when, with tunic

and trident, he appeared as a fighter, and was chased across the
    arena,
a Roman of nobler birth than the Manlii or the Marcelli,
yes, or the scions of Catulus and Paulus, or the Fabian family,
or all the onlookers there in their front-row places, including
the man who provided the show where Gracchus cast his net.)

That there are such things as spirits of the dead and infernal
    regions,
the river Cocytus, and the Styx with inky frogs in its waters,   150
that so many thousands cross the stream in a single skiff,
not even children believe, unless they're still in the nursery.
But let's suppose it's true. What does Curius feel,
or the Scipios twain? What do Fabricius and the shade of
    Camillus,
and Crémera's legion and the valiant lads who fell at Cannae—
the dead of all those wars—when a ghost like this descends
from the world above? They'd insist on purification, if sulphur
and torches were to be had, and a laurel-twig dipped in water.
There, alas, we process in disgrace. Granted, our armies
have pushed beyond the Irish coast and the recently captured   160
Orkneys, and also Britain with its paltry ration of darkness.
But things go on at the centre of our victorious nation
which are not done by our conquered foes. They tell us,
    however,
that a Zálaces born in Armenia, even less manly than our
jeunesse dorée, has given himself to a passionate tribune.
That's what external relations involve. He came as a hostage;
but Rome is where 'men' are produced. If lads from abroad are
    permitted
a longer stay in the city, they'll never be short of lovers.
They'll get rid of their breeches along with their daggers and
    whips and bridles,
and then return to Artáxata carrying our teen-age morals.   170

SATIRE 3
The Evils of the Big City

Sad as I am at the fact that my dear old friend is leaving,
I applaud his decision to make his home in derelict Cumae,
thus providing the Sibyl with a solitary fellow townsman.
That's the gateway to Baiae, a charming coast with delightful
seclusion. I'd choose Próchyta's rocks before the Subúra.
When have you ever seen a place so dismal and lonely
that it doesn't seem worse to live in fear of continual fires,
collapsing houses, the countless threats of a savage city,
not to speak of poets reading their work in August.
As the whole of his house was being loaded on a single waggon,   10
he lingered beside the damp old arch of the Porta Capena.
At the place where Numa used to meet his sweetheart at night-
    time,
where now the grove, with its holy spring and temple, is rented
to Jews, whose paraphernalia consists of a hay-lined chest
(every tree is obliged to pay its rent to the people;
and so, with the Muses evicted, the wood has taken to begging),
we wander down the hill to Egeria's valley and a grotto
unlike the real thing. How much more palpably present
the fountain's spirit would be, if a grassy border surrounded
the water, and no marble profaned the native tufa!   20

Here Umbricius began: 'There is no room in the city
for respectable skills,' he said, 'and no reward for one's efforts.
Today my means are less than yesterday; come tomorrow,
the little left will be further reduced. So I'm going to make for
the place where Daedalus laid aside his weary wings.
While my greyness is new, and my ageing frame is fresh and
    upstanding,
while Láchesis still has thread to spin and I make my way

on my own two feet without the need of a stick to support me,
it's time to leave home. Let Artorius live there, and Catulus too;
let those remain who are able to turn black into white,   30
happily winning contracts for temple, river, and harbour,
for draining flooded land, and carrying corpses to the pyre—
men who auction themselves beneath the owners' spear.
Once these fellows were blowers of horns, a regular feature
of shows in the provinces, cheek-puffers known in the country
        townships.
Now they present their *own* productions, winning applause
by killing whoever is given the crowd's "thumbs down". They
        return
and lease latrines—and why stop at that? For they are the sort
that Lady Luck will take from the gutter and raise to the summit
of worldly success, whenever she feels like having a joke.   40

What can I do in Rome? I can't tell lies; if a book
is bad I cannot praise it and beg for a copy; the stars
in their courses mean nothing to me; I'm neither willing nor able
to promise a father's death; I've never studied the innards
of frogs; I leave it to others to carry instructions and presents
to a young bride from her lover; none will get help from me
in a theft; that's why I never appear on a governor's staff;
you'd think I was crippled—a useless trunk with a paralysed
        hand.
Who, these days, inspires affection except an accomplice—
one whose conscience boils and seethes with unspeakable
        secrets?   50
If someone tells you a *harmless* secret, he doesn't imagine
you have a hold over him; nor does he try to buy your silence.
Verres will love that man who knows he can prosecute Verres
whenever he likes. But all the sand of shady Tagus
and the gold it carries seaward would never compensate you
for losing your sleep and anxiously taking ephemeral gifts,
and always remaining a source of fear to your powerful friend.

I now proceed to speak of the nation specially favoured
by our wealthy compatriots, one that I shun above all others.
I shan't mince words. My fellow Romans, I cannot put up with   60

a city of Greeks; yet how much of the dregs is truly Achaean?
The Syrian Orontes has long been discharging into the Tiber,
carrying with it its language and morals and slanting strings,
complete with piper, not to speak of its native timbrels
and the girls who are told by their owners to ply their trade at the
    race-track.
(That's the place for a foreign whore with a coloured bonnet.)
Romulus, look—your bumpkin is donning his *Grecian* slippers,
hanging *Grecian* medals on a neck with a *Grecian* smudge.
He's from far-off Ámydon, *he*'s from Sícyon's heights,
these are from Andros and Samos and Tralles, or else Alabanda.   70
They make for the Esquiline, or the willows' hill, intent on
    becoming
the vital organs and eventual masters of our leading houses.
Nimble wits, a reckless nerve, and a ready tongue,
more glib than Isaeus'. Tell me, what do you think he *is*?
He has brought us, in his own person, every type you can think
    of;
teacher of grammar and speaking, geometer, painter, masseur,
prophet and tightrope-walker, doctor, wizard—your hungry
Greekling knows the lot; he'll climb to the sky if you ask him.
In fact, it wasn't a Moor, nor yet a Sarmatian or Thracian,
who sprouted wings, but a man born in the centre of Athens.   80
I must get away from them and their purple clothes. Shall our
    friend, here,
sign before me as a witness and recline above me at dinner—
one who was blown to Rome by the wind, with figs and
    damsons?
Does it count for nothing at all that I, from earliest childhood,
breathed the Aventine air and was fed on the Sabine berry?

What of the fact that the nation excels in flattery, praising
the talk of an ignorant patron, the looks of one who is ugly,
comparing the stalk-like neck of a weakling to Hercules'
    muscles
as he holds the giant Antaeus aloft well clear of the ground,
admiring a squeaky voice which sounds as wretched as that   90
of the cock, which seizes his partner's crest in the act of mating?
We, of course, can pay identical compliments; yes, but

they are *believed*. No actor from elsewhere is half as good
when playing Thais, or the wife, or Doris who's clad in no more
      than
her tunic. Why, the woman herself appears to be speaking,
not an actor at all; you'd swear that under the tummy
all was smooth and even, except for a tiny chink.
In Greece, however, Antíochus would not be thought an
      exception,
nor Strátocles, nor Demetrius along with the dainty Haemus;
the whole country's a play. You chuckle, he shakes with a louder 100
guffaw; he weeps if he spots a tear in the eye of his patron,
yet feels no grief; on a winter day if you ask for a brazier,
he dons a wrap; if you say 'I'm warm', he starts to perspire.
So we aren't on equal terms; he always has the advantage
who night and day alike is able to take his expression
from another's face, to throw up his hands and cheer if his patron
produces an echoing belch or pees in a good straight line,
or makes the golden receptacle clatter as its bottom flips over.

The man holds nothing sacred; nothing is safe from his organ,
not the lady of the house, nor the virgin daughter, nor even   110
her still unbearded fiancé, nor the hitherto clean-living son.
If none of these is at hand, he'll debauch his patron's grandma.   112
And since I have started to talk of the Greeks, forget the
      gymnasia;   114
think of a crime committed by a philosophical big-wig.
A Stoic brought about Barea's death. Though advanced in
      years,
he informed on his friend and pupil. Now *he* was born by the
      river
where a feather fell from the nag that sprang from the Gorgon's   120
      blood.
There's no room here for any Roman; the city is ruled by
some Protógenes or other, some Díphilus or Hermarchus.
A man like that never shares a friend (it's a national trait);
he keeps him all for himself. So when he has put in his patron's
ready ear a drop of his own and his country's poison,
I am pushed from the door; gone are my years of service.
Nowhere on earth does the loss of a client matter less.

Besides (not to flatter ourselves) what use is a poor man's
    attention
and service here if, when he goes to the trouble of dressing
and hurrying out in the dark, a praetor meanwhile is urging
his lictor to go full speed ("the childless are long since up")
for fear Albina and Modia may be greeted first by his
    colleague?   130
A free-born Roman's son concedes the inner position
to a rich man's slave. The latter pays as much as a tribune
of a legion earns in a year to Calvina or Catiena
to shudder on top of her once or twice; but you, however,
when you fancy Chíone's looks, will have to stop and think
    twice
before helping the dolled-up harlot down from her chair.
Produce a witness in Rome as good as the man who assisted
the Idaean goddess ashore, let Numa himself come forward,
or him who rescued the frightened Minerva from the burning
    temple,
they are interested first in his money (the *last* question concerns   140
his integrity): how many slaves does he keep, how many acres
of land does he own, how large and how many the plates on his
    table?
Whatever amount of cash a person has in his strong-box,
that's the extent of his credit. If a poor man swears by the altars
of Sámothrace and of Rome, people assume that he's flouting
the gods and their thunderbolts, with the consent of the gods
    themselves.
That same man, moreover, provides a cause and occasion
for universal amusement if his cloak is ripped and muddy,
if his toga is a little stained, and one of his shoes gapes open
where the leather is split apart, or if several scars are apparent   150
where coarse new thread proclaims that a wound has been sewn
    together.
Of all that luckless poverty involves, nothing is harsher
than the fact that it makes people funny.
                    "Shame on you!" says the speaker.
"Kindly leave the cushioned seats reserved for the knights,
if your means are less than the law requires. You will give your
    place

to brothel-keepers' boys, who first saw the light in some
    bawdy-house.
The debonair son of an auctioneer can sit and applaud here,
on his right a fighter's well-dressed lad, on his left a trainer's."
Thus decreed the brainless Otho, who assigned us our places.
Who is accepted as a son-in-law here, if he doesn't have funds   160
to match his fiancée's dowry? When is a poor man named
as an heir, or consulted by aediles? Citizens lacking in substance
should long ago have banded together and marched out of
    town.

It's hard for people to rise in the world when their talents are
    thwarted
by living conditions of cramping poverty. At Rome, however,
their task is especially hard; dingy lodgings are costly,
costly are servants' stomachs; a meagre supper is costly.
It's shaming to eat off earthenware; but you wouldn't despise it
if suddenly whisked away to a Marsian or Sabine table.
There a cloak with a coarse blue hood would be quite sufficient.   170
We may as well face the truth. In most of Italy no one
puts on a toga until he's dead. On grand occasions,
when a public holiday is being held in a grassy theatre,
and the well-known farce, so long awaited, returns to the
    platform
(the peasant child in its mother's arms cowers in fear
when confronted by the gaping mouth of the whitened mask),
even then you will see similar clothes being worn
by the stalls and the rest alike; as robes of their lofty office,
the highest aediles are content to appear in plain white tunics.
Here the style of people's clothes is beyond their means.   180
Too much tends to be borrowed here from another's account.
That is a universal failing. All of us live
in pretentious poverty. Why elaborate? Nothing in Rome
is ever free. What does it cost you, once in a while,
to call on Cossus or win a tight-lipped glance from Veiento?
The beloved of one is having his beard, of another his hair cut;
the house is full of cakes; for each there's a "contribution".
"Here, just take it, and keep your yeast!" As clients we have to
pay our fee and swell the savings of well-dressed servants.

Who is afraid, or was ever afraid, of his house collapsing   190
in cool Praeneste, or among Volsinii's tree-clad hills,
in Gabii, so plain and simple, or in Tibur's lofty fastness?
Here we live in a city which, to a large extent,
is supported by rickety props; that's how the landlord's agent
stops it falling. He covers a gap in the chinky old building,
then "sleep easy!" he says, when the ruin is poised to collapse.
One ought to live where fires don't happen, where alarms at
    night
are unknown. Ucalegon's shouting "Fire!" and moving to safety
his bits and pieces; your third floor is already smoking;
you are oblivious. If the panic starts at the foot of the stairs,   200
the last to burn is the man who is screened from the rain by
    nothing
except the tiles, where eggs are laid by the gentle doves.
Cordus possessed a bed too small for Prócula, a handful
of little pots adorning his sideboard, below them a tiny
mug, and, supporting the whole, a marble Chiron couchant.
A chest, now far from new, contained some volumes of Greek;
and illiterate mice were busy gnawing the deathless verses.
Cordus had nothing. Quite. But still, the unfortunate fellow
lost that nothing—every bit of it. Then, as a final
straw on his heap of woe, when he hasn't a stitch and is begging   210
for scraps, no one will help him with food or lodging or shelter.
If Asturicus' mansion is gutted, the nobles appear in mourning,
their ladies with hair dishevelled; the praetor adjourns his
    hearing.
Then we lament the city's disasters and rail at fire.
Before the flames are out, one comes forward with marble,
or an offer of building materials; another with nude white
    statues;
another presents a masterpiece of Euphránor, and bronzes
of Polyclítus, once the glory of Asian temples.
He gives books and shelves, and a Minerva to stand in the
    middle;
he a coffer of silver. More, and superior, items   220
are showered on Persicus the childless magnate, who not
    without reason
is now suspected of having set fire to his own house.

If you can tear yourself from the races, an excellent house
can be bought outright at Frúsino, or Fabratéria, or Sora
for the price you pay these days as yearly rent for a hell-hole.
There you will have a plot, with a well so shallow that water
can be drawn without a rope and sprinkled over your seedlings.
Live wedded to the hoe, and tend your well-kept garden,
until you can give a feast to a hundred Pythagoreans.
It is some achievement in any place, however remote,   230
to become the proud possessor of a solitary lizard.
Here most invalids die from lack of sleep (but the illness
itself is caused by food which lies there undigested
on a feverish stomach); who ever obtained a good night's rest
in rented lodgings? It costs a fortune to sleep in the city.
That's the root of the trouble. The coming and going of
     waggons
in the narrow winding streets, the yells at a halted herd,
would banish sleep from even a seal or the emperor Drusus.
If duty calls, as the crowd falls back, the rich man passes
quickly above their faces in a large Liburnian galley,   240
reading or writing or taking a nap as he speeds along.
(The closed windows of a litter can make the occupant drowsy.)
Yet he'll arrive before us. As we hurry along we are blocked
by a wave in front; behind, a massive multitude crushes
my pelvis; *he* digs in with an elbow, *he* with a hard-wood
pole; then *he* hits my head with a beam, and *he* with a wine-jar.
My legs are caked with mud; from every side I am trampled
by giant feet; a soldier stamps on my toe with his hob-nails.
Look at all that smoke; a crowd is having a picnic.
A hundred guests, each with a portable kitchen behind him.   250
Córbulo could hardly carry so many enormous utensils,
so many things on his head, as that unfortunate slave-boy,
who keeps his head erect and fans the flame as he runs.
Freshly mended tunics are ripped; a giant fir-tree
on a swaying cart comes bearing down; another waggon
carries a pine; they nod overhead and threaten the people.
For if the axle transporting Ligurian marble collapses,
tipping its mountainous load down on the hordes beneath,
what is left of their bodies? Who can locate their limbs
or bones? Each casualty's corpse is crushed out of existence,   260

just like his soul. Meanwhile at home, unaware of what's
   happened,
they're washing dishes, puffing at the fire, making a clatter
with greasy scrapers, laying out towels and filling the oil-flask.
The staff is busy with various tasks; but he is already
sitting on the bank, a new arrival, dreading the frightful
ferryman; vainly he waits for the bark of those muddy waters,
poor devil, having no coin to offer between his teeth.

Consider now the various other nocturnal perils:
how far it is up to those towering floors from which a potsherd
smashes your brains; how often leaky and broken fragments   270
fall from the windows; and with what impact they strike the
   pavement,
leaving it chipped and shattered. You may well be regarded as
   slack,
and heedless of sudden disaster, if you fail to make your will
before going out to dinner. There's a separate form of death
that night in every window that watches you passing beneath it.
So hope, and utter a piteous prayer, as you walk along
that they may be willing to jettison only what's *in* their slop-pails.
Your drunken thug who has failed, by chance, to record a
   murder
pays the price; he spends the night as Achilles did
when mourning his friend; he lies on his face and then on his
   back.   280
For sleep, a brawl is needed. But however wild the youth,   282
and however heated with wine, he carefully skirts the figure
protected by a scarlet cloak and an endless line of attendants,
and a swathe of light which is cut by flaming lamps of brass.
He despises *me*; for I am escorted home by the moon,
and the light of a guttering candle, whose wick I carefully tend
and conserve. Now this is how the horrible fight begins
(if fight it is, where you do the punching and I just take it):
he stands in my way and tells me to halt. One has to obey him;   290
for what can you do when you're in the power of a madman,
   who also
is stronger than you are? "Where have you been?" he bellows,
   "And whose

beans and plonk have given you wind? Well, who is the cobbler
you've sat with scoffing the tops of leeks and a boiled sheep's
   head?
No answer, eh? You'd better talk, or I'll put the boot in!
Come on then, where's your pitch? What synagogue do you go
   to?"
Whether you try to converse or to steal away without speaking,
it's all the same. They will beat you up; then, highly indignant,
take you to court. A poor man's rights are confined to this:
having been pounded and punched to a jelly, to beg and implore   300
that he may be allowed to go home with a few teeth in his head.

That is not all you have to fear. When your house is shut,
when your shop is secured by chains, when every shutter is
   fastened,
and all is silent, there will still be somebody there to rob you.
Sometimes a villain will suddenly do the job with a dagger.
Whenever the Pontine marshes and the Gallinarian forest
are, both of them, rendered safe by armed patrols, such people
converge in a body on Rome, as though on a game reserve.
What forge, what anvil, is not beset with heavy chains?
Most of our iron is used for fetters; hence we are threatened   310
with a shortage of ploughs and a serious dearth of hoes and
   mattocks.
Happy, one feels, were our distant ancestors, happy the ages
which lived of old beneath the rule of kings and tribunes,
in the days when a single jail sufficed the capital city.

In addition to these, I could give you several other reasons.
But the mules are calling and the sun is setting; it's time to be off.
The driver has long been waving his whip to show he's ready.
Good-bye, then; now and again spare me a thought; and
   whenever
you manage to get out of Rome for a break, and return to
   Aquinum,
ask me up from Cumae to visit Helvius' Ceres   320
and your Diana. I'll don my boots and come to your chilly
district, to hear your satires—unless they would feel
   embarrassed.'

SATIRE 4

The Emperor's Fish

Here is Crispinus again (indeed I shall often be bringing him
onto the stage), a monster of vice without a redeeming
virtue, a sickly fop, though strong enough when it comes
to lechery; only the unmarried are spared his lewd attentions.
What matter, therefore, the length of the colonnades where he
    wearies
his mules, the size of the shady groves in which he is driven,
the number of mansions he owns, or his acres close to the
    Forum?
A villain is never happy, least of all a seducer
(polluted at that) with whom a Vestal recently slept,
thus dooming herself to be entombed with her heart still
    beating.   10

Now to less serious matters. (But if anyone else had done
what I'm going to relate, he would have been condemned by the
    censor.
An act which would have disgraced X or Y was in order
for Crispinus. What can you do when the person himself is
    appalling
and more repulsive than any charge?) He purchased a mullet
for six thousand—in fact exactly a thousand a pound,
as those who go in for fishing stories would probably put it.
I'd happily praise his clever move, had he used the present
to grab the most favoured place in the will of a childless dotard,
or (a better ploy) had given it all to a high-born mistress   20
who rode in a cavernous litter with screens on its picture
    windows.
Nothing like that; he bought it for himself. We see things done

which the modest and frugal Apicius balked at. Did you,
   Crispinus,
you who once wore a loincloth made of your native papyrus,
pay that money for scales? The fisherman might have been
   purchased
at a smaller price than the fish. For that, a sizeable holding
may be had in the provinces; yes, and a larger still in Apulia.
Just imagine what banquets then were guzzled by his Highness,
the emperor himself, when so many thousands (the merest
   fraction,
no more than a side-dish of one of his ordinary dinners)   30
were belched up by the purple-clad clown of the royal palace.
Now he is chief of the knights, but he used to shout as he peddled
his fellow townsmen, Alexandrian fish, from a damaged cargo.

Begin, Calliope—and do sit down, it isn't a matter
for singing; the theme is a true event; recount it, ye maidens
of Pieria—and may I win some credit for calling you maidens.
In the days when the last of the Flavian line was tearing to pieces
a half-dead world, and Rome was slave to a bald-headed Nero,
off the temple of Venus, which stands above Doric Ancona,
an Adriatic turbot of wonderful size was caught.   40
It stuck there, filling the bag of the net, no smaller than those
which the ice of Maeotis covers and then, when broken at last
by the sun, releases to be swept to the mouth of the Pontic flood,
torpid with sloth and fattened by the long cold of the winter.
The owner of the boat and net resolved to present the monster
to the highest priest. For who would dare to put on display
or buy such a fish, when the shores were filled with crowds of
   informers?
The public inspectors of seaweed, now so widely deployed,
would at once have brought an action against the ill-clad
   boatman,
quite prepared to assert that this was a runaway turbot   50
which had long been fattened in Caesar's fish-pond; having
   escaped
from there, it should by rights be returned to its former owner.
If we accept Palfurius' view or Armillatus',
every rare and beautiful creature within the ocean,

wherever it swims, is the emperor's property. So, to prevent it
going to waste, it will be presented. The deadly autumn
was yielding to frost, patients were hoping for quartan fevers,
and the catch was keeping fresh in the howling blasts of winter.
But the man sped on, as though pursued by a southerly breeze.
When he reached a point above the lakes, where the ruins of
   Alba   60
preserve the Trojan flame and worship a smaller Vesta,
his entry was blocked for a little while by a gaping crowd.
Then a path was cleared, and the gates swung open on easy
   hinges.
The senators, still shut out, beheld the morsel's admission.
Ushered into Atreides' presence, the Picene spoke:
'Accept a gift too great for a commoner's oven; let this
be a holiday; come, expand your tummy with an excellent feed,
and eat a turbot preserved to adorn your glorious epoch.
He *wished* to be caught!' Could anything have been more
   blatant? No matter;
his comb began to rise. When power which is virtually equal   70
to that of the gods is flattered, there's nothing it can't believe.

However, no dish of the requisite size could be found for the
   turbot.
So the privy council was summoned. He hated them all, and
   their faces
carried the pallor that goes with a great and sickening friendship.
'Quickly,' shouted Liburnus, 'he has taken his seat already!'
Snatching up his cloak, Pegasus headed the scramble,
recently installed as bailiff over the terrified city.
(Well, what else were the prefects then? The best and most
   honest
jurist among them, Pegasus, vainly held that in spite of
the terrible times every case should be handled by Justice   80
without her sword.) Then came the aged agreeable Crispus,
a gentle soul, whose style of speaking closely reflected
his character. None would have given more useful advice to a
   monarch
ruling nations by land and sea, had he been able
under that plague, that disaster, to offer honest proposals

and to combat cruelty. But what more vicious than the ear of a
    tyrant
on whose caprice depended the life of a friend who was meaning
simply to chat about the rain, or the heat, or the showery spring?
In consequence, Crispus never struck out against the current;
nor was he ever that noble type of Roman subject   90
who could freely state his opinions and risk his life for the truth.
Thus he survived for eighty winters and as many summers,
protected by that armour, even in such a court.
Next in the rush came Acílius, a man of similar age,
with his son, who little deserved the cruel and premature death
which lay in store to be dealt by the sword of his master. (For
    long, though,
the combination of age and birth has seemed like a portent.
Better to be little brother to a towering son of the soil.)
It did the unfortunate man no good to strip like a hunter,
and, standing close, to spear Numidian bears in the Alban   100
arena. Nowadays everyone's wise to the ploys attempted
by the aristocracy. No one's impressed by the ancient cunning
of Brutus; it is easy to fool a king with an old-world beard.

Next, looking just as ghastly in spite of his humble background,
came Rubrius, charged with an earlier crime which must not be
    mentioned,
and yet with all the nerve of a sodomite writing satire.
Montanus (the Stomach) also arrived, slowed down by his belly;
then Crispinus, reeking with perfume applied that morning,
more overpowering than a pair of funerals; also Pompeius,
a crueller man, who could slit a throat with the softest whisper; 110
and Fuscus who then was studying war in his Tuscan villa,
saving his flesh to provide a feast for the Dacian vultures.
The prudent Veiento came, along with the deadly Catullus,
who burned with passionate love for a girl he had never seen—
a major, remarkable freak even in times like our own.   115
He should have been one of the beggars who blow obsequious
    kisses   117
as they throng the wheels of carriages jolting down to Arícia.
No one was more amazed at the turbot. Facing left,
he was voluble in its praise. The creature, however, was lying   120

on his right. So too he would cheer with gusto at the cut and
   thrust
of Cilix, and at the contraption that whisks boys up to the
   awning.
Veiento rose to the challenge, and, like a priest of Bellona
goaded to frenzy, broke into prophecy: 'There,' he intoned,
'you have a gigantic omen of great and glorious victory.
You will take some monarch prisoner; or else Arvíragus will
   tumble
from the pole of a British chariot. Like him, the creature is
   foreign;
look at the spikes that march up his spine!' The only omission
on Fabricius' part was to give the turbot's age and birthplace.

'So what do you recommend? Cut him in pieces?'   130
                                     'Ah spare him
that indignity!' pleaded Montanus, 'Make him a platter
fit to encircle his massive bulk with its thin defences—
a dish that calls for a mighty Prometheus to burst on the scene.
Make haste, bring hither clay and wheel. From this day forward,
Caesar, I pray you have potters on hand within your
   headquarters!'
The motion was carried; it suited a man who had been familiar
with the old imperial court's extravagance—Nero carousing
at midnight, the second hunger that grew as Falernian heated
the lungs. Within my lifetime, none has had greater skill
in the art of eating. He knew from the very first bite of an oyster   140
whether it hailed from Circeii, or the rocks of the Lucrine Lake,
or whether it saw the light in a bed at Richborough, England.
He could also tell at a glance what shore a sea-urchin came from.

The council ended. The members rose, and were duly
   dismissed—
men whom the mighty leader had dragged to his Alban fortress,
all in a state of terror, commanded to hurry as though
they were going to hear a dispatch concerning the savage
   Sygambri,
or the Chatti, perhaps; as though from distant parts of the world
disastrous news had just come in on the wings of panic.

Yes, and how much better, had he spent on these silly
     amusements   150
all those savage years when he plundered Rome of her noblest
and most distinguished souls with none to avenge or punish!
But though he could stain his hands with the Lamiae's blood,
     when he started
to arouse the workers' fears, from that point on he was doomed.

SATIRE 5

A Tyrannical Host

If you are still unashamed of your plan, and retain your
    conviction
that the highest good is to live from the crumbs of another's loaf,
if you can stand for what Sarmentus or even the worthless
Gabba would not have endured at Caesar's graded table,
I'd be wary of taking your word, although you gave it on oath.
Nothing I know calls for less expense than the belly. However,
suppose you lack the little it takes to fill the void,
is there no room on the pavement? No bridge, or even a minor
share in a mat? Do you set such store by being insulted;
is your hunger so famished? Would it not be less degrading to
    shiver   10
where you are, and to nibble at the mouldy crust that's thrown
    to a dog?

Get this clear at the start: an invitation to dinner
counts as payment in full for all your previous service.
The reward of such great friendship is food. Your patron
    records it;
yes, he records it, however infrequent. Eventually, after
neglecting a client for two months, he decides to invite him,
to prevent the third place on the couch from lying empty.
'Come and join us,' he says. It's a dream come true! Can you ask
for more? Why, Trebius now has a reason for interrupting
his sleep, and leaving his shoes untied in a panic, in case   20
the crowd of morning callers has made the rounds already,
as the stars are fading, or at that hour when the frosty waggon
of the sluggish herdsman wheels its journey across the sky.

But what a dinner! Wine which a woollen swab would refuse
to mop up; before your eyes a guest turns into a dervish.

Wrangling starts the proceedings; soon a fight will be raging
between you and a squad of freedmen, with Saguntine crockery
flying around; you yourself will be hurling goblets,
and, when hit, be stanching your wounds with a bloody napkin.
His Lordship's wine was bottled in the year of a long-haired
    consul;   30
he has in his hand a grape that was trodden in the War with the
    Allies.
Though he'd never send a spoonful to a friend who had
    indigestion,
tomorrow *he* will be drinking something grown on the Alban
or the Setine hills (over the years its date and district
have vanished under layers of soot on the ancient jar),
the kind that Thrasea and Helvidius would drink, wearing
    garlands,
on the birthdays of the Bruti and Cassius. The generous cups
    which Virro
holds in his hand are overlaid with Helios' daughters,
and studded with beryl. Gold is never entrusted to you,
or, when it is, a guard at once is stationed behind you   40
to count the jewels and watch what your sharpened nails are up
    to.
One can't blame Virro; his splendid jasper is widely admired.
He, like many another, transfers the stones from his fingers
to his cups—stones which the youth who was once preferred to
    Iarbas,
that jealous prince, would mount on the outer side of his
    scabbard.
You will drain a four-nosed vessel, which got its name
from a Beneventan cobbler; now it is badly cracked,
and should be offering its broken glass in exchange for matches.

If the food and wine have brought a fever to the master's
    stomach,
sterilized water is ordered, more cool than the Getic snows.   50
Did I complain just now that you had a different wine?
Your *water* is different! And the service? You will receive your
    cup

from a Saharan footman, or the bony hand of a black-faced
    Moor,
a character whom you would rather not meet in the middle of
    the night
when driving uphill past the tombs on the *Via Latina*.
The flower of Asia waits on the host, bought for a figure
beyond the total assets of the valiant Tullus and Ancus,
beyond (to be brief) the paltry junk of all the kings
of early Rome. So catch your African Ganymede's eye,
when you need a drink. A lad who cost so many thousands   60
cannot pour for a pauper. Oh well, such insolence goes
with youth and beauty. But when will the other get round to
    you?
When will he come, when you've called him, with water, hot or
    cold?
No doubt he resents obeying a long-standing client, and the fact
    that
you give orders, and that you recline while he is serving.
All the major houses are full of arrogant servants.
Here's another. Grumbling audibly, he hands you some bread
which is almost unbreakable—mouldy lumps of heavy
    dough,
which rattle your molars and resist every attempt at biting.
The kind reserved for the master is soft and snowy white,   70
kneaded from the finest flour. Your hand shoots out—restrain
    it!
The bread-pan must be respected. But suppose you feel a bit
    naughty,
there's always a voice from above which insists that you put it
    back:
'You impertinent fellow! Kindly use the proper basket
when helping yourself. You must know the colour of your own
    bread!'
('This, if you please, was the honour for which I daily
    abandoned
my wife and struggled up the Esquiline's freezing slope,
as Jupiter raged above with his equinoctial blizzards,
sending the rain running in rivulets down my cloak.')

That lobster there, adorning the dish on its way to the master—   80
look at the length of its body and how it is walled around
with choice asparagus; see how its tail looks down on the party
as it enters, borne aloft by the hands of a towering waiter.
You are served with a prawn, hemmed in by half an egg,
crouched on a tiny saucer, a meal fit for a ghost.
His Lordship drowns his fish in Venafran, but this anaemic
cabbage that's coming to you will smell strongly of lamp-oil.
The oil judged fit for *your* stomach has been imported,
carried up river by one of Micipsa's sharp-nosed canoes,
which explains why no one in Rome will enter the bath with
     Boccar.   90
It even ensures protection against the deadliest vipers.
The master will eat a mullet dispatched from Corsica, or from
Tauromenium's rocks, now that our local waters
are all fished out and exhausted. Gluttony's on the rampage;
the nearest grounds have been swept clean by the market's non-
     stop
trawling. Tyrrhenian fish are not allowed to grow up.
The provinces therefore supply our kitchens; from there is
     imported
what Laenas the legacy-hunter can buy (to be sold by Aurelia).
Virro is served with a lamprey, the hugest yet to come forth
from Sicily's straits. For when the wind from the south is
     resting,   100
sitting idly in his cell and drying his soaking wings,
daring nets will defy the risks of Charybdis' channel.
Waiting for you is an eel, the long thin water-snake's cousin,
or a greedy Tiber bass, covered with blotches, himself
a slave reared by the banks, and fed on the flood of the sewer,
who can find his way right up to the drain of the central Subura.

I'd like a word with the host, if he'd deign to lend an ear:
'No one expects what used to be sent to their humbler friends
by Seneca or Piso the Good, or the gifts which Cotta was wont
to bestow (for then the honour of giving was prized more highly   110
than titles and symbols of office). All we ask is this:
that you treat us as fellow-citizens. Do that, and then you can be,
like many another, rich to yourself and poor to your friends.'

In front of him is a goose's liver, and (as big as a goose)
a capon, and also a foaming boar, fit for the blade
of the blond Meleager. Next on his menu are truffles,
    provided
it's spring and the thunder everyone prays for swells the feast.
'O land of Libya,' Alledius says, 'you can keep your harvests,
and unyoke your teams of oxen, so long as you send us truffles.'
Meanwhile, just to ensure that your cup of anger is brimming,   120
watch the carver waving his arms like an Indian dancer,
flashing his knife until he has finished all of his teacher's
programme. Yes, for of course it's a matter of vital importance
what flourish is right for slicing a hare and what for a hen.
If you dare to open your mouth, as if you possessed the triple
name of a free-born Roman, you'll be lugged outside by the
    heel,
as Cacus was when Hercules clubbed him. When will Virro
drink your health or accept the goblet bearing the imprint
of your lips? Which of you, pray, is so utterly reckless,
so dead to shame, as to say 'Cheers!' to his Lordship? There's
    many   130
a thing that cannot be said by folks with holes in their mantle.
Suppose you were handed 'four hundred' by a god, or a mere
    human-being
resembling a god and kinder than fate—hey presto! from
    nothing
you'd suddenly find you were one of Virro's dearest friends.
('Give some to Trebius, serve it to Trebius; brother, you'd care
    for
a bit of the loin?') Cash! It's cash that wins such attention,
cash that makes you his 'brother'. But if you mean to end up
as a big-wig, or as a big-wig's boss, no tiny Aeneas
must play within your halls or, even more charming, a
    daughter.
Close, warm-hearted, friends are created by a barren wife.   140
But if your Mycale now gave birth, and of a sudden deposited
a trio of sons in their father's arms, then Virro would beam
at the chattering brood; he would order jackets of racing green,
and kindly dispense little nuts on request and shiny coppers,
whenever an infant parasite came to his dinner table.

Doubtful fungi are served to friends of no importance;
to the master, a mushroom just like those which Claudius ate,
before the one prepared by his wife put an end to his eating.
For himself and friends of equal status, Virro will order
fruit to be handed round whose scent is a meal in itself,   150
the kind that used to grow in Phaeacia's endless autumns,
or such as you might believe was filched from the African
    sisters.
You are regaled with a rotten apple, of the kind that is gnawed
by a creature upon the Embankment, who learns in shield and
    helmet
through fear of the whip to throw a spear from a hairy she-goat.

Perhaps you imagine that Virro is simply saving money.
No, he does it to make you suffer. What farce or slapstick
is greater fun than a whining glutton? His whole intention,
depend on it, is to reduce you to tears of helpless rage,
to make you sit there grinding your teeth throughout the
    evening.   160
To you, you're a free person, the guest of a wealthy patron.
He thinks you have been enslaved by the smell of his kitchen;
and he's not far wrong. For who is so destitute as to endure him
a second time—assuming he wears the childhood *bulla*
of Tuscan gold, or even a poor man's knot of leather?
The hope of a lavish dinner—that's what attracts you: 'Ah now
    then,
he'll give us a bit of the hare's carcass or the haunch of pork;
what's left of the chicken will come our way.' So all of you draw
your bread-sticks, holding them clean and ready, waiting in
    silence.
He knows what he's doing, treating you like that. For if you can
    stomach   170
every insult, then serve you right. Sooner or later
you'll shave your head and let it be pummelled; you will not
    shrink
from a flogging. You deserve just that kind of dinner and that
    kind of friend.

SATIRE 6

Roman Wives

Chastity lingered on earth, they say, in the reign of Saturn.
She was long to be seen in the days when a freezing cave
   provided
a tiny home, complete with hearth and household gods,
and enclosed both herds and owners within a communal gloom,
in the days when a mountain wife would spread her woodland
   couch
with leaves and straw and the skins of beasts who lived in the
   district.
She wasn't at all like Cynthia, or like that other lady
whose lustrous eyes were dimmed and spoiled by the death of a
   sparrow.
Giving her breasts, with plenty to drink, to her mighty babes,
she was often more uncouth than her acorn-belching husband.   10
People, of course, lived differently then, when the world was
   young
and the sky was new—people born from the riven oak
or freshly fashioned from mud, who had no proper parents.
Some, if not many, traces of Chastity's former presence
may have survived under Jove, before the Lord of Olympus
had yet acquired a beard, before the Greeks were ready
to swear on another's life, when fruit and cabbages flourished
untroubled by thieves, and no one bothered with garden walls.
Then, little by little, Justice withdrew to heaven,
and Chastity with her. The two sisters departed together.   20

Postumus, old and hallowed by time is the custom of rattling
your neighbour's bed, defying the spirit that guards a marriage.
Other crimes came later, produced by the age of iron.
It was the silver age that beheld the first adulterers.

And yet, in a time like ours, you are preparing a contract
with terms for a binding marriage; by now you're under the
   comb
of the senior stylist; perhaps you've placed a ring on her finger.
Postumus marrying? You used to be sane; no doubt about that.
What Fury, then, with her maddening snakes is hunting you
   down?
Can you bear to be the slave of a woman, when so much rope is
   at hand,   30
when those vertiginous top-floor windows are standing open,
and when the Aemilian bridge nearby offers assistance?
If none of these means of deliverance seems to have any appeal,
don't you think it better to sleep with a little boy-friend?
A boy-friend doesn't argue all night or ask you for presents
as he lies beside you, or complain that you are not giving a
   hundred
percent and are not producing the requisite panting and puffing.

Ursidius supports the Julian law; he intends to bring up
a darling heir, though he thereby forfeits the bearded mullets
and fattened doves—all bait from the legacy-hunting market.   40
Will wonders never cease? A woman is willing to marry
Ursidius. He who was once the most notorious lecher,
a man who often crouched in the chest of imperilled Latinus,
is now inserting his stupid head in the noose of marriage.
Not only that; he wants a wife with old-fashioned morals!
Call the doctor! His veins are carrying too much blood.
And how fastidious! Anyone having the luck to discover
a pure-lipped lady should fall before the Tarpeian shrine
in awe and gratitude, and offer Juno a gilded heifer
(few indeed are worthy to touch the fillets of Ceres,   50
few whose kisses would not be shunned by their father), and
   hang
a wreath on the doorway, with clusters of ivy over the lintel.
Is Hiberina content with a single man? More prospect
of inducing the lady to be content with a single eye!
'There are great reports, however, of a girl who is living on her
   father's
farm.' Let her live in Gabii or Fidenae as she lived in the country;

then I'll believe the story about her father's plot.
Anyhow, who says that nothing has ever occurred on a hillside
or in a cave? Are Mars and Jupiter so decrepit?
In all our arcades, can you point to a single woman who is
    worthy   60
of your attention? Is there, in all the tiers of our theatres,
one that you could pick out and love without misgiving?
As soft Bathyllus dances Leda, with sinuous gestures,
Tuccia cannot control her bladder; Apula squeals;   64
Thymele watches, and Thymele learns like a country girl.   66
Others, whenever the curtains are quietly stowed away,
when the theatre's locked and empty, and only the courts are
    heard,
when the People's games are over, and Cybele's are far in the
    future,
sadly fondle Accius' mask and his staff and loincloth.   70
Urbicus, in an Atellane farce, produces laughter
by miming Autonoë; Aelia loves him, but has no money.
Some pay a lot to undo the pin of a comic actor;
others will not allow Chrysógonus to sing; while Hispulla
adores a tragedian. Well, do you think they'd love a Quintilian?
You're taking a wife, so that she'll make the harpist Echíon
a father, or Gláphyrus perhaps, or Ambrosius (both of them
    pipers).
Let us erect a platform along the narrow street,
adorn the doors and doorways with whole, magnificent, laurels,
so that Lentulus' high-born babe in his tortoise-shell cradle   80
may look like Euryalus, crossed with a bruiser from the arena.

When Eppia abandoned her senator husband to follow a troop
to Pharos and the river Nile and Lagus' notorious city,
even Canópus condemned the monstrous morals of Rome.
Without a thought for her country, ignoring home and husband
and sister too, she callously left her weeping children,
left (an even greater surprise) the games and Paris.
Although as a little girl she had been surrounded with comfort,
had slept in a quilted cradle, pillowed on family down,
she scorned the sea; she had long since scorned her reputation—   90

a loss of little account among the padded litters.
And so she endured with steadfast heart the Tyrrhenian billows,
and then the Ionian's echoing roar; she never faltered
as one stretch of water succeeded another. When the reason for
    meeting
danger is right and proper, women are timid. Their hearts
freeze with fear; their legs shake; they cannot stand upright.
When the dangerous action involves disgrace, they face it
    unflinching.
To go aboard at a husband's bidding is a cruel duty;
the smell of the bilge is sickening, the sky wheels giddily round.
The one who travels with a lover has a steady stomach. While
    the other   100
vomits on her husband, *she* has meals with the crew and
    wanders
about the boat, happily hauling the roughest ropes.
Where, however, was the youthful beauty that inflamed and
    enchanted
Eppia? What did she see to make her accept the name
of 'the fighter's floozie'? By now her darling Sergius had started
to scrape his chin, and a wounded arm gave hope of retirement.
His face had also numerous flaws: a weal on his forehead,
chafed by his helmet, an enormous wen in the middle of his
    nose,
and the severe complaint of a constantly weeping eye.
But he *was* a *gladiator*. That's what makes each one an Adonis;   110
that she prized above country and children, sister and husband.
Yes, the steel is the thing they like. Had this very Sergius
received his discharge, he would soon have come to resemble
    Veiento.

Are you disturbed by Eppia's doings in a private household?
Look at our quasi-divinities; think of what Claudius had to
endure. As soon as the wife perceived her husband was sleeping,
she would steal away from him, taking with her a single maid,   119
and actually bear to prefer a mat to her bed in the palace.   117
The imperial harlot ⟨did not blush⟩   118
. . . . to don a hooded cloak at the dead of night.
No, with a yellow wig concealing her raven locks,   120

she made for a brothel warm with the stench of a much-used
    bedspread,
and entered an empty cell (her own). Undressing, she stood
    there
with gilded nipples under the bogus sign of 'The She-wolf',
displaying the womb which gave the lordly Britannicus birth.
She smilingly greeted all who entered, and asked for her
    'present'.   125
Then, when the brothel's owner allowed the girls to go home,   127
she lingered as long as she could before closing her cell
and sadly leaving, still on fire, with clitoris rigid.
At last she returned, exhausted, but not fulfilled, by her men;   130
and with greasy grimy cheeks, and foul from the smoke of the
    lamp,
she carried back to the emperor's couch the smell of the
    whorehouse.

Why should I tell of philtres, spells, and deadly concoctions
given to stepsons? Women commit more serious crimes
at the *bidding* of sex; lust itself is the least of their sins.

'But why does Caesennia's husband attest she's a model wife?'
She brought him a million: that's what the statement of chastity
    cost.
He is not haggard from Venus' quiver, nor fired by her torch;
the dowry it was that kindled his ardour and furnished the
    arrows.
Her freedom is paid for; no need to conceal her notes and
    glances.   140
A wealthy woman who marries a miser is as good as single.

Why, you ask, does Bibula fire Sertorius' passion?
If you want the truth, it isn't a wife he loves, but a face.
Just let a couple of wrinkles appear, let her skin become dry
and start to sag, let her teeth turn black and her eyes go puffy—
'Pack your bags', a freedman will cry, 'and be on your way.
You get on our nerves, forever blowing your nose; hurry up
and be off; your successor is someone without a perpetual
    sniffle.'

Till then she's in favour; she rules the house and pesters her
    husband,
asking for shepherds, Canusian sheep, and Falernian vineyards.   150
Why stop at that? She demands his servants and even his chain-
    gangs.
What a neighbour possesses, and she doesn't, has to be
    purchased.
In the month of December, when Jason the trader is hidden from
    sight,
and canvas stalls are placed in front of his crew and their
    weapons,
large vases of crystal are carried away, to be followed
by huge vessels of fluorspar, and then a legendary diamond,
enhanced by Queen Berenice's finger; the savage Agrippa
gave it once to be worn by his own incestuous sister
in a land where kings, barefooted, observe the rites of the
    sabbath,
and pigs, by a kindly tradition, are allowed to reach old age.   160

'From all the crowds of women, can you not find one who is
    decent?'
Suppose she is beautiful, graceful, wealthy, fertile, and also
has ancient ancestors dotting her hallway; suppose she is purer
than any Sabine with streaming hair who stopped a war—
a rare bird, as strange to the earth as a black swan;
who could endure a wife who was such a paragon? Better,
better, I say, a common slut than you, Cornelia,
mother of the Gracchi, if you combine with your massive
    virtues
a disdainful expression, and count your triumphs as part of your
    dowry.
Take your Hannibal, please; take your Syphax, who lost   170
that battle in his camp; take all of Carthage; and then, take off!

'Healer, have mercy, I beg you. O goddess, lay down your
    arrows!
The children are innocent. There—shoot your shafts at their
    mother!'
That was Amphíon's cry; but the Healer drew his bowstring,

and she led to the grave her flock of young, and also their father.
For Niobe claimed to surpass Latóna in her lofty line,
and to be more prolific than the great white sow of Alba.
Are beauty and dignity worth so much, if they're always
    enlisted
to humiliate *you*? For there's no joy to be had in the rarest
and highest qualities when a woman, spoilt by an arrogant
    temper,   180
brings with her aloes rather than honey. Who is besotted
to such an extent that, although he praises his wife to the skies,
he does not dread her and shun her seven hours out of twelve?
Some things, indeed, are small; but husbands cannot abide
    them.
One of the most revolting is the myth that no one is pretty
until she has changed from a Tuscan into a Greekling, from girl
of Sulmo to daughter of Cecrops. Everything happens in Greek. 187
In this they express their fears and troubles, their joy and anger; 189
in this they confide their heartfelt secrets; what more can I say? 190
they *couple* in Greek. Very well, one may grant those habits to
    girls;
but you, eroded as you are by a series of eighty-five years,
do *you* still use Greek? Such language is simply not decent
on an old woman's lips. Whenever that naughty endearment
    pops out—
Zoē kai psychē—you are using in public an expression
which should be confined to the sheets. What organ fails to be
    stirred
by a coaxing lascivious phrase? It has fingers. Still (to prevent
    you
preening yourself), though you make it sound more enticing
    than Haemus
or even Carpóphorus, the sum of the years is etched on your
    face.

If you don't intend to love the woman who was your betrothed   200
and is now your lawfully wedded wife, why marry at all?
Why waste money on a meal? Or hand out pieces of cake
to the bloated guests when the company's drifting away? Not to
    mention

the reward for the wedding night (there, on a splendid salver,
Dacia's and Germany's conqueror gleams on coins of gold).
If your love for your wife is pure and simple, and your heart is
    devoted
to her alone, then bow your head and prepare your neck
for the yoke. No woman has any regard for the man who loves
    her.
She may be passionate; still, she loves to fleece and torment him.   210
And so, the better a husband is, and the more attractive,
the smaller the benefit that he receives from having a wife.
You will give no gift without your spouse's permission;
    no item
will be sold when she says no, or bought if she is against it.
She will prescribe your affections. A friend who was known to
    your door
when his beard first grew, now late in life will be turned away.
While pimps and fighters' trainers do what they please when
    making
a will, and while the arena enjoys a similar right,
she will dictate that some of your rivals figure as heirs.

'Put that slave on a cross!'
                       'What crime has he done to deserve it?
What witnesses are there? Who's his accuser? Give him a
    hearing.   220
When a human life is at stake, no delay is excessive.'
'You fool! Is a slave human? What if he *hasn't* done wrong?
That is my wish, my *order*; my will is reason enough.'
Thus she rules her man; but soon she resigns her dominion
and passes through a succession of homes, with her veil in
    tatters,
and then flies back, refilling the dinge in the bed she deserted.
The doors so recently decked, the house with its coloured
    awnings,
and the boughs still fresh and green on the threshold—all are
    abandoned.
And so the tally grows: that makes eight husbands exactly
in five Octobers, a feat which should be carved on her
    tombstone.   230

As long as her mother's alive, harmony is not to be hoped for.
She will train her to strip a man of all his possessions;
she will train her to deal with seducers' letters, replying
in a style which contains nothing naïve or candid; and she
will trick your guards or buy their silence. When perfectly
 healthy,
she sends for Archígenes, tossing the covers as though in a fever.
Meanwhile, all by himself, the adulterer lurks in hiding;
chafing at the delay, he silently pulls his foreskin.
Do you really expect a mother to teach respectable habits
which are quite unlike her own? Besides, it is sensible business   240
for a filthy old woman to train her child to be filthy too.

There's hardly a case that comes to court that is not inspired
by a woman. Manilia will be the plaintiff, if not the defendant.
They prepare the briefs on their own, and explain to Celsus
how to open his speech and how to make his points.

Purple tracksuits, and mud from the ring where women wrestle,
are familiar sights. And who hasn't seen a wounded tree-stump,
repeatedly hacked by a wooden sword and bashed by a shield?
She goes through all the drill, and (although a lady) is fitted
to blow a trumpet at Flora's festival—unless she is hatching   250
a bolder plan and aims to fight in the real arena.
What sense of shame can be found in a woman wearing a helmet,
who shuns femininity and loves brute force? (In spite of it all,
 though,
she'd hate to become a man—our pleasure is so much fainter.)
If an auction is held of your wife's effects, how proud you will be
of her belt and arm-pads and plumes, and her half-length left-leg
 shin-guard!
Or if, instead, she prefers a different form of combat,
how pleased you'll be when the girl of your heart sells off her
 greaves!
(These are the women who sweat in a dress of frilly muslin,
whose pampered skin is chafed by the flimsiest piece of gauze.)   260
Hear her grunt while she practises thrusts as shown by the
 trainer,
wilting under the weight of the helmet; notice the size

of the puttees wrapped around her hams, and the coarseness of
   their fibre.
Then laugh when she lays down her arms and picks a chamber-
   pot up.
Tell me, ladies whose grandsire was Lepidus or blind Metellus
or Fabius Maw, what 'fighter's floozie' ever affected
clothes like these? Did Asýlus' wife ever gasp at a tree-stump?

The bed which contains a bride is always the scene of strife
and mutual bickering. There's precious little sleep to be had
   there.
She turns on her husband, worse than a tigress robbed of her
   cubs.   270
She pretends to be injured, covering up her own misdeeds.
She rails at his slave-boys, or invents a mistress to weep about.
Floods of tears are always at hand; they stand at the ready,
within the reservoir, waiting to hear the word of command;
then they flow as she tells them. You, poor worm, are delighted,
complacently thinking it's love. You set about drying her tears
with your lips, little aware of what you'd find in her letters
if you ever unlocked the desk of that whore who pretends to be
   jealous.
Suppose you catch her in bed with a slave or a wealthy knight:
'Please, Quintilian, supply a defence in this situation.'   280
'I'm stumped; supply it yourself.'
                                                         'Long ago we agreed,'
she says, 'that you could do as you liked, and that I should be
   able
to please myself. You can rant and rave till the sky falls;
I am a *person*!' There's nothing to equal women's effrontery
when caught in the act. Their guilt endows them with wrath and
   defiance.

'How do such monsters arise?' you ask. 'What source do they
   come from?'
In earlier days the humble position of Latium's women
kept them chaste. Their tiny cabins were saved from corruption
by heavy work, short hours of sleep, and hands that were chafed

and calloused by Tuscan wool, by Hannibal's imminent
    presence   290
before the city, and their menfolk guarding the Colline Gate.
Now we are paying for a lengthy peace. More deadly than
    armies,
luxury has fallen upon us, avenging the world we conquered.
Every crime and act of lust has become familiar
since the demise of Roman poverty. Following that,
our ancient hills have been flooded by Sybaris, Rhodes, and
    Miletus,
and by that city of garlands—drunken, licentious, Tarentum.
Filthy lucre paved the way for the importation
of foreign morals. Flabby riches have rotted our age
with revolting decadence. When Venus is drunk she's open to
    anything.   300
Past caring which is her head and which is her tail
is the woman who after midnight munches enormous oysters;
who makes the unguents foam by adding Falernian neat,
and drinks from a perfume shell, while the ceiling reels above
    her
and the table rises to meet her with its lanterns showing double.
You needn't wonder now why Maura pulls a grimace   306
and sniffs with contempt as she passes Chastity's ancient altar.   308
Here at night they leave their litters and empty their bladders,
filling with powerful jets the lap of the goddess's image;   310
they take it in turns to ride, as the moon looks down on their
    antics;
then they go home. When daylight comes and you go to visit
your powerful friends, you have to tread in your spouse's urine.

The secrets of the Good Goddess are scarcely a secret. The pelvis
is stirred by the pipe, and Priápus' maenads are swept along,
frenzied by horn and wine alike, swinging their hair
in a circle, and howling. Then what a yearning for sex erupts
in their hearts; what cries are emitted as their lust pulsates; what
    rivers
of vintage liquor come coursing down their drunken legs!
Tossing her garland in, Saufeia challenges harlots   320
trained in a brothel, and takes the award for undulant hips;

she in turn admires Medullina's rippling buttocks.
The prize is between the ladies; their birth is matched by their
     valour.
Nothing is done by way of illusion; in every performance
the real thing is enacted—a sight that would warm the blood
of old king Priam himself, or the ancient organ of Nestor.
Then, as their itch can't wait any longer, every disguise
is stripped from the women. The chorus is heard throughout the
     grotto:
'The time is here! Let in the men!' If her lover's asleep,
his son must don a cloak and hood and hurry to join her.   330
If that's no good, the slaves are assaulted; what if there isn't
a slave at hand? They'll hire the man who delivers the water.
If *he* is sought in vain, and no human aid is forthcoming,
then she'll dispose her rump to take the weight of a donkey.
Would that the ancient rites, or at least the public observances,
might take place without such foul desecration! But every
Moor and Indian knows which 'lady lutanist' carried
a penis longer than both the *Anticatos* of Caesar
to a place which even a mouse, aware that his testes will witness
against him, leaves in a hurry, where every picture portraying   340
the form of the other sex must be decently covered.
Who in those days sneered at the gods? Or who would have
     dared
to laugh at the earthenware bowls and the black basins of Numa,
or at the brittle pots that came from the Vatican hill?
Today what altar is without a Clodius skulking around it?   345
Nowadays all of them, high or low, have the same lust.   349
The woman who treads the black stone blocks is not any better   350
than the one who rides on the shoulders of tall Syrian porters.

In order to watch the games, Ogulnia hires a dress;
she hires a retinue, a chair, a cushion, some personal friends,
a conniving nurse, and a fair-haired slave-girl to carry notes.
The same woman presents what is left of the family plate,
down to the very last ewer, as a gift to some beardless athlete.
Many at home are hard up, but none pays due regard
to her poverty. They never think of adjusting themselves to the
     limits

which it assigns and imposes. Men, however, in time
think of their practical interests. Taking their cue from the ant,   360
some eventually learn to avoid cold and hunger.
Extravagant women are never aware of their dwindling assets.
As though the coins continued to burst into teeming life
in their empty box, and the pile, when drawn on, never
    diminished,
they give not the slightest thought to what their pleasures are
    costing.
In a house where a tutor of obscenity lives, free to indulge   O1
in his antics, hinting at every vice with his restless hand,
the others, you will find, are all debauched and no better than
    perverts.
These are allowed to pollute the food, and to take full part in
the family's meals; cups are washed which ought to be broken
when touched by a tongue or a bearded mouth with those
    proclivities.
The home of a fighter's trainer is cleaner and better than yours.
There the ones with a lisp are required to keep right away from
those with a normal voice. Why even the nets are divided
from the tunics that signal disgrace. The one who fights in a
    loincloth   O10
hangs his shoulder-guard up, along with his thrusting trident,
in a separate locker. The school's remotest quarters are given
to the most despised; they have even a different chain in prison.
Your wife, however, expects you to share a drinking cup
with creatures whom even a yellow-haired whore in a
    crumbling graveyard
would refuse to join, though the wine itself were Surrentine or
    Alban.
On *their* advice they suddenly take, or leave, a husband;
to these they turn for light relief when depressed or worried;
with their tuition they learn to waggle their hips and buttocks
(the rest, the teacher himself can tell). You cannot, however,   O20
always trust him. Although he sets off his eyes with soot,
and dresses in yellow and wears a hair-net, he's still an
    adulterer.
The more effeminate his voice, and the more he goes in for
    resting

his hand on his rounded hip, the more you should have him
   watched.
In bed he will prove most virile; there the ballet is forgotten.
'Thais' puts off her mask to reveal the accomplished Triphallus.
'Who are you fooling? Save the pretence, and let's have a wager.
I bet you're a genuine man; I *bet* you. Do you admit it?
Or are the maids to be sent to the torturer's stall? I know
the advice my old friends give and their prudent
recommendations: O30
"Bolt your door and keep her in." But who is to guard
the guards themselves? They are paid in kind for concealing the
   shady
tricks of the naughty girl. Complicity promises silence.
One's wily wife anticipates this, and begins with them.'

There are some women who take a delight in non–combatant
   eunuchs   366
with their girlish kisses and beardless faces (another advantage:
they do not necessitate drugs to procure abortions). The highest
pleasure ensues when a hot-blooded lad, with jet-black fringe
and genitals fully mature, is taken to visit the surgeon.   370
When testicles, then, are allowed to drop and encouraged to
   ripen
until they've become a pound apiece, the cut of a scalpel
from Heliodorus involves no loss, except for the barber.   373
(Slavedealers' boys are pathetically scarred by a real mutilation; 373A
they feel ashamed of the bag and the half-grown pod they've
   been left with.)   373B
The one whom his mistress has had castrated enters the baths;
seen from afar and noticed by all, he is able to challenge
the god who is guardian of vine and plot. He will do no damage
if he sleeps with his mistress. But Postumus, never entrust to a
   eunuch
a Bromius who is just mature and due for a haircut.

If she likes music, none of the pins will stay in place
of those who sell their voice to the praetor. She constantly
   handles   380
instruments. Over the tortoise-shell lyre her rings of sardonyx

glitter; the quivering quill rhythmically strikes the strings,
the quill that was used by the tender Hedýmeles. This she will
   fondle,
consoling herself; she will even kiss the beloved fetish.
A lady (one of the Lamiae, boasting the Appian name)
offered to Janus and Vesta meal and wine, and enquired
whether her Pollio might hope to win the Capitol crown,
and might promise that to his lyre. What more could the woman
   have done
had her husband been seriously ill or the doctors despaired of
   saving
the life of her little son? She stood at the altar, and thought it   390
no disgrace to veil her head on behalf of a harp;
she repeated the words prescribed, and blanched as the lamb was
   laid open.
Father Janus, oldest of the gods, tell me, I pray you,
do you answer people like her? You've plenty of leisure in
   heaven.
In fact, from what I can see, there's nothing for you to do there.
One consults you about a comic actor, another
commends a tragedian; the augur will soon get varicose veins.

Better to be mad about music, however, than brazenly hurry
all over the town, facing the meetings of men, and engaging
uniformed generals in conversation in her husband's presence,   400
without any trace of embarrassment and with no milk in her
   breasts.
That kind of woman knows what's happening throughout the
   world—
what Thrace and China are up to, what secrets a stepmother
   shares
with the son, and who's in love, and for whom the ladies are
   scrambling.
She will tell you who made the widow pregnant, and in which
   month;
with what endearments each woman makes love, and in what
   positions.
She is the first to observe a comet that presages ill
for a Parthian or an Armenian king; she snaps up the latest

rumours and tales at the city gate, and fabricates others.
The Niphátes has flooded whole communities, the fields have
  vanished   410
under water, cities are tottering, lands subsiding—
that's what she tells to whoever she meets at every corner.

No less vicious a habit, however, is found in the woman
who, with a curse, seizes her poor, unassuming neighbour
and punishes him with a whip. For, if her peaceful slumbers
are broken by barking, 'Quick,' she screeches, 'bring me a
  cudgel,
at once!' And she orders first the owner to be given a thrashing,
and then the dog. She's a terror to meet, with her glowering
  face,
as she makes for the baths in the evening. She orders camp and
  containers
to be moved in the evening. She loves to sweat amid all the
  uproar.   420
Then, when her arms drop limp, worn out by the heavy dumb-
  bells,
the clever masseur presses his fingers into her fringe
and brings from the top of the lady's leg an explosive reaction.
All this time her luckless guests are falling asleep
or fainting with hunger. At last she arrives, red in the face,
thirsty enough to tackle the jar which stands beside her
bulging with three full gallons; she lowers a couple of pints
before her dinner to arouse a raging hunger, for shortly
up it comes and slaps the floor with her stomach's contents.
Streams run over the marble pavement; the gilded basin   430
reeks of Falernian. For like the gigantic serpent which toppled
into a vat, she drinks and vomits. No wonder her husband
is sickened and only controls his bile by shutting his eyes.

But more offensive is the one who on taking her place at dinner
gushes in praise of Virgil, forgiving the doomed Elissa;
compares and evaluates poets; holds the scales of judgement,
placing Maro in one of the pans and Homer in the other.
Professional critics withdraw; rhetoricians are bested; the party
falls silent, and neither lawyer nor crier ventures to speak,

nor another woman; so great a torrent of words descends.   440
You'd swear so many pots and bells were clashing at once
that no one now need wake the trumpet or weary the cymbal;
she on her own will manage to succour the struggling moon.
Philosophers tell us that one can have too much of a good thing.
Hence the woman who wants to appear too learned and fluent
should wear a tunic that doesn't reach below the knee,
slaughter a pig to Silvanus, and enter the baths for a quarter.
Make sure the woman reclining beside you doesn't affect
a rhetorical style, or brandish phrases before unleashing
a clinching argument; let her not know the whole of history,   450
or understand every word that she reads. For myself, I abhor
the woman who is always consulting and thumbing Palaemon's
    Grammar,
so precise in observing the laws and rules of speech,
and, like a scholar, quoting lines that I've never heard of.
Are these things matters for men? Let her correct the speech
of an ignorant friend; but a husband's slips should pass without
    comment.

A woman denies herself nothing and considers nothing
    disgraceful
once she surrounds her neck with an emerald choker, and once
she fastens those heavy pearls onto her sagging ear-lobes.
No more unbearable thing exists than a wealthy woman.   460
. . . .
Meanwhile her face is a hideous and laughable sight, as she pads
    it
with layers of bread; it reeks of heavy Poppaean ointments
in which the lips of her luckless husband become embedded.
(Her skin is clean when she meets her lover. When does she ever
care to look pretty at home? Nard is obtained for her lovers,
for them she buys whatever the slender Indians send us.)
At length she uncovers her face, removing the outer plaster.
Slowly she comes into view. She washes in special milk.
(To ensure a supply she would take in her train a herd of asses,
even if banished to the chilly clime of the Hyperboréans.)   470
But that which is coated and warmed with so many odd
    preparations

(applied and removed), that which is dressed with lumps of
    baked
and moistened dough—what shall we call it? A face, or an ulcer?

It is worth the trouble to study in detail what such women
do to put in the day. If during the night the husband
has turned his back, the wool-maid is done for; the hairdressers,
    too,
are stripped of their tunics; the Liburnian chair-man is told he is
    late
and is forced to pay for another's sleep. One has an ash-plant
split on his back, another is raw from a whip, and a third
from a strap. Some women pay their beaters an annual stipend.   480
'Hit him!' she says, and smears her face or chats with her friends,
or examines the width of a golden stripe on a coloured dress.
'Whip him!' she cries, and studies a page of the lengthy day-
    book.
'Whip him!' she cries; and then, when the floggers are weary,
    'Get out!'
she screams in a terrible voice, once the 'enquiry' is over.
Her house is ruled with the cruelty of a Sicilian court.
If she has made a date and wants to be specially *soignée*
and is now in a hurry and, for some time, has been due at the
    park
(or, a more probable place, the temple of 'Isis the Madam'),
then her coiffeuse, the unfortunate Psecas, will have to submit   490
to having her hair torn out, her shoulders and breasts uncovered.
'Why is this curl sticking up?' And at once the strap of bull-hide
comes down to punish the heinous crime of the errant ringlet.
What has Psecas done? How can the girl be blamed
if you dislike the shape of your nose? On the left is another,
drawing and combing the hair, and twisting it into a curl.
Sitting in council is a maid of her mother's, promoted to wool
having seen much service with curlers. She will be asked her
    opinion
first; thereafter, those below her in age and skill
will deliver theirs, as though a matter of honour or life   500
were at stake; such anxious thought goes into the quest for
    beauty.

So many the tiers she piles on her head, so many the storeys
with which she builds it up, Andrómache seems to confront
    you.
From behind she's smaller; you'd think she was somebody else;
    so imagine
the effect, if she happens to be short in the leg and (unless she
    resorts
to wearing risers) looks as though she'd be dwarfed by a Pygmy,
and has to lift herself up on her toes to receive a kiss!

Meanwhile she never gives her husband a thought. No mention
is made of the sums she costs him. She might as well be a
    neighbour,
except that she does have a personal tie with his friends and
    servants—   510
she hates them all; and she wrecks his finances. Look at what's
    coming—
the troupe of frenzied Bellona and the Mother of the Gods,
    including
a giant eunuch (revered by his smaller degenerate friend).
He snatched up a sherd and severed his genitals long ago,
foregoing his sex. Now he drowns the shrieking mob and their
    timbrels,
his common cheeks enclosed in the flaps of a Phrygian bonnet.
In portentous tones he warns her to fear September, and with it
the wind from the south, unless she has offered a hundred eggs
and presented him with the plum-coloured dress she's no longer
    wearing.
(Thus any sudden or serious threats will enter the clothes,   520
and she, with a single act, will have made her peace for a year.)
On a winter's morning she will break the ice and enter the
    Tiber,
plunging into the water thrice and dipping her fearful
head right into the eddies. Emerging, half-dressed and shaking,
she will crawl across the entire field of Tarquin the Proud
on her bleeding knees; if milk-white Io tells her to do so,
she will make her way to sweltering Meroe, beyond the border
of Egypt, in order to fetch some water that she may sprinkle
in Isis' temple, which stands right next to the ancient sheepfold.

She believes she received her orders direct from the voice of the
    goddess—   530
a likely soul and mind for the gods to talk to at night-time!
Hence the highest, most special, honour is paid to the one
who, followed by creatures in linen robes with shaven heads,
trots along as Anubis, and mocks at the wailing crowd.
He intercedes whenever a woman has failed to refrain
from sex with her husband on days which ought to be honoured
    as holy,
when a heavy penalty is due to be paid for polluting the mattress,
and when Isis' silver serpent is seen to nod its head.
Anubis' tears ensure, along with his ritual murmurs,
that Osiris will not refuse to forgive the sin—provided,   540
of course, he is bribed with a big fat goose and a little cake.

When he has moved on, a palsied Jewess puts down her hay-box
and comes a-begging, whispering secretly into her ear.
She interprets the laws of Jerusalem, *she* is the priestess
of the tree, who truly conveys the will of highest heaven.
She too gets something, but less, for the Jews will sell you
whatever view of a dream you like for a couple of coppers.
An Armenian or Syrian diviner will promise a youthful lover,
or else a large bequest from a childless millionaire,
once he has handled and studied the lungs of a still-warm
    pigeon.   550
He will probe inside the ribs of a chicken, or a puppy's innards,
or sometimes even a child's; he may then inform on his client.

An even greater trust is placed in Chaldaeans; whatever
an astrologer says, they fondly believe is drawn from the
    fountain
of Ammon, now that the Delphic oracle speaks no more,
and men are condemned to face a future shrouded in darkness.
Most esteemed is the one who has been most often in exile.   557
Faith in his skill is enhanced, if he has served a lengthy sentence   560
in a barracks prison, with manacles clanking on both his arms.
No Chaldaean has genius without a criminal record.
He needs to have barely survived, to have just succeeded in
    being

sent to the Cyclades; then to have languished on tiny Seríphos.
Your Tanaquil inquires about her mother who is dying of
   jaundice:
how long will she last? (Already she has a report on *you*!)
When will she bury her sister and uncles? Will her lover survive
when she is gone? (What greater boon could the gods
   vouchsafe?)
Yet she at least cannot tell what the gloomy planet of Saturn
portends, or under what sign joyful Venus emerges,   570
which months of the year are assigned to loss, and which to
   profit.
Be sure to keep out of the way of that type, too; you will see her
carrying round in her hands, like a ball of scented amber,
a well-thumbed almanac. She no longer consults, but rather
she herself is consulted. When her husband is leaving for camp
or home, she will not go too, if Thrasyllus and his sums detain
   her.
When she decides to travel a mile, a suitable hour
is produced from her book; if there's an itch in the corner of her
   eye
when she rubs it, she studies her horoscope before sending for
   ointment.
Suppose she is ill in bed, there is one right time and one only,   580
it seems, for taking food—the time Petosíris lays down.
If she is less well off, she will wander between the pillars
at the racetrack, drawing cards for her fortune and letting the
   seer
inspect her palm and forehead, while popping her lips as
   instructed.
The rich receive their replies from a Phrygian augur, or one
imported ⟨at great expense from the land where the crocus
   grows   586
or, it may be,⟩ from an expert in reading the starry heavens,
or a greybeard who purifies public sites that are struck by
   lightning.   587
The fate of the poor is settled on the track or out on the rampart.
A woman with neck uncovered, wearing a long gold chain,
inquires in front of the towers and the pillars supporting the
   dolphins   590

whether to break with the publican and marry the rag and bone
   man.

Women like her, however, experience the dangers of childbirth,
and cope with all the strains of nursing which their station
   imposes.
It's rare for a gilded bed to contain a woman in labour;
so efficacious now are the drugs and skills of the female
who renders women sterile, and is paid for murdering people
within the womb. Be glad, you wretch, and give her the potion,
whatever it is, yourself. For if she were willing to swell
and disturb her belly with leaping babies, you might discover
that you were the father of an Ethiopian, that you'd made your
   will   600
for a coloured heir whom you'd shudder to see first thing in the
   morning.
I need not speak of spurious children, of the joys and prayers
so often deluded at filthy latrines, of the priests and pontiffs
who are fetched from there to bear, in spite of their true identity,
the name of Scaurus. Brazen Fortune stands there at night,
and smiles on the naked babies. She hugs them close to her
   bosom
and cuddles them; then she passes them on to our noble houses,
preparing to relish her private joke. She loves them, imposing
herself upon them; and ensures that, as hers, they always
   prosper.

One man gives her magical spells, another will sell her   610
Thessalian potions which so impair her husband's sanity
that she can slipper his buttocks. That's what induces your
   dotage,
your darkness of mind, and the total amnesia of what you did
quite recently. That, however, can be endured, provided
you don't go raving mad, like Nero's famous uncle,
for whom Caesonia poured the membrane ripped from the
   forehead
of a staggering foal. Who will not take her cue from an empress?
The structure had gone, and the world was sinking in blazing
   ruins;

it was just the same as if Juno herself had robbed her husband
of his reason. So, when compared with that, Agrippina's   620
    mushroom
doesn't appear so deadly. For *it* put a stop to the heart-beats
merely of one old man, sending his shaky head,
and his lips drooling with streams of slobber, away to heaven.
Caesonia's philtre, however, clamoured for fire and iron,
tearing and torturing fathers and knights in a bloody shambles;
such was the havoc wrought by a foal and a single poisoner.
Women detest a rival's children; let nobody cavil
or call it wrong. Why, now it is lawful to murder a stepson.
I'm warning orphans as well: if you own a sizeable fortune,
watch out for your lives; don't trust anything served at table.   630
Those blackening cakes are highly spiced with a mother's
    poison.
Let somebody else be the first to munch what she who bore you
offers you; get your nervous tutor to test the drinks.

You think this is fiction? That my satire has donned theatrical
    boots,
that going beyond the bounds and law of earlier writers
I am raving in Sophocles' gaping style a lofty song
of things unknown to Rutulian hills and Latin skies?
Would it were all a dream. But Pontia cries 'It was me!
I confess; I got some aconite and administered it to my children.
The murder was detected and is known to all; but *I* am the
    culprit!'   640
Two, do you say, at a single meal, you venomous viper,
two at a sitting?
                        'Yes, and seven, had there been seven!'

Let us believe what tragedy says concerning Procne
and the cruel woman of Colchis; I won't dispute it. They too
dared to commit some monstrous crimes in their generation—
but not for the sake of cash. Extreme atrocities tend
to cause less shock when fury incites the female to outrage,
and when, with their hearts inflamed by madness, they are
    carried down

like boulders wrenched from a mountain ridge as the ground
   collapses
and the vertical face falls in from beneath the hanging cliff-top.   650
I cannot abide the woman who assesses the profit, and coolly
commits a hideous crime. They watch Alcestis enduring
death for her man, but if they were offered a similar choice
they would gladly let their husband die to preserve a lapdog.
Every morning you meet Eriphýles in dozens, and also
daughters of Danaus; every street has a Clytemnestra.
Whereas, however, Tyndáreus' daughter wielded an oafish
and awkward two-headed axe which needed both her hands,
now the job is done with the tiny lung of a toad—
though it may need steel if your son of Atreus is now immune,   660
as the thrice-defeated monarch was, through Pontic drugs.

SATIRE 7

The Plight of Intellectuals

Writing's hope and incentive depend entirely on Caesar.
For he alone in the present time has looked with favour
upon the dejected Muses, when distinguished and famous poets
were reduced to applying for a lease on Gabii's dingy bath-house
or a city bakery, and others considered it no disgrace
or shame to become auctioneers; when Clio had bidden farewell
to the vales of Aganippe and made for the salerooms in search of
    a meal.
For if there's no sign of a penny within the Piérian grove,
you have to take on the name and life-style of Harry the
    Hammer,
and sell whatever the embattled auction sells to the crowd   10
of bystanders—winejars, three-legged stools, book-cases,
    trunks,
and Paccius' *Alcíthoë*, along with the *Thebes* and *Tereus* of
    Faustus.
At least that's better than saying in front of a judge 'I saw'
what you didn't see at all. Leave that to our Asian knights   14
whose slippers disgrace them by showing the weals on their
    naked ankles.   16
No one, however, in future, if he weaves melodious tunes
into a web of vocal art, or chews the laurel,
will have to submit to a kind of work that demeans his calling.
Fall to it, my lads. Our leader's favour is looking around,   20
urging you on, eager to encourage those who deserve it.
But if you expect support for your fortunes from anywhere else,
and, in that hope, are filling your pages of yellow parchment—
quick, Telesinus, go and obtain some kindling wood,
and then present your poetic creations to Venus' husband,
or close your books and lay them aside for the tunnelling worm.

Break your pen, poor fellow, destroy those sleepless battles,
you who are fashioning lofty poems in your tiny attic,
with the aim of winning a garland of ivy and a famished bust.
There is no hope beyond that. The miserly magnate has learned   30
to admire and praise accomplished writers—and do nothing
    about it,
like children with Juno's bird. Meanwhile, the time of life
is passing, which could put up with the sea, the spade, and the
    helmet.
Then weariness enters the heart, and age, with its literary skill
and without a rag to its back, curses itself and its Muse.

Here are his tricks. To avoid giving *you* any money, that patron,
for whose service you have left the temple of the Muses and
    Apollo,
composes verses himself, and is second only to Homer
(well *he*'s a thousand years older). If the heady prospect of fame
leads you to give a recital, he lends you a damp-mottled
    building,   40
a house pressed into service although it has been locked for
    years,
with a door which makes a noise like a herd of frightened pigs.
He's good at supplying freedmen to sit at the end of each row,
and at placing his attendants' booming voices around the hall;
but none of your lordships will ever provide the cost of the
    benches,
or the tiers of seats which are raised aloft on a rented framework,
or the front-row chairs which must be returned when the show
    is over.
We still keep at it, however, driving furrows along
the powdery dust, and turning the shore with our barren
    plough.
For if you try to break free, you are held in a noose by the craving 50
to excel as a writer, which becomes a chronic disease in your
    heart.   52

But the peerless poet, who has no ordinary vein of talent,
who does not go in for extracting goods for the market to sell,
or strike an already familiar song from the common mint—

the sort of man I cannot point to, but only feel—
he is the product of a mind released from anxiety, and free
of any bitterness, a mind that loves the woods and is worthy
to drink from the Muses' fountain; whereas disconsolate
   Hardship
cannot sing in a Piérian grotto or grasp the thyrsus,   60
for she lacks the money which, day and night, the body requires.
Horace's stomach is full when he cries 'All hail!' to Bacchus.
Where can genius find room, except in the heart that trembles
at song alone, and is carried away by the lords of Cirrha
and Nysa, excluding all but that one compulsive concern?
It calls for a lofty soul, that is not disturbed by the thought
of buying a blanket, to behold horses and chariots and the sight
of gods and the terrible face of the Fury as she crazed the
   Rutulian.
If Virgil had been without a slave-boy and decent lodgings,
the snakes would have dropped from her hair; and her trumpet,
   bereft of sound,   70
would have blared forth no menacing note. So how can we ask
that Rubrénus Lappa should rise to the heights of the ancient
   buskin,
when his Atreus pawns his coat, along with his cup and saucer?
Impoverished Numitor has nothing to give his client; he does
have enough for gifts to Quintilla; nor did he lack the funds
to buy a lion (already tamed), who had to be fed
with masses of meat. I suppose a beast is less expensive,
and it takes so very much more to fill a poet's guts.
Lucan may well be content with fame, as he lies at ease
in his marble gardens. What use, however, to the haggard Saleius   80
and Serranus is glory, no matter how great, if it's *only*
   glory?
When Statius has made the city happy by fixing a day,
there's a rush to hear his attractive voice and the strains of his
   darling
Thebaid. He duly holds their hearts enthralled by his sweetness;
and the people listen in total rapture. But when, with his verses,
he has caused them all to break the benches in their wild
   excitement,
he starves—unless he can sell his virgin *Agave* to Paris.

Paris also confers positions of military power,
and puts the gold of six months' service on a poet's finger.
What the nobles refuse, a dancer will grant. Do you throng the
    halls   90
of our great patrician houses, of Bárea and the Camerini?
It's *Pelopéa* who appoints our prefects, *Philoméla* our tribunes.
But you shouldn't resent a bard who wins his bread from the
    stage.
Who will be Maecenas today? Who Proculéius?
Who a Fabius, or a second Lentulus, or another Cotta?
Genius then was fairly rewarded. A pallor brought profit
to many, and so did abjuring wine for the whole of December.

Next I address the writers of history: what about *your* work?
Is it any more fruitful? More time and oil is wasted.
A thousand columns are full, and as no end is in prospect   100
you see the mounds of papyrus growing—along with the cost.
That is prescribed by the subject's size, and the law of the genre.
What harvest, however, accrues? What crop from the land you
    have tilled?
Who will pay a historian as much as a newsreader earns?

'Well, they're a lazy lot, too fond of their couch in the shade.'
Tell me, then, what barristers earn from their civil practice,
and from those briefs that stand at their side in bulky bundles.
They brag, above all when a creditor's listening, or if they are
    tapped
more urgently still on the shoulder by a man with a fat account-
    book
who has come to claim a debt from an unreliable client.   110
Then their capacious bellows puff out limitless lies,
and their robes are beslobbered. If you want to assess their actual
    profits,
in one scale place the total wealth of a hundred lawyers,
in the other simply that of the Lizard, who drives for the Reds.
The council is now in session; you rise, a ghastly Ajax,
to uphold endangered freedom before a panel of yokels.
Strain your lungs till they burst, poor fellow, so that when
    you're exhausted

your stairs may be proudly framed by branches of verdant palm.
And what do you earn by your voice? A bit of dried ham, or a jar
of miniature tunnies, some ancient onions (the monthly ration   120
of a Moor), or five flagons of wine brought from up-river.
Suppose, after speaking at four hearings, you are given a
      sovereign;
by the terms of the contract you have to deduct the attorney's
      share.
'The maximum fee will go to Aemilius, and I spoke better.'
Yes, because in his forecourt there stands a chariot of bronze,
with a team of four, which carries an ancestor high in triumph,
while he, astride a gallant charger, aims from afar
a sagging spear—a one-eyed statue preparing for battle.
That is how Pedo fails and Matho is ruined; that end
awaits Tongilius, who takes a rhinocerus flask to the baths   130
and creates a disturbance with his muddy mob. He is carried
      through town
in a long litter by Thracian bearers, intent on acquiring
slave-boys and silver plate, fluorspar vases, and villas.
And yet this self-advertisement works. The expensive clothes   135
of purple and violet sell the barrister; therefore it pays him
to live in the loud flamboyant style of wealthier people;   137
his exotic purple, with its Tyrian thread, secures him credit.   134
Our spendthrift city sets no limit to squandering money.
Rely on eloquence? Nowadays no one would give two hundred
to Cicero himself, unless he flashed a massive ring.   140
The first question a litigant asks is whether you run to
eight slaves and a dozen clients, with a litter behind you
and burghers in front. That is why Paulus would hire a sardonyx
when pleading in court, and why he commanded a higher fee
than Gallus or Basilus. Eloquence rarely appears in rags.
When can Basilus hope to produce a weeping mother?
Who would give Basilus a hearing, however well he spoke?
Go to Gaul, or better still to that nurse of lawyers,
Africa, *if* you want your tongue to earn you a living.

Do you teach declamation? What an iron stomach Vettius needs   150
when a long succession of pupils gets rid of the cruel tyrant!
What one has just read out from his desk, another goes through

on his feet, declaiming the same material in similar phrases.
Cabbage, re-hashed *ad nauseam*, does for the wretched teacher.
What kind of case is it, how do we handle it, what is the crucial
point at issue, what shots will be fired from the opposite side?
That's what they all want to hear, but no one is willing to pay
   for.
'You ask for money? But what have I learned?'
                                 'No doubt it's the teacher's
fault that our young Arcadian bumpkin feels not a spark
of intellectual power in his skull, when at five-day intervals   160
he pounds his "Hannibal the Terrible" into my aching head,
no matter what the question at issue (should he strike at the city
straight from Cannae, or after the thunderstorm should he play
   safe
and order his rain-soaked cohorts to do an about turn?).
State your price, and I'll pay on the nail, whatever it costs,
if only his father could hear him as often as I do.' Whereat
six, or more, teachers of rhetoric shout 'Hear hear!',
and turn to genuine cases. 'The rapist' is left high and dry;
not a word on 'the pouring of the poison', 'the evil ungrateful
   husband',
or 'the pestle and mortar that cure those who have long been
   blind'.   170
But in fact, if he takes my advice, he will grant himself a
   discharge
and start on a new career—I mean the man who descends
from rhetoric's ivory tower to join in the fray of the lawcourts
for fear he may miss the paltry sum that it takes to purchase
a corn coupon (for that is the fattest fee he will get).
Ask what Chrysógonus and Pollio earn for teaching music
to the sons of the rich, and you'll shred Theodorus' *Art of
   Speaking*.

Six hundred thousand for the baths, and more for the covered
   walk
where the master can drive on rainy days. Well, is he to wait
for the sky to clear, and allow his pair to be spattered with mud?   180
Much better here, where the mule stays clean, with his hooves a-
   sparkle.

In another part of his grounds he bids a diningroom rise
with high Numidian columns to catch the winter sunshine.
Whatever the house may cost, someone will come to arrange
the dishes, and someone to flavour the food with an expert
    touch.
Amongst such items, two thousand (and that's a generous
    figure)
will be quite enough for Quintilian. In a father's scale of
    expenses
nothing is lower than his son.
                              'In that case, how did Quintilian
come by those large estates?'
                              Cases of rare good fortune
should be left aside. The lucky man is handsome and brave;   190
the lucky man has a crescent sewn on his black leather shoes;
the lucky man is outstanding as a speaker and javelin-thrower,   193
and he sings superbly—when he hasn't a cold. For it all
    depends
on what stars may be there to greet you, when you start to utter
your first infantile cries and are still red from your mother.
If Fortune wishes, you'll turn from a teacher into a consul;
and if she wishes, you'll turn from a consul into a teacher.
Think of Ventidius; and think of Tullius. What else do they
    show,
except the amazing power of the stars and mysterious fate—   200
fate, which bestows a crown on slaves and a triumph on
    prisoners?
But the lucky man is harder to find than a white crow,
while many have rued the futile and profitless Chair of
    Speaking.
Witness Thrasýmachus' end, and that of Secundus Carrínas;
the latter too appeared in rags in the streets of Athens,
which ventured to offer him nothing except a cooling hemlock.
God grant that the earth lie soft and light on the shades of our
    forebears,
that fragrant crocus may bloom on their urn in eternal spring.
They believed no less respect was due to a teacher
than to a parent. When Achilles (no longer a child) was learning   210
the lyre in his native hills, he had to beware of the cane;

and would never have dared to laugh at the tail of his music
    master.
But Rufus and the rest are now chastised by their own
    students—
Rufus, so often called 'The Allobroges' answer to Cicero'.
Scholars like Céladus, say, or Palaemon, never succeed
in pocketing what their teaching deserves. And before they
    receive it,
whatever it is (and it's less than the pay of a rhetoric teacher),
the pupil's attendant, an insensitive soul, nibbles some off it;
then the cashier takes a slice for himself. Don't worry,
    Palaemon;
resign yourself to certain 'reductions', just like a pedlar   220
who is wrangling over a winter mat or a snow-white blanket,
provided there's *some* return for sitting from midnight on
in a hole which would not be endured by a smith or a fellow who
    teaches
apprentices how to card wool with a slanting metal comb;
provided there's *some* return for smelling all those lamps
(one for every boy in the class) while Flaccus went dark
all over, and Maro was covered by a layer of filthy soot.
And yet you rarely obtain your fee without recourse
to a tribune's enquiry. You, the parents, should of course insist
on the strictest standards: the teacher's grammar has to be
    faultless;   230
he must read the stories in books, and know each one of the
    writers
like the back of his hand; so that, if a person happens to ask him,
when he's on the way to the public baths (or Phoebus'
    establishment),
he may name Anchises' nurse, come out with the name and
    birthplace
of Anchémolus' stepmother, state to what age Acestes lived,
and how many jars of Sicily's wine he gave to the Phrygians.
Make sure that he moulds the children's characters, just as a
    sculptor
models a face from wax with his thumb. Make sure that in fact
he's a father to the group, to stop them playing indecent tricks
and doing it to each other. With so many pupils, it's hard   240

to watch the hurried movements of hand and eye at a climax.
'These are your duties,' he says. 'But, at the end of the session,
you'll get as much cash as the crowd demands for a winning
    fighter.'

SATIRE 8

True Nobility

What use are family trees? Dear Ponticus, what's the advantage
in being judged by the length of your blood, in displaying the
    portraits
of forebears—an Aemilianus standing high in his chariot,
a Curius of whom only half survives, or perhaps a Corvinus
minus his arms, or a Galba deprived of nose and ears?
What is gained by being entitled to exhibit pontiffs
on your ample chart, and to reach right back through many a
    branch
to grimy masters of horse, with perhaps a dictator included,
if under the Lepidi's eyes your life is evil? What good are
the statues of all those warriors, if you spend the night in
    gambling   10
before the Numantini, and don't go to bed until dawn—
the time when the generals of old would be moving camp and
    standard?
Why should a Fabius, born in Hercules' house, take pride
in the Great Altar and the Gallic title, if he's greedy and silly,
if he's altogether more pampered than a Eugánean lamb,
if, by having his buttocks smoothed with Cátina's pumice,
he affronts his hairy progenitors, and if, through dealing in
    poison,
he disgraces his clan, and his own statue is publicly smashed?
Though you deck your hall from end to end with ancient waxes
on either side, *virtue* is the one and only nobility.   20
So be a Paulus or Cossus or Drusus—in moral integrity.
Prize that moral integrity above your ancestors' portraits.
When you are consul, let *that* walk ahead of your very rods.
First you must show me the goods of the spirit. Do you
    deserve

by your words and deeds to be counted blameless and valiant for
    justice?
I accept your status, and salute you as Gaetúlicus or as Silánus.
Whatever your ancient line, if you prove a rare and distinguished
citizen, then you will be a boon to your happy country,
and all will gladly cry what the people of Egypt cry
when the new Osiris is found. For who would call anyone noble   30
who disgraced his family, and claimed renown for nothing,
    apart from
his famous name? If somebody owns a dwarf, we call him
'Atlas'; a negro, 'Swan'; a bent and disfigured girl,
'Europa'. Curs that are listless, and bald from years of mange,
and lick the rim of an empty lamp for oil, are given
the name of 'Leopard', 'Tiger', 'Leo', or whatever beast
inspires fear by its terrible roars. Take very good care, then,
that *this* is not why you are called 'Créticus' or 'Camerínus'!

For whom are these words of warning? I am talking to you,
    Rubellius
Blandus. Your head is swollen by belonging to Drusus' line,   40
as if *you* had done anything to make yourself noble, or deserved
    any credit
for having a blue-blooded Julian lady as mother, instead of
a woman who weaves for hire beneath the windy embankment.
'You are trash,' you say, 'the very commonest rabble.
Not one of you can point to the country where his father was
    born.
But I'm a descendant of Cecrops.' Bravo, and long may you
    glory
is such a pedigree! Yet, in the lowest dregs you'll encounter
a Roman of eloquence; one who will often plead the case
of an ignorant aristocrat. From the masses will come a toga'd
    figure
who can pick his way through the knots and riddles of law and
    statute.   50
From there comes the keen young soldier who takes as his goal
    the Euphrates
or the eagles that are set to guard the conquered Batávi. But you
are a mere 'descendant of Cecrops', just like a limbless Herm.

In fact there is one point only in which you have the advantage:
while he has a head of marble, you are a *living* statue.

Tell me, o scion of the Trojans, in the case of dumb animals,
    who
considers them highly bred unless they are strong? For that
we admire the flying horse, whose easy victories send
deafening roars of excitement echoing round the race-course.
The thoroughbred horse, whatever his pasture, is the one whose
    speed   60
takes him clear of the others, and whose dust is first on the track.
Coryphaéus' progeny, however, or that of Hirpínus, is
    auctioned
as low-grade stock if Victory seldom rides on his pole.
No respect for pedigree there, no favour obtained
through the ghosts of the dead. Those who lack the speed of
    their sires
and are only good for turning a mill, must change their owners
for a paltry sum, and gall their necks by pulling a waggon.
So if we're to venerate *you*, and not your possessions, provide us
first with something to carve on your record, apart from the
    honours
we pay, and have always paid, to those who gave you your
    status.   70

So much, then, for the youth who, as tradition assures us,
was puffed full of arrogance, all on account of his kinship with
    Nero.
In men of that class a concern for others is rarely encountered;
but in your case, Ponticus, I should be sorry if you were valued
for your family's prowess, and not for achieving something
    yourself
to be proud of in future. It's feeble to lean on the fame of others;
remove the supporting columns, and the roof will come
    crashing down;
the vine on the ground misses the elm to which it was married.
Be a brave soldier, a faithful guardian, and also an honest
judge. Or if, in a case where justice hangs in the balance,   80
you appear as a witness, then, though Phálaris bids you deny

the truth, brings in his bull, and dictates the lies to be told,
count it the worst disgrace to prefer survival to honour,
and, for the sake of life, to lose the point of living.
The man who deserves to die is dead, though he dine on a
    hundred
Gauran oysters and soak in a bath of Cosmus' perfumes.

When at last the province, to which you have long looked
    forward,
receives you as governor, put a rein and curb on your anger,
and on your greed; take some pity on the poor provincials.
What you see is the bones of their state, sucked dry of the
    marrow.   90
Keep in mind what the laws prescribe, what the senate lays
    down,
what honours await the good, how just was the bolt which
    blasted
Tutor and Capito, Cilicia's pirates, down to ruin,
when the senate condemned them. Yet what was gained by their
    condemnation?
Find an auctioneer, Chaerippus, to sell your rags,
since Pansa is stripping you now of whatever Natta left.
Then hush! On top of all that, it's madness to lose your boat-
    fare.

Once, when our allies were newly conquered and still were
    thriving,
things were different. To be sure, they groaned with pain at their
    losses;
but their private houses were full of goods; masses of money   100
remained untouched. They had Spartan cloaks and Coan
    purples.
They had Phidias' ivories, with Myron's bronzes and
    Parrhasius' pictures—
wonderfully life-like; Polyclitus' marbles were all around;
there was hardly a table without its piece of Mentor's silver.
Then Dolabella and the greedy Antonius, then the unholy
Verres set about smuggling home in their tall-hulled ships
peace-time trophies which far exceeded the spoils of war.

Now we can steal no more from our allies, on taking a croft,
than a few yoke of oxen, a handful of mares along with the
　　stallion,
and the actual gods of the hearth—if there's a decent statue,　110
or a single Lar in his little shrine. Perhaps you despise
people who prize such items highly (for these are their
　　treasures).
Well, you are right to despise the indolent sons of Rhodes,
and Corinth reeking with perfume (for what would you have to
　　fear
from the resined youth of a country where everyone's legs are
　　smooth?).
But hairy Spain, and the land of Gaul, and Illyria's coast—
be sure to stay clear of *them*; and leave those reapers alone
who feed the capital, setting it free for shows and races.
(The effects of your crime would be dire, and where's the profit?
　　For now that
Marius has stolen their money-belts, there are no fat Africans
　　left.)　　120
Beware, above all, of inflicting a grave injustice on people
who are brave as well as wretched. You can take their gold and
　　silver,
every bit of it; you will not remove their shield and sword,
their spear and helmet. When men have been robbed, they still
　　have weapons.

Those last words are not a mere epigram. No, they're the truth.　130
Believe me, I'm reading you one of the Sibyl's leaves.
If your staff is above reproach, no long-haired boy is permitted
to sell your verdicts, and no complaint is attached to your wife
(if she doesn't look forward to swooping down through the
　　towns and districts,
pouncing on cash with her crooked claws, just like a Celaeno),
you may trace your line to the woodpecker king; and if you
　　hanker
after loftier names, you may count the entire formation
of Titans—yes, and Prometheus himself—among your
　　forebears.　　133
But if ambition and lust sweep you impulsively on,　　135

if your rods are broken across the bloody backs of our allies,
if you take a delight in blunted axes and weary headsmen,
then the renown of those very ancestors stands in your way,
and holds a shining torch above your infamous deeds.
The higher a criminal's place in the world, the more universal   140
is the odium which he incurs for every vice of the soul.
Tell me, if you're a forger of wills, how does it help
that you do it in a temple your grandfather built, or in front of a
   statue
proclaiming your father's triumph? What use is birth if, at night-
   time,
you muffle your head in a Gallic cloak and set out on adultery?
The fat Lateranus hurtles past his family's ashes
and bones in a flying gig, and he himself, yes he
himself applies the brake to the wheel, does our muleteer
   consul—
by night, to be sure, but the moon looks down, and the stars
   bear witness,
watching intently. Later, when his term of office is ended,   150
then Lateranus will take up his whip in broad daylight.
Not in the least uneasy at meeting an elderly friend,
he will greet him first with a flick of his switch; he'll even unbind
a truss of hay and shake out barley for his weary mules.
Till then, while he slays 'a woolly victim and a reddish bullock'
as Numa prescribed, he swears before the altar of Jove
by Épona alone, whose picture is daubed on the stinking stables.
But when he decides to visit again the all-night bistro,
a Syrian Jew, wet with the perfume he has plastered on,
comes bustling up, a Syrian Jew from Palestine Gate,   160
playing 'mine host', calling him 'sir' and 'your honour'; behind
   him
comes barmaid Cýane, dress tucked up and flagon at the ready.
To excuse his misconduct, someone will say 'well we did the
   same
when we were lads'. Very well; but you stopped, I take it, and
   didn't
persist with your folly. Escapades should be just a phase.
Some kinds of silliness ought to be shed with your earliest beard.
Boys will be boys. But when Lateranus passed underneath

the awnings' coloured signs on his way to the bath-house bar,
he was old enough to defend Armenia's and Syria's rivers,
and also the Rhine and Danube. Men of that age have the vigour   170
to protect the person of Nero. Send your lieutenant, Caesar,
to Ostia, send him. But look for him first in a roomy bodega.
You will find him lying cheek by jowl beside an assassin,
enjoying the company of sailors, thieves, and runaway slaves,
on his right a hangman and a fellow who hammers coffins
    together,
on his left the silent drums of a sprawling eunuch priest.
Here is Liberty Hall. The cups are shared and the couches
are not reserved; everyone's equally close to the table.
Ponticus, what would you do if you chanced on a slave like
    him?
You'd pack him off to Lucania, I warrant, or a Tuscan chain-
    gang!   180
But our Trojan elite excuse each other; so forms of behaviour
are allowed to Brutus and Vólesus which would bring disgrace
    to a cobbler.

Alas, one can never cite so foul and shameful an instance
that something even worse does not remain to be mentioned.
When all his money was squandered, Damasippus proceeded to
    hire
his voice to the stage, playing the screaming *Ghost* of Catullus,
while the agile Lentulus played Lauréolus' part to perfection;
(if you ask me, he deserved a proper cross). But the people
themselves are partly to blame. With a brazen contempt for
    propriety,
they sit and watch the puerile antics of Rome's patricians;   190
they listen to Fabian fools, and manage to laugh at Mamerci
getting a drubbing. Who cares what such figures are paid in
    exchange
for their social existence? They sell it, although no Nero compels
    them.
They sell it, without a thought, at the games of the lofty praetor.
Yet imagine the headsman's sword was here, and the stage was
    there.
Which is the better? Would anyone choose, from fear of death,

to be Thýmele's jealous husband, or the clown Corinthus'
  partner?
And yet, when an emperor plays the harp, is it strange that a
  noble
should act in a farce? The one step left is the fighters' school.
Rome has known even that disgrace: a Gracchus fighting,   200
not in a 'fisherman's' gear, nor yet with shield and sabre   201
(he rejects those kinds of outfit); no, he wields a trident!
He casts the hovering net with a flick of the wrist; but on missing 204
his target he turns his uncovered face to the crowd, and
  displaying
his features to all he runs for his life across the arena.
There's no mistaking his tunic with the stripe of gold that
  stretches
down from its throat, or the ribbon that streams from his conical
  hat.
The 'chaser', therefore, who was ordered to enter the arena with
  Gracchus
endured a disgrace which was harder to bear than any wounds.   210

Give the people a free vote; without hesitation
every decent man would prefer Seneca to Nero.
To punish that creature in a fitting manner, a single ape,
a single snake, and a single bag would not have sufficed.
His crime was that of Agamemnon's son, but cases are altered
by motives. The latter, at the behest of heaven itself,
was avenging a father slain as the wine was flowing; he never
defiled himself by strangling Electra or shedding the blood
of his Spartan wife; he never mixed a poisoned cocktail
for his own relations; never sang the part of Orestes,   220
or wrote a Trojan epic. What crime cried louder for vengeance
on the part of Verginius' men or those of Vindex and Galba,
of all that Nero committed in his savage and bloody reign?
These are the achievements, these the arts of our high-born
  sovereign,
one who enjoyed demeaning himself on a foreign stage
by his horrid singing, and winning a garland of Grecian parsley.
Deck your forefathers' busts with the prizes won by your voice;
before Domitius' feet lay down the trailing robe

of Thyestes, or else the mask of Antigone or Melanippe,
and hang your harp on your own colossal statue of marble!   230

What could you hope to find more high than Catiline's birth
or that of Cethégus? Yet *they* conspired to attack our homes
and temples at night, with steel and flame, as though they
    belonged
to the heirs of the trousered Narbonese or the sons of the
    Senónes;
they dared an outrage grave enough for 'the shirt of discomfort'.
But a consul was on the alert, and threw their banners back.
A man who was new to office, a provincial knight from
    Arpínum,
a commoner just arrived in Rome, posted detachments
throughout the frightened city; took thought for every hill.
Thus, within the walls, the toga conferred upon him   240
renown and honour no less than Octavian won off Leucas,
or upon Thessaly's plains when, with his dripping sword,
he forged a chain of death. But Rome was a free republic
when she called Cicero her country's parent and her country's
    father.
Another son of Arpínum worked in the Volscian hills
for a daily wage, toiling behind another's plough.
Later, the centurion's knotty staff would break on his head,
when he was slow or lazy in digging the camp's defences.
Yet *he* took on the Cimbri, at a time of national peril,
and he was the one who brought salvation to the terrified city.   250
And so, as the ravens (who had never encountered such massive
    corpses)
glided down to glut themselves on the slaughtered Cimbri,
his noble colleague was given a smaller share of the bays.
The souls of the Decii, yes, their very names were plebeian;
they, however, were deemed enough by the gods below
and by Mother Earth to serve as quittance for all the legions,
and all the auxiliary troops, and all the youth of Latium.   257
One born of a slave attained to Quirínus' crown   259
and his mantle and rods. He was the last of our righteous kings,   260
whereas the sons of the consul himself plotted to open
the bolts of the gates to the banished tyrants, acting like traitors,

when they ought to have done some valiant deed to establish
   freedom,
a deed which Mucius, or Cocles, or the lass who swam the Tiber
(then the bounds of the Roman empire) could have admired.
A slave who was fit to be mourned by ladies divulged the secret
plot to the senate. The sons received their just deserts
from the lash and the axe, then for the first time sanctioned by
   law.

I'd rather Thersites had been your father, provided that you
resembled Aeacus' grandson and could wield the weapons of
   Vulcan,   270
than that Achilles begat you, and you were another Thersites.
However far back you care to go in tracing your name,
the fact remains that your clan began in a haven for outlaws.
The first of all your line, whatever his name may have been,
was either a shepherd—or else a thing I'd rather not mention.

SATIRE 9

The Woes of a Gigolo

Tell me, Naevolus—why, whenever we meet, do you wear
a gloomy scowl, like Mársyas when he had lost the contest?
Why do you have the expression that Ravola had when I caught
  him
with his beard still damp from brushing Rhodope's crotch, and I
  gave him
the kind of thrashing one gives to a slave found licking a pastry?
Your face is as tragic as that of Creperéius Póllio, who,
though he goes around offering triple interest, can't find a
  person
fool enough to take him on. Why, all of a sudden,
so many wrinkles? You used to ask little of life, and would play
the provincial squire, an amusing guest who would make
  remarks   10
with a trenchant wit, urbane as anything born in the city.
Now all is changed. Your expression is grim; your hair is dry
and as wild as a forest; your skin has totally lost that gloss
produced by bandages plastered with hot Bruttian pitch;
hairs are sprouting all over your dirty neglected legs.
What does this mean? You're as thin as a patient in whom a
  quartan
fever has long resided, ensuring a regular roasting.
You can tell the mental pain that lurks in a sick man's body;
it's the same with joy. The face derives its smiles and frowns
from within. And so you seem to have altered your style of
  behaviour,   20
and to be going against your previous way of life.
Recently, as I recall, you would hang around Isis' temple,
and Peace's Ganymede, and the Palatine shrine of the immigrant
  mother,

and Ceres too (for women are there in every temple).
Aufidius himself was no better known as a hunter of wives;
and (what you don't divulge) you would also mount their
    husbands.

'Many have made a profit from this kind of life, but I
have had no return for my efforts. Now and again I am given
a greasy cloak to protect my toga (rough and coarse,
and loose in texture, thanks to the comb of a Gallic weaver),   30
or a piece of brittle silver from an inferior vein.
Men are governed by fate, including those parts which are
    hidden
beneath their clothes. For if the stars are not in your favour,
the unheard of length of your dangling tool will count for
    nothing,
even though, when you're stripped, Virro stares at you
    drooling
and sends you a continuous stream of coaxing billets-doux.
As Homer said, it's the queer himself that lures a man on.
And yet, what creature is more grotesque than a miserly
    pervert?
"I paid you this; I gave you that; and then you got more."
As he tots it up he wriggles his rump. Well, set out the
    counters;   40
send for the slaves and the abacus. Put down five thousand in all
as paid to me. And then put down my heavy exertions.
Do you think it's nice and easy to thrust a proper-sized penis
into a person's guts, encountering yesterday's dinner?
The slave who ploughs a field has a lighter task than the one
who ploughs its owner. But you, of course, used to think
    yourself
a pretty young lad, fit to become a butler in heaven.
Will people like you show any kindness to a humble attendant
or to a client, when you will not pay for your sick diversions?
There is the type to whom you should send big amber balls   50
on his birthday, or perhaps a green umbrella in showery weather
in early spring, when he drapes himself on a chaise longue,
fingering the stealthy presents which Ladies' Day has brought
    him!

Tell me, my sparrow, for whom are you keeping those hills and
   estates
in Apulia, those kites which are weary from flying across your
   pastures?
Your Trifoline land with its fertile vineyards, the ridge above
   Cumae,
and Gaurus' cratered hill provide you with ample reserves.
(Does anyone seal more vats of wine that will last for longer?)
How much would it cost to present an acre or two to the organs
of your worn-out client? But as things are, that child in the
   country   60
with his mother and little cottage and playmate pup—is it
   better
that he should be left in your will to a friend who bashes the
   cymbals?
"It's impertinent of you to beg," he says. But my rent is
   shouting
"Beg!" and my slave joins in, as solitary as Polyphemus'
enormous eye, which let the cunning Ulysses escape.
He's not enough; a second will have to be purchased, and both
of them fed. So what shall I do when the blizzards blow, I ask
   you,
what shall I say to my lads in December, when their feet and
   shoulders
are chilled by the cold north wind? "Hold on, and wait for the
   cicadas"?

Even though you conceal and ignore everything else,   70
don't you attach any value to the fact that, had I not been
a loyal and devoted client, your wife would still be a virgin?
You know right well how often you begged that favour—the
   tones
employed, the promises made. Why the girl was actually
   leaving
when I caught her in my arms. She had torn up the contract and
   was moving out.
I barely managed to save the situation; it took me all night,
while you were wailing outside. The bed is my witness, and
   you—

you must have heard the creaking of the bed and the mistress's
    moaning.
A tottering crumbling marriage just on the verge of collapse
has, in the case of many a house, been saved by a lover.   80
Why prevaricate? How can you frame a respectable answer?
Does it count for nothing, nothing at all, you ungrateful
    swindler,
that, thanks to me, you possess a little son and daughter?
You rear them as yours, and you like to proclaim in the daily
    gazette
the proofs of your manhood. Hang a garland over your door;
now you're a father! I've given you the means of silencing
    gossip.
Thanks to me, you have parent's rights; you are listed as heir,
you receive whole legacies, and juicy bequests which celebates
    forfeit.
As well as bequests, you'll enjoy many another advantage,
if I bring your family up to three.'   90
                          You have every reason
to feel resentful, Naevolus. But what does he say in reply?
'He turns a deaf ear and looks for another two-legged donkey.
I'm telling you this in total confidence; so keep it secret;
just lock my protests quietly away inside your memory.
It's fatal to antagonize someone who smooths his body with
    pumice.
The man who has recently told me his secret is angry, and hates
    me.
He suspects I've given away what I know. He will not scruple
to use a dagger, lay open my head with a bludgeon, and set
my door alight. You mustn't dismiss or ignore the fact that,
for wealth like his, the price of poison is never too high.   100
So keep these things to yourself, like the council of Mars in
    Athens.'

Corydon, Corydon, alas! Do you think a rich man's secret
is ever preserved? If his slaves keep quiet, his horses and dog
will talk, and his doorposts and statues. Fasten the shutters, and
    cover
the chinks with curtains; close the door and remove the light;

have all the guests withdraw; let no one sleep within earshot.
Nevertheless, all that he did at second cock-crow
will be known before dawn to the local barman, along with
    whatever
confections the pastrycook may have dreamt up with the aid of
    the carver
and the chief chef. They'll stop at nothing in inventing charges   110
against their master; for they use such slanders to take revenge
on the straps. And there'll always be someone to track you down
    in the street
and insist on befuddling your luckless ears with his drunken
    stories.
They are the people you ought to urge to keep dark the matters
on which, just now, you pledged me to silence. But they would
    rather
betray a secret than drink stolen Falernian vintage
in the quantities that Saufeia would swill when conducting a
    service.
There are many reasons for living aright, the best one being   118
that then you can treat with disdain the wagging tongues of your
    servants.   120
The tongue is always the vilest part of a worthless slave.   121
'The advice you have just been giving is sound, but rather
    general.   124
What should I do right now, in view of my wasted years
and the ruin of my hopes? As a fleeting flower, the paltry portion
of our sad and straitened life is hurrying on to finish
its course. As we drink our wine, as we call for perfume and
    garlands
and girls—old age, unnoticed, is creeping stealthily up.'

Courage! So long as these hills stand firm, you will never be
    short   130
of a passive friend to support you. From every corner of the
    world
they all converge on Rome in carriage and ship—the fraternity
that scratches its head with a single finger. A second and greater
hope remains: ⟨like others, seek out a rich old woman⟩,
you'll be her darling, provided you crunch up plenty of rockets.   134A

'Quote these cases to luckier souls. My Clotho and Lachesis
are well content if my organ provides for my belly's needs.
O little household gods of mine, whose aid I am wont
to secure with meal, or grains of incense and a simple garland,
when shall I net a sum that will save me, when I am old,
from the beggar's mat and crutch? An income of twenty
    thousand   140
from a well-secured principal; some plain silver (a few little
    pieces,
which censor Fabricius, however, would ban), a couple of
    brawny
Moesian porters to take me upon their shoulders, and let me
ride serenely above the crowd at the noisy racetrack.
I would like, in addition, a stooping engraver, and also an artist
quick at producing numerous portraits. That is sufficient.
When shall I ever be merely "poor"? A pitiful prayer
without much hope. When Fortune is prayed to on my behalf,
she always stops her ears with wax obtained from the vessel
which was pulled away from Sicily's songs by unhearing
    oarsmen.'   150

SATIRE 10

The Futility of Aspirations

In all the countries that stretch from Cadiz across to the Ganges
and the lands of dawn, how few are the people who manage to
  tell
genuine blessings from those of a very different order,
dispelling the mists of error! For when do we have good
  grounds
for our fears or desires? What idea proves so inspired that you do
  not
regret your attempt to carry it out, and its realization?
The gods, in response to the prayers of the owners, obligingly
  wreck
entire households. In peace and in war alike, we beg
for things that will hurt us. To many the art of speaking is fatal,
and their own torrential fluency. In a famous instance, an athlete   10
met his end through trusting in his strength and his marvellous
  muscles.
More, however, are smothered by heaps of money, amassed
with excessive care, and by fortunes exceeding other men's
  wealth
by as much as the giant British whale outgrows the dolphin.
Hence it was, in those terrible times, that on Nero's orders
Longinus' house and the over-rich Seneca's spacious park
were closed, and the Lateran family's splendid mansion
  besieged
by an entire company. A soldier rarely enters an attic.
When you make a journey by night, if you carry even a handful
of plain silver items, you will go in fear of the sword   20
and barge-pole; you will quake at the shadow of a reed that
  sways in the moonlight.
The traveller with nothing on him sings in the robber's face.

As a rule, the first prayer offered, and the one that is most
    familiar
in every temple, is 'money': 'let my wealth increase,' 'let my
    strong box
be the biggest of all down town'. But aconite never is drunk
from an earthenware mug; *that* is something to fear when you're
    handed
a jewelled cup, or when Setine glows in a golden wine-bowl.
In view of that, you may well approve of the two philosophers:
one of them used to laugh whenever he closed the door
and stepped into the street; his opposite number would weep.   30
While harsh censorious laughter is universal and easy,
one wonders how the other's eyes were supplied with moisture.
Demócritus' sides would shake with gales of incessant laughter,
although in the towns of his day there were no purple- or scarlet-
bordered togas to be seen; no rods or litters or platforms.
What *would* he have made of a praetor standing there in his car,
lifted high in the air amid the dust of the race-track,
dressed in the tunic of Jove himself, with a curtain-like toga
of Tyrian embroidery draped on his shoulders, and a crown so
    enormous
in its circumference that no neck could support its weight;   40
in fact it is held by a public slave who sweats with exertion.
(He rides in the same chariot to restrain the official from hybris.)
And don't forget the bird that is perched on his ivory staff,
on this side trumpeters, on that a train of dutiful clients
walking in front, and the snow-white Romans beside his bridle
who have been transformed into friends by the dole thrust into
    their purses.
In his day too, in all the places where people gathered,
he found material for laughter. He showed by his excellent sense
that men of the highest quality who will set the finest examples
may be born in a land with a thick climate, peopled by
    boneheads.   50
He used to laugh at the masses' worries, and at their pleasures,
and sometimes, too, at their tears. For himself, when Fortune
    threatened,
he would tell her go hang, and make a sign with his middle
    finger.

So what in fact are the useless or dangerous things that are
    sought,
for which one must duly cover the knees of the gods with wax?
Some are sent hurtling down by the virulent envy to which
their power exposes them. Their long and impressive list of
    achievements
ruins them. Down come their statues, obeying the pull of the
    rope.
Thereupon, axe-blows rain on the very wheels of their chariots,
smashing them up; and the legs of the innocent horses are
    broken.   60
Now the flames are hissing; bellows and furnace are bringing
a glow to the head revered by the people. The mighty Sejanus
is crackling. Then, from the face regarded as number two
in the whole of the world, come pitchers, basins, saucepans, and
    piss-pots.
Frame your door with laurels; drag a magnificent bull,
whitened with chalk, to the Capitol. They're dragging Sejanus
    along
by a hook for all to see. Everyone's jubilant. 'Look,
what lips he had! What a face! You can take it from me that I
    never
cared for the fellow. But what was the charge that brought him
    down?
Who informed, who gave him away, what witnesses proved it?'   70
'Nothing like that. A large, long-winded letter arrived
from Capri.'
                'Fine . . . I ask no more.'
                             But what's the reaction
of Remus' mob? It supports the winner, as always, and turns on
whoever is condemned. If Nortia had smiled on her Tuscan
    favourite,
if the elderly prince had been caught off guard and sent to his
    death,
that same public, at this very moment, would be hailing Sejanus
as Augustus. Long ago, the people cast off its worries,
when we stopped selling our votes. A body that used to confer
commands, legions, rods, and everything else, has now
narrowed its scope, and is eager and anxious for two things only: 80

bread and races.
        'I hear that a lot are going to die.'
'No question about it. The kitchen is sure to be hot.'
                                'My friend
Bruttidius looked a bit pale when I met him beside Mars' altar.
I've an awful feeling that the mortified Ajax may take revenge
for being exposed to danger. So now, as he lies by the river,
let's all run and kick the man who was Caesar's enemy.
But check that our slaves are watching; then no one can say we
    didn't,
and drag his terrified master to court with his head in a noose.'

Such were the whispers and the common gossip concerning
    Sejanus.
Do *you* want to be greeted each morning, as Sejanus was;   90
to possess his wealth; to bestow on one a magistrate's chair,
to appoint another to an army command; to be seen as the
    guardian
of Rome's chief, as he sits on the narrow Rock of the Roedeers
with his herd of Chaldaeans? Of course you would like to have
    spears and cohorts,
the cream of the knights, and a barracks as part of your house.
    Why *shouldn't* you
want them? For even people with no desire to kill
covet the power. But what is the good of prestige and prosperity
if, for every joy, they bring an equal sorrow?
Would you sooner wear the bordered robe of the man that you
    see there
being dragged along, or be a power in Fidénae or Gabii,   100
adjudicating on weights and quantities, or a ragged aedile
smashing undersize measuring cups in empty Ulúbrae?
You acknowledge, then, that Sejanus never succeeded in
    grasping
what one should really pray for. By craving ever more honours
and seeking ever more wealth, he was building a lofty tower
of numerous storeys; which meant that the fall would be all the
    greater,
and that when the structure gave way, its collapse would wreak
    devastation.

What cast down the likes of Pompey and Crassus, and him
who tamed the people of Rome and brought them under the
   lash?
It was the pursuit of the highest place by every device,   110
and grandiose prayers, which were duly heard by malevolent
   gods.
Few monarchs go down to Ceres' son-in-law free from
bloody wounds; few tyrants avoid a sticky death.

Glorious eloquence, such as Demosthenes and Cicero had—
that is desired from the start, and through Minerva's vacation,
by the youngster who worships the thrifty goddess, as yet with a
   coin,
and who has a slave in attendance to mind his diminutive satchel.
Yet eloquence proved the undoing of both those statesmen; and
   both
were carried to ruin by the large and copious flood of their genius.
Thanks to his genius, one had his hands and head cut off.   120
(The rostrum was never stained with a petty advocate's blood.)
'O fortunate state of Rome, which dates from my consulate!'
He could have scorned Mark Antony's swords, had all his
   sayings
been like that. So—better to write ridiculous poems
than that inspired Philippic (the second one in the set)
which is universally praised. An equally cruel death
removed the man whose fluent power excited the wonder
of Athens, as he used his reins to drive the crowded assembly.
The gods in heaven frowned on his birth, and fate was against
   him.
His father, with eyes inflamed by the soot of the glowing metal,   130
sent him away from the coal and tongs, and the anvil that
   fashions
swords, and all the filth of Vulcan, to a rhetoric tutor.

The spoils of war—a breastplate nailed to the trunk of a tree
shorn of its branches, a cheekpiece dangling from a shattered
   helmet,
a chariot's yoke with its pole snapped off, a pennant ripped
from a crippled warship, a dejected prisoner on top of an arch—

these, it is thought, represent superhuman blessings, and these
are the things that stir a general, be he Greek, Roman, or
    foreign,
to excitement; they provide a justification for all
his toil and peril. So much stronger is the thirst for glory   140
than for goodness. (Who, in fact, embraces Goodness herself,
if you take away the rewards?) Often states have been ruined
by a few men's greed for fame, by their passion for praise and for
    titles
inscribed in the stones protecting their ashes—stones which the
    boorish
strength of the barren fig-tree succeeds in splitting apart;
for even funeral monuments have their allotted life-span.
Weigh Hannibal; how many pounds will you find in that
    mighty
commander? This is the man too big for Africa—a land
which is pounded by the Moorish sea and extends to the
    steaming Nile,
then south to Ethiopia's tribes and their different elephants.   150
He annexes Spain to his empire, and dances lightly across
the Pyrenees; then nature bars his path with the snowy Alps;
by vinegar's aid he splits the rocks and shatters the mountains.
Italy now is within his grasp; but he still presses on.
'Nought is achieved,' he cries, 'until I have smashed the gates
with my Punic troops, and raised our flag in the central Subura!'
Lord, what a sight! It would surely have made an amazing
    picture:
the one-eyed general riding on his huge Gaetulian beast.
So how does the story end? Alas for glory! Our hero
is beaten. He scrambles away into exile, and there he sits   160
in the hall of the monarch's palace, a great and conspicuous
    client,
until it shall please his Bithynian lord to greet the day.
That soul which once convulsed the world will meet its end,
not from a sword, or stones, or spears, but from an object
which, avenging Cannae, will take reprisal for all that
    bloodshed—
a ring. Go on, you maniac; charge through the Alpine wastes
to entertain a class of boys and become an oration!

A single world is not enough for the youth of Pella.
He frets and chafes at the narrow limits set by the globe,
as though confined on Gýara's rocks or tiny Seríphos.   170
Yet, when he enters the city that was made secure by its potters,
he will rest content with a coffin. It is only death which reveals
the puny size of human bodies. People believe
that ships once sailed over Athos, and all the lies that Greece
has the nerve to tell in her histories: that the sea was covered with
    boats,
and the ocean provided a solid surface for wheels. We believe
deep rivers failed, that streams were all drunk dry by the
    Persians
at lunch, and whatever Sostratus sings with his soaking pinions.
Yet in what state did the king return on leaving Salamis—
the one who would vent his savage rage on Corus and Eurus   180
with whips, an outrage never endured in Aeolus' cave,
the one who bound the earth-shaking god himself with fetters
(that, indeed, was somewhat mild; why he even considered
he deserved a branding! What god would be slave to a man like
    that?)—
yet in what state did he return? In a solitary warship, slowly
pushing its way through the bloody waves which were thick
    with corpses.
Such is the price so often claimed by our coveted glory.

'Jupiter, grant me a lengthy life and many a year!'
Whether you are hale or wan, that is your only prayer.
Yet think of the endless and bitter afflictions that always attend   190
a long old age. First and foremost, look at the face—
misshapen and hideous beyond recognition; instead of skin,
you see a misshapen hide, baggy cheeks, and the kind
of wrinkles that are etched on the aged jowls of an African ape,
where Thábraca stretches its shady forests along the coast.
Young men vary in numerous ways—A is more handsome
than B and has different features; C is more sturdy than D.
Old men are all alike—trembling in body and voice,
with a pate that is now quite smooth, and the running nose of an
    infant.

The poor old fellow must mumble his bread with toothless
    gums.   200
He is so repellent to all (wife, children, and himself),
that he even turns the stomach of Cossus the legacy-hunter.
He loses his former zest for food and wine as his palate
grows numb. He has long forgotten what sex was like; if one
    tries
to remind him, his shrunken tool, with its vein enlarged, just lies
    there,
and, though caressed all night, it will continue to lie there.
As for the future, what can those white-haired ailing organs
hope for? Moreover, the lust that, in spite of impotence,
    struggles
to gain satisfaction, is rightly suspect. And now consider
the loss of another faculty. What joy does he get from a singer,   210
however outstanding, or from the harpist Seleucus and others
who as harpists or pipers always shine in golden mantles?
What does it matter where he sits in the spacious theatre,
when he can barely hear the sound of the horns or the fanfare
of trumpets? The slave announcing a caller's arrival or telling
the time is obliged to shout in his ear to make himself heard.
Again, so little blood remains in his chilly veins
that he's only warm when he has a fever. All kinds of ailments
band together and dance around him. If you asked their names
I could sooner tell you how many lovers Oppia has taken,   220
how many patients Thémison has killed in a single autumn,
how many partners have been swindled by Basilus, how many
    minors
by Hirrus, how many men are drained in a single day
by the tall Maura, how many schoolboys are debauched by
    Hamillus.
I could sooner count the country houses now possessed
by the fellow who made my stiff young beard crunch with his
    clippers.
Here it's a shoulder crippled, there a pelvis or hip;
this man has lost both eyes, and envies the fellow with one;
that takes food with bloodless lips from another's fingers.
He used to bare his teeth in greed at the sight of a dinner;   230
now he merely gapes like a swallow's chick when its mother

alights with a beakful, going without herself. And yet,
worse than any physical loss is the mental decay
which cannot remember servants' names, nor the face of the
    friend
with whom he dined the previous evening, nor even the
    children,
his very own, whom he raised himself. By a cruel will
he forbids his flesh and blood to inherit, and all his possessions
go to Phíalë. So potent the breath of that artful mouth
which stood on sale for many years in the cell of a brothel.
Suppose his mind retains its vigour, he still must walk   240
in front of his children's coffins, and bear to gaze on the pyre
of his beloved wife or brother and on urns full of his sisters.
This is the price of longevity. As people age, the disasters
within their homes for ever recur; grief follows grief;
their sorrows never cease, and their dress is the black of
    mourning.
The king of Pylos, if you place any trust in mighty Homer,
stood for a life which was second only to that of a crow.
No doubt he was happy. Postponing death for three
    generations,
he began to count his years upon his right hand's fingers;
he drank new wine at many a harvest. But listen a little,   250
I urge you, to the bitter complaints which he makes at the laws
    of fate
and his own protracted thread, as he watches the beard of the
    valiant
Antílochus blazing, and appeals to all his friends who are there
to tell him why *he* should have survived to the present age,
and what crime he has committed to deserve so long a life.
Peleus did the same as he mourned the death of Achilles;
and so did the other, who rightly lamented the Ithacan
    swimmer.
Troy would still have been standing when Priam went down to
    join
the shades of Assaracus—Cassandra and Polyxena, tearing their
    garments,
would have led the ritual cries of lament, while Hector, along
    with   260

his many brothers, would have shouldered the body and carried
  it out
with magnificent pomp amid the tears of Ilium's daughters—
had Priam died at an earlier time, a time when Paris
had not as yet begun to build his intrepid fleet.
Therefore what boon did his great age bring him? He lived to see
everything wrecked, and Asia sinking in flame and steel.
Then, removing his crown, he took arms, a doddering soldier,
and slumped by the altar of highest Jove like a worn-out ox,
which is scorned by the ungrateful plough after all its years of
  service
and offers its scraggy pathetic neck to its master's blade.   270
His was at least the end of a human being; the wife
who survived him became a vicious bitch, snarling and barking.

I hasten on to our countrymen, passing over the king
of Pontus, and Croesus too, whom the righteous Solon
  exhorted
in eloquent words to watch the close of a long-run life.
Exile, prison walls, the dreary swamps of Minturnae,
begging for bread in the ruins of Carthage—it all resulted
from living too long. What could nature, what could Rome
have brought forth upon earth more blest than that famous
  man,
if, after leading around the city his host of captives   280
and all the parade of war, he had breathed his last at the moment
of greatest glory, when poised to leave his Teutonic car?
With kindly foresight, Campania gave a desirable fever
to Pompey; however, the public prayers of numerous cities
prevailed; so Pompey's fortune and that of the capital saved
his life—but only to cut it off in defeat. Such mangling
Lentulus missed; Cethégus avoided that fate and was killed
without mutilation; Catiline lay with his corpse entire.

When she passes Venus' temple, the anxious mother requests
beauty—in a quiet voice for her sons, more loudly for her
  daughters,   290
going to fanciful lengths in her prayers. 'So I do,' she says,
'what's wrong with that? Latona delights in Diana's beauty.'

But Lucretia discourages people from praying for looks of the
    kind
which she had herself. Verginia would welcome Rutila's hump
and bestow her own appearance on *her*. It's the same with a son;
if he possesses physical charm, his parents are always
in a state of wretched anxiety. For it's true that beauty and virtue
are rarely found together. Although he may come from a home
which instils pure habits and is just as strict as the Sabines of old,
although generous Nature may add with a kindly hand   300
the gift of an innocent heart and a face that burns with modest
blushes (what greater boon can a boy receive from Nature,
who has more authority than any caring parent or guardian?),
he is not allowed to become a man. A wealthy seducer
with brazen effrontery actually dares to approach the parents.
Such is the confidence placed in bribes. No *ugly* youngster
was ever castrated by a despot within his barbarous castle.
Nero would never rape a stripling with bandy legs
or scrofula, or one with a swollen belly and a crooked back.
I challenge you now to rejoice in your son's good looks! And
    greater   310
hazards still are ahead. He'll become a lover at large;
then he will have to fear whatever reprisals a furious
husband may take. (He can hardly hope to have better luck
than the ill-starred Mars; he too will be caught in the net.)
    Moreover,
such anger sometimes exacts more than is granted to anger
by any law. Thus one is cut down by a dagger; another
is cut up by a bloody whip; some make room for a mullet.
Your young Endymion will fall for a married lady and become
her lover. And then, once he has taken Servilia's cash,
he will do it to one for whom he cares nothing, stripping her body 320
of all its jewellery. For what will any woman deny
to her clammy crotch? She may be an Oppia or a Catulla,
but when she's rotten, *that* is the centre of all her conduct.
'What harm is beauty to one who is pure?' Ask rather what profit
was gained by Hippolytus, or by Bellerophon, from his stern
    convictions.
            〈Phaedra and Sthenoboea〉

She blushed with shame at the rebuff, as though despised for her
    looks;
Sthenoboea, too, was just as incensed as the woman of Crete.
They lashed themselves, both, to fury; a woman is at her most
    savage
when goaded to hatred by an injured pride.

                         Decide what advice
you think should be offered to the man whom Caesar's wife is
    determined   330
to marry. He's a fine fellow of excellent birth, and extremely
handsome; but the luckless wretch is being swept to his death
by Messalína's eyes. She has long been sitting there, all prepared
in her flaming veil; a purple bed stands open to view
in the grounds. A dowry of a million will be paid in the old
    ancestral
manner; a priest will come with people to witness the contract.
Perhaps you thought all this was a secret known to a few?
Not at all; she insists on a proper ceremony. State your decision.
Unless you're willing to obey her commands, you must die
    before dusk.
If you go through with the crime, there will be a respite until   340
what is known to all and sundry reaches the emperor's ear.
He'll be the last to hear of his family's shame; in the meantime
do what you're told, if you rate a few days' extra life
as highly as that. Whatever you judge to be the more easy
and better course, that fine white neck must bow to the sword.

Is there nothing, then, that people should pray for? If you want
    some advice,
you will let the heavenly powers themselves determine what
    blessings
are most appropriate to us and best suit our condition;
for instead of what's pleasant, the gods will always provide
    what's fitting.
They care more for man than he cares for himself; for we   350
are driven by the force of emotion, a blind overmastering
    impulse,

when we yearn for marriage and a wife who will give us
    children; the gods,
however, foresee what the wife and children are going to be like.
Still, that you may have something to ask for—some reason to
    offer
the holy sausages and innards of a little white pig in a chapel—
you ought to pray for a healthy mind in a healthy body.
Ask for a valiant heart which has banished the fear of death,
which looks upon length of days as one of the least of nature's
gifts; which is able to suffer every kind of hardship,
is proof against anger, craves for nothing, and reckons the trials   360
and gruelling labours of Hercules as more desirable blessings
than the amorous ease and the banquets and cushions of
    Sardanapállus.
The things that I recommend you can grant to yourself; it is
    certain
that the tranquil life can only be reached by the path of goodness.
Lady Luck, if the truth were known, you possess no power;
it is we who make you a goddess and give you a place in heaven.

SATIRE 11

A Simple Life-style

If Atticus eats an excellent dinner, he's said to be princely;
if Rútilus does, he's mad. For what is greeted with louder
guffaws by the public than a poverty-stricken Apicius? Every
meeting-place, all the baths, every assembly and play-house
is full of Rutilus. For, at a time when he's young and strong,
hot-blooded, and fit to bear arms, they say he is going to sign
a contract accepting the trainer's tyrannical terms and
    conditions.
The tribune doesn't compel him to do so, but nor does he stop
    him.
To many another also, the only reason for living
lies in the palate. So the creditors, whom they have given the
    slip,   10
can always be seen waiting to catch them at the market entrance.
The richest and costliest dinners are devoured by the poorest of
    all,
whose ruined life, with its gaping holes, is about to collapse.
But first they scour air, earth, and water for dainty morsels.
Where greed is concerned, the cost is no object; in fact you will
    find,
if you look more closely, the higher the price the greater the
    pleasure.
They do not balk at raising money, soon to be squandered,
by pawning their plate or melting down a statue of mother.
Their last four hundred goes to supply a gourmet's trimmings
for an earthenware supper. Then it's the hash of the fighters'
    school.   20
So a lot depends on who gives the meal. What in Rutilus' case
is reckless waste, in that of Ventidius at once acquires
a respectable name, deriving esteem from his fortune.

                                                        For me,
there is every reason to despise the type who knows how much
    higher
Atlas is than the other Libyan mountains and yet
is unable to tell the difference between a purse and a strongbox
bound in iron. 'Know thyself' has been sent from heaven—
a motto which should be fixed in the mind and thought upon,
    whether
you are looking for a wife or seeking a place in that honoured
    body,
the senate. Thersites never claimed Achilles' breastplate;   30
Ulysses donned it, and then became a public disgrace.
If you aspire to defend a case of the highest importance
which could go either way, examine yourself and be candid:
are you a powerful speaker, or a windbag like Curtius and
    Matho?
A man should take stock of himself, and bear that balance in
    mind
in matters great and small. So when you are buying a fish,
take care not to set your heart on a salmon when there's only a
.   kipper
in your pocket. For if your purse continues to shrink as your
    gullet
expands, just how do you think it's all going to end,
when your family fortune and assets have been swallowed up by
    that belly   40
which devours interest, silverware, flocks, and acres alike?
In the case of such owners, the last possession to leave the family
is the ring; when his finger is stripped, Pollio has to beg.
It is not an untimely funeral pyre and an early grave
that a wastrel fears; no, death is less of a horror than age.
These are the usual stages: money is raised in Rome,
and the creditors see it squandered. Then, when only a trifling
sum is left and the money-lender is turning pale,
it's time for a change of scene, and they're off to Baiae's oysters.
It is now no worse to leave the city square as a bankrupt   50
than to move your address to the Esquiline out of the stifling
    Subura.
The only grief that exiles feel, and their only sadness,

is this: they have to survive for a year without the races.
Not enough blood is left in their cheeks to produce a blush;
Shame is jeered as she leaves the city, and few detain her.

You will be able to check today, dear Persicus, whether
in my life and conduct I fail to practise those high-sounding
    precepts,
praising pulse though at heart a glutton; ordering porridge
when people are listening, but whispering 'cakes' in my
    servant's ear.
Now that you've promised to come to dinner, you will find in
    me   60
an Evander; you will be the hero of Tiryns, or else
the lesser guest, though he was also akin to the gods.
The latter was raised to the stars by water, the former by fire.
Here is the menu, supplied without the help of the market:
from my farm at Tivoli a kid will come, the tenderest and
    plumpest
of all the herd, one which has never tasted grass
or dared as yet to nibble the twigs of the humble willow,
one which is fuller of milk than blood, and with him, from the
    hillside,
asparagus picked by the farmer's wife after leaving her spindle.
There will also be fine large eggs, still warm in their packing of
    straw,   70
along with the hens that laid them, and grapes which have been
    preserved
for half the year and are just as fresh as they were on the vine;
Signia and Syria provide the pears and, sharing their baskets,
are apples that rival those from Picénum and keep their
    fragrance.
You needn't have any worries; they are quite reliable, now that
the cold has dried the bitter juice which they had in the autumn.

That was the kind of dinner, quite lavish by then, which the
    senate
would eat in days gone by. Curius picked his greens
in his plot and cooked them himself on his tiny hearth. Such a
    menu

is now despised by a filthy labourer digging a ditch   80
in chains. (He remembers the taste of tripe in a stuffy tavern.)
The ancient way was to keep in store for special occasions
a side of salted pork, which hung from a wickerwork frame,
and to serve a flitch of bacon as a birthday treat to relations,
with some fresh meat besides, if a sacrifice chanced to provide it.
A kinsman, honoured thrice with the title of consul, a man who
had held command over armies and had wielded the power of
    dictator,
would make for home rather sooner than normal to attend such
    a banquet,
carrying his mattock at the slope after subduing a mountain.
When people trembled before the Fabii and stern old Cato,   90
and before such men as Scaurus and Fabricius, when even a
    censor
feared the harshness that might result from his colleague's
    austerity,
nobody thought it a matter for grave and serious attention
what kind of turtle, swimming then in the ocean's waves,
might make a splendid and noble prop for our Trojan élite.
Couches were small, their sides were plain, and only the
    headrest
was bronze; it showed the garlanded head of a common donkey;
beside it the lively country children would romp and play.   98

The soldier was rough, and untrained to admire the art of
    Greece.
                                                                    100
When, after the sack of a city, he found in his share of the spoil
cups produced by famous artists, he would break them up
to give his horse the pleasure of trappings, and to set designs
on his helmet, so that the foe might see at the moment of death
Romulus' beast grown tame, as imperial destiny ordered,
the Quirinal twins within the cave, and the naked image
of Mars, as, grasping his shield and sword, he swooped from
    above.
And so they would serve their porridge on plates of Tuscan
    ware.
What silver they had would shine on their weapons, and
    nowhere else.

(To covet such riches you would have to be somewhat jealous
    by nature.)   110
Help was also closer at hand from the mighty temples.
At the time when the Gauls were advancing on Rome from the
    edge of the ocean,
a voice was heard at midnight throughout the silent city;
for the gods were playing the role of prophet. These were the
    warnings
he gave us, this was the care which Jove devoted to Latium
when he was made of clay and still unspoiled by gold.
In those days men were accustomed to seeing Italian tables,
made from our native trees; wood was there for the purpose
whenever an easterly gale uprooted an ancient walnut.

Now, however, the rich derive no pleasure from dining,   120
turbot and venison lose their flavour, perfume and roses
seem to stink, unless an enormous circular table
rests on a mass of ivory—a rampant snarling leopard
made of the kind of tusk that comes from Syene's gate,
or from the speedy Moor, or the Indian duskier still,
or is shed by the monstrous beast in some Nabatéan glade
as being too large for his head to carry. This stimulates
    hunger
and promotes digestion; for a table with silver feet is to them
like an iron ring on the finger. That is why I avoid
the snobbish guest who compares his host to himself and
    despises   130
a simple style of living. I do not possess an ounce
of ivory; neither my dice nor any of my pieces are made
of that material; why even the very handles of my knives
are bone. Yet that never spoils the taste of my savoury dishes,
nor is my slice of chicken any the worse for that.

Nor shall I have a carver to whom the whole of the workshop
has to defer, a pupil of Dainty the maestro, for whom
a large sow's belly and hares and boars and Scythian pheasants
and tall flamingoes and antelopes, yes and Moorish gazelles—
a sumptuous banquet of elmwood dummies—are all
    dismembered   140

with blunted knives, while the clatter resounds throughout the
    Subura.
My own young server has never been taught to filch a slice
of venison, or a guinea-fowl's wing; he has been a novice
all his days, and has only pinched an occasional chop.
Commonplace cups, which cost a few pence, will be handed
    round
by a country lad whose clothes are designed to keep him warm.
He is not from Phrygia or Lycia; he was not obtained from a
    dealer
at a fancy price. So when you order, order in Latin.
Their clothes are all alike; their hair is short and uncurled;
it is neatly combed today only because of the party.   150
This is the son of a hardy shepherd; this of a ploughman.
He sadly misses the mother he has not seen for years,
and longs to return to the cabin and kids that he knew so well.
The boy has an honest well-bred face, and similar manners,
such as one ought to encounter in those with a crimson stripe.
His voice is unbroken; as yet, his armpits need no plucking;
he doesn't take to the bath-house pubescent testicles; his penis
is not so large that it has to be shyly concealed with an oil-flask.
He will serve you wine bottled among those very mountains
from which he comes and beneath whose summit he used to
    play.   160

Perhaps you expect a group of girls who, singing together,   162
will start a lascivious Spanish dance, and then, encouraged
by the diners' applause, will sink to the floor with shimmying
    buttocks—   164
a stimulant, that, to jaded appetites, used by the rich man   167
as a sharp aphrodisiac; the tension he feels goes on increasing
till he ends by wetting himself in response to sight and sound. 170
A modest house has no room for such nonsense. So leave the
    clatter
of castanets, and words that are shunned by the naked whore
who stands in a stinking brothel; leave the enjoyment of filthy
expressions and all the arts of lewdness to the one who moistens
with spits of wine his circular floor of Spartan marble.

That is a privilege granted to rank. Gambling is shameful;
adultery, too, is shameful to ordinary people; when *these* chaps
go in for the same diversions, they are hailed as smart and jolly.
The entertainment at this evening's party will be very different.
The *Iliad*'s author will be recited, and Maro's poem   180
which, with its lofty music, challenges his for the crown.
With verse like that, what matter about the voice of the reader?

But now put off your worries and all the concerns of business.
Treat yourself to a rest, because there's nothing to stop you
spending the livelong day at ease; not a word of the money
that people owe you; and don't be consumed with an inner fury
if your wife goes out first thing in the morning and returns at
    night
with her flimsy diaphanous dress damp and suspiciously
    creased,
her hair in a mess, and her face and ears still flushed with
    excitement.
Take off whatever upsets you before you enter my door;   190
leave at home your slaves and the objects they break and lose;
and leave, above all, those friends who never acknowledge your
    kindness.

The grandstands, meanwhile, are observing the rite, imported
    from Ida,
of Cybele's napkin. The praetor (himself a prey to the horses)
sits in state like a general in triumph. And if I may say so
without offending a populace proud of its countless numbers,
today the whole of Rome is inside the Circus. The shouting
swells to a deafening roar. I assume the Greens have won;
for, if they had lost, then you would see this city of ours
stunned and stricken, as it was on the day when the consuls were
    vanquished   200
in the dust at Cannae. Watching the races is fine for
youngsters—
the cheering, the risky bets, the chic young woman beside you.
My wrinkled skin would rather absorb the April sunshine
and forgo public events. You can make for the baths already

with a clear conscience, although there's still a full hour to go
till noon. And yet you can't do that for several days
in a row; because even so charming a life engenders enormous
boredom. The less we indulge our pleasures the more we enjoy
    them.

SATIRE 12

Welcome to a Survivor

Today, Corvinus, is dearer to me than the day I was born.
An altar of festal turf is ready to welcome the victims
vowed to the gods. For the Queen I am bringing a snowy lamb,
and a similar fleece for the goddess armed with the Moorish
    gorgon.
But the frisky animal set aside for Tarpeian Jove
is pulling the long rope tight and fiercely tossing its head;
for that's a spirited calf, just ready for temple and altar,
ripe for a sprinkling of wine. He's ashamed to tug any more
at his mother's teats, and he butts at oaks with his budding
    horns.
If I had money enough at hand to reflect my feelings,   10
I should bring a bull as fat as Hispulla, whose very size
would make him slow. He would not have been reared in local
    pastures;
his blood would point to the verdant meadows beside the
    Clitumnus,
and his neck would call for a tall attendant to wield the blade.
That would mark the return of my friend, who is still quite
    shaken
after his recent horrors, and amazed at having survived.

For he managed to escape not only the threats of the sea, but also
the lightning's strokes. The sky was screened by a solid curtain
of pitch-black cloud, when a fiery flash shivered the yardarms.
Everyone thought that *he* had been hit; soon, thunderstruck,   20
they came to hold that no sinking ship was so awful a sight
as a wreck with blazing sails. Every detail was there,
just as appalling as when a raging tempest develops
in a poem. And now another crisis occurred: pray listen,

and pity the man again, although the rest is part
of the same experience—dreadful indeed, but known to many,
and one recorded on votive tablets in countless shrines.
(As everyone knows, it is Isis who saves our painters from
        starving.)
That was the kind of disaster which fell on my friend Catullus.
Since the hold was now half full of water, and the mast was
        unsteady   30
because of the waves which were pounding against each side of
        the vessel,
the grizzled old skipper at last perceived that all his skill
counted for nothing; so he started to do a deal with the winds
by lightening ship, adopting the ploy of the beaver who renders
himself a eunuch, resolved to escape though it means the loss
of his testicles. (Well he knows the price of the drug in his groin.)
'Get rid of all my things—yes, all of them!' shouted Catullus.
He was willing to throw overboard even his finest possessions—
purple clothes, just right for men like the soft Maecenas,
and other garments made from a flock which the noble nature   40
of the grass has tinted (though credit is also due to the excellent
water with its secret properties, and to Baetica's climate).
He also jettisoned silver plate, including salvers
wrought for Parthenius' use, and a three-gallon mixing bowl
which might have been made for the thirsty Pholus, or Fuscus'
        wife,
and metalwork baskets, a thousand dishes, and many engraven
goblets tossed by the cunning king who purchased Olynthus.
What other man these days, and in what part of the globe,
could bear to prefer his life to his plate, and his soul to his
        money?   49

When most of the useful articles too had gone overboard,   52
a loss which failed to bring relief, the captain was forced
by the grave and imminent peril to unstep the mast with an axe;
and so the crisis was eased. It is surely a desperate plight
when the only way to strengthen a ship is by making it smaller!
So go and commit your lives to the breezes, placing your trust
in a plank of timber; all that comes between you and death
is four fingers of pinewood, or seven if extra thick!

In future, along with your bag of bread and your pot-bellied
    flagon,   60
be sure to take an axe—for use in case of storm.
But happier times were ahead for our sailor. Cheerfully turning
to a more auspicious task, the Parcae set about spinning
a thread of the whitest wool with their kindly hands. And then,
as his fate prevailed over wind and ocean, the sea sank down
to a level calm, and a wind sprang up that was little stronger
than a gentle breeze. Before it ran the pitiful craft,
jury-rigged with clothes stretched out and, set on the prow,
its one surviving sail. As the southerly wind subsided,
the hope of life returned along with the sun. Into view   70
came the lofty peak which Iulus loved and preferred for his
    home
to Lavinia's town. It received its name from the fair white sow
famed for her wondrous belly, so joyfully hailed by the
    Phrygians,
with its thirty teats—a sight which none had ever beheld.

At last it enters the harbour built to enclose the sea—
the Tuscan lighthouse, and the arms which run right out to mid-
    ocean
leaving Italy far behind, and then curve inward;
you will find it a greater marvel than any similar harbour
given by nature. So the master steers his crippled vessel
for the inner basin, enclosed in a sheltered bay, where a Baian   80
skiff could sail. And there the sailors shave their heads,
and, safe ashore, recount their escape in voluble detail.

Away my lads. Not a word or thought should be out of place.
Festoon the shrines with garlands; sprinkle handfuls of meal
on the sacred knives, and adorn the soft green turf of the altars.
I'll follow shortly; and then, when the major rite has been duly
performed, I shall come back home where the tiny images,
    gleaming
with brittle wax, are being decked with delicate wreaths.
Here I shall worship my household Jove, offering incense
to the family gods, and scattering pansies of many a hue.   90

Everything is gleaming. Lofty branches grow from the
    doorway,
which happily joins in the service with lanterns lit at daybreak.

In case all this, Corvinus, makes you uneasy, the Catullus
on whose return I am gratefully building these altars possesses
three little heirs. You would wait some time if you wanted to see
anyone spending a sickly hen, just closing its eyes,
on so sterile a friend. In fact a hen is too dear; why even
a *quail's* never killed for a man with children. But if Gallitta
or Paccius, who are rich and childless, have even the slightest
    fever,
the porches are covered from end to end with tablets, affixed   100
in the proper form. Some will promise a hundred—oxen,
that is, for elephants aren't to be had, not even for cash.
The animal does not breed in Latium, or anywhere else
with a climate like ours. Some, it is true, are grazing today
in Turnus' country, deep in Rutulian forests; but these
have been brought from the dark man's land to form the
    emperor's herd.
They refuse to serve any ordinary subject; for their ancestors
    used to
obey the commands of Hannibal of Tyre and the Molossian
    monarch
and our Roman generals, carrying cohorts of men on their
    backs.
No small part of the war were those towers that went into battle.   110
In principle, though, Pacuvius Hister would have no scruples,
nor would Novius, in leading an ivory tusker to the altar.
Before Gallitta's Lares would fall the only victim
worthy of such divinities and of those who court their favour.
If given the chance, the former will vow to slaughter the tallest
from his herd of slaves (for they as a rule are the most attractive);
he will even place sacrificial wreaths on the heads of his younger
servants (boys and girls); should he have an Iphigenia
of marriageable age at home, he will offer *her* on the altar,
though he cannot hope she'll be switched for a doe, as she is in
    the play.   120

I applaud my fellow Roman; indeed I wouldn't compare
a thousand ships to a legacy. For if the invalid cheats
the goddess of death, he'll be trapped in the creel and cancel his
    will
in view of Pacuvius' signal service; and perhaps with a phrase
will appoint him heir to all his possessions. The latter will strut
proudly in front of his vanquished rivals. And so you perceive
the handsome dividend gained by killing a maid of Mycenae.
Long live Pacuvius! I pray he may live as long as Nestor.
May he own as much as Nero plundered, amassing mountains
of gold. And may he love not a soul, and be loved by no one!   130

SATIRE 13

A Consolation

A deed that sets a bad example never brings joy
to the doer. The first effect is this: no guilty party
is acquitted by his own conscience, not even if he has bribed
the praetor to rule in his favour with the aid of a cheating urn.
What do you think, Calvinus, that people feel in regard to
this recent wrong—the crime of betraying a trust? However,
you are not, as it happens, so badly off in financial terms
that the weight of a moderate loss will sink you. What you've
    experienced
is not an unusual sight; your lot is familiar to many;
it is now quite commonplace, drawn from the middle of
    fortune's pile.   10
Let's keep our grief within reasonable bounds. A man's
    resentment
shouldn't be *over*-heated, or exceed the injury suffered.
You can barely support the smallest and tiniest speck
of even the lightest misfortune. Look at you—inwardly
    seething,
all because your friend will not repay you the sum
which he swore to look after. Does this come as a shock to a man
who was born when Fonteius was consul, and won't see sixty
    again?
Have you derived no profit from your long acquaintance with
    life?

Great, indeed, is Philosophy. She conquers fortune, and teaches
her pupils to do the same in her sacred books; but we also   20
count as happy those who have learned in the school of life
to accept life's hardships and not attempt to throw off the yoke.
What holiday, pray, is so holy that it fails to bring to light

theft, dishonesty, and fraud; profits achieved through every
illegal device; cash acquired by dagger or pill-box?
The good, indeed, are rare. Count them; they're barely as many
as are the gates of Thebes or the mouths of the wealthy Nile.
We are living today in the ninth era—a period worse
than the age of iron; one so evil that Nature herself
has found no metal base enough to use for its name.   30
Should we appeal to gods and men for protection so loudly?
You would think Faesidius was pleading in court to the cheers of
   his vocal
dole-queue! Tell me, my aged friend, who should be in nappies,
are you not aware of the strong attraction of another's money?
Are you not aware that people laugh at your gullible nature,
when you ask a person to keep his word and to show a belief
that a holy power is present in temples and blood-stained altars?
That is what life was like among the native inhabitants
before the coup which ousted Saturn and made him exchange
his crown for a farmer's sickle; then Juno was still a wee lassie,   40
and Jove a caveman on Ida without official status.
No dinners were held above the clouds by the heavenly host;
nobody served the drinks, like the Trojan boy or the lovely
wife of Hercules; nor did Vulcan, quaffing his nectar,
wipe from his arms the filth of his workshop in Lipara's cavern.
A god had lunch on his own. There was no such mob of
   immortals
as there is today. The starry sky was content with a handful
of deities, and therefore leant more lightly on luckless Atlas.
The gloomy realm of the vast abyss had not been assigned
to the pitiless Pluto along with his Sicilian spouse.   50
No wheel was there, no Furies or stone, no black avenging
vulture. In the absence of royalty, the ghosts had a jolly time.
Wickedness, in that far-off age, brought shock and
   amazement.
People thought it a heinous outrage calling for death,
if a young man failed to rise for a senior citizen, or
a boy for a bearded youth, regardless of whether the former
had more wild strawberries at home and a larger pile of acorns.
Such was the honour of being just four years older; so closely
was a lad's first down on a par with the hoary head of an elder.

Now, if a friend does *not* disavow a sum entrusted, 60
if he duly returns the battered purse with its rust intact,
his honesty is seen as a portent; the Tuscan books are consulted;
and atonement must be sought by killing a garlanded lamb.
If I happen to find a totally honest man, I regard
that freak as I would a baby centaur, or a shoal of fish
turned up by the plough to its own surprise, or a mule in foal.
I am disconcerted, as if it had rained a shower of stones,
or a swarm of bees had settled in an elongated cluster
on top of a temple roof, or a river had flowed to the sea
sweeping along a marvellous flood of swirling milk. 70

You moan about oaths denied and the loss of ten thousand. But
      what if
a man through a similar trick has been robbed of two *hundred*
      thousand
lodged without witness, or another has lost a sum so huge
that when every corner was full his chest could hardly contain it?
It's a simple straightforward matter to deny what the gods have
      witnessed,
provided no human is in on the secret. Notice how loudly
he disclaims the deed; look at the strength of that fraudulent face.
He swears by the rays of the sun and Jove's Tarpeian bolts,
by the heavy lance of Mars and the darts of the seer of Cirrha,
by the quiver and shafts of the maiden goddess who leads the
      chase, 80
and the trident wielded by Neptune, lord of the Aegean wave.
He includes, in addition, Hercules' bow and the spear of
      Minerva,
and all the weapons stock-piled there in the arsenal of heaven.
If he's a father, he cries 'May I eat the pitiful head
of my son, first boiled, then drenched with Egyptian vinegar
      dressing'.

Some attribute every event to the play of fortune.
They hold that the sky revolves without a guiding spirit,
and that nature itself brings round the phases of day and year.
So without compunction they lay their hands on any altar. 89
Another believes in the gods and still commits perjury, thinking 91

'Let Isis decide whatever she pleases about my body;
let her blast my sight with her angry rattle, on this condition,
that, blind as I am, I may keep the cash I deny receiving.
Consumption, festering ulcers, the loss of half a leg—
they are all worth while. If Ladas were poor, he would certainly
        covet
the rich man's gout, unless he needed Antícyra's cure
or Archígenes' skill. For speed of foot doesn't earn any money;
nor is there any meat on a sprig of Olympic olive.
Great it may be, but the wrath of the gods is certainly slow.   100
So if they have it in mind to punish *all* the guilty,
when will they get to me? Besides, I may find the divinity
hears appeals; such acts are often forgiven. The same
crimes are committed by many people with different results.
One receives a cross for his villainy, another a crown.'

That is how he rallies his mind when it trembles with fear
at a dreadful deed. When you call him to swear in a sacred shrine,
he will walk in front, and even nag you and drag you along.
For when colossal effrontery urges a spurious case,
many accept it as honest assurance. The man is presenting   110
a *farce*, like that of the witty Catullus with its runaway clown.
But you, poor devil, protest in a voice that would drown the
        roars
of Stentor—as loudly, indeed, as Mars in Homer 'How *can* you,
Jupiter, hear such lies without a murmur? Now really,
you ought to give utterance, whether you be of bronze or
        marble.
Otherwise, why should people unwrap the holy incense
and place it upon your glowing coals with slices of calves'
liver and white pork sausages? As far as I can discover,
there's nothing to choose between statues of you and Vagellius'
        image!'

Here are some words of comfort that even a layman may offer—   120
one who has never read the Cynics, or the rules of the Stoics
(who apart from their shirt are Cynics too), or admired
        Epicurus,
who took such pleasure in the plants he grew in his tiny garden.

Puzzling cases ought to be treated by medical experts;
but *you* can safely trust your pulse to a student of Philip's.
If in the whole wide world you cannot point to so vicious
a crime, I'll say no more. Go ahead and beat your breast
with your knuckles bunched, and slap your face with the flat of
      your hand.
For, after a loss like that, you are bound to close your door.
Cash calls forth a more plangent cry and a louder wail   130
throughout the house than the death of a loved one. In such a
      bereavement,
nobody feigns distress, or stops at ripping the neckline
of his clothes, or compels his eyes to squeeze a reluctant drop.
Tears are genuine when they fall at the loss of money.

But if every court is found to be full of complaints like yours;
if, when a contract has been read ten times by the other party,
they declare the signature false and the entire document void,
despite the fact that the handwriting's theirs, like the signet ring
(a peerless gem of sardonyx, kept in an ivory case);
then, my precious friend, do you claim a position apart from   140
the common run, as if *you* were the son of a royal hen,
while we were a worthless brood hatched from lower-class
      eggs?
Your injury's not so great. It calls for moderate anger,
if you cast your eye on more serious crimes. Think, for example,
of the hired assassin, or the raging fire deliberately started
by a match, when a man's hall door suddenly bursts into flames.
Think of the people who enter an ancient temple and rob it
of massive cups incrusted with numinous rust—the donations
of whole communities, and crowns presented by early kings.
If no such items are there, you will find a petty profaner   150
who will scrape the gilt off Hercules' thigh or even the face
of Neptune, and carefully prise gold leaf from Castor's body—
why not, when the usual thing is to melt the Thunderer
      wholesale?
Think of those engaged in preparing and selling poisons,
of the one who ought to be sent to sea in an ox's hide,
sharing the bag with an innocent ape whose fate is sealed.
Yet these are merely a fraction of the crimes that Gallicus hears

as City Prefect from break of day till the sun goes down.
If you wish to know the moral state of the human race,
a single court is all you need. Just spend a few days there;   160
I challenge you then, when you come away, to complain of your
    luck.
Who is surprised by a swollen throat in the Alps, or a breast
in southern Egypt larger than the chubby baby that sucks it?
Does anyone gape when he sees a German's sky-blue eyes,
and the yellow curls which he greases, twisting them into a
    horn?   165
When the Thracian cranes swoop down to attack in a raucous
    cloud,   167
the Pygmy warrior in his tiny armour rushes to meet them.
But soon he is overpowered by his foe, and snatched aloft
and away by the crooked claws of those cruel birds. If you saw it 170
in this country you'd split your sides; but over there,
where the nation's army, to a man, is less than a foot in height,
because such battles are an everyday sight, nobody laughs.

'What? Is this barefaced liar, this godless cheat, to get off
scot free?'
            Suppose he is clapped in irons and hurried away
this very minute and killed in the manner that we dictate
(What more could anger demand?); the loss remains, and the money
you lodged is gone for good. Whatever comfort you gain
from the blood of that headless trunk will be spoiled by the hate
    that comes with it.
'But revenge is an excellent thing, sweeter than life itself.'   180
That is what non-philosophers say. You sometimes see them
blazing inside for a trivial reason, or none at all.   182
Chrysippus would not agree, nor the gentle-hearted Tháles,   184
nor the great old man who used to live near sweet Hymettus.
He would never have given his accuser a drop of the hemlock
which he had to drink in his cruel cell. It is always a small   187–9
and mean and feeble mind that takes a delight in vengeance.   190
You can see the proof in the following fact: no one exults
in revenge more keenly than a woman.

                    In any case, what makes you think

they have got away, when the consciousness of their terrible
    crime
holds them in fear, flogging them raw with a soundless whip,
and the mind is a torturer laying on an invisible lash?
It is, indeed, a savage punishment, far more cruel
than any devised by the fiendish Caedicius or Rhadamanthus,
to carry within you, night and day, an accusing witness.
The Pythian priestess once replied to a certain Spartan
that one day he would be punished because he had felt inclined   200
to hold on to a sum received in trust and to cloak the offence
by perjury. For he had asked what the deity's attitude was,
and whether Apollo advised him to carry out the swindle.
He therefore returned the money, from fear not honesty. Still,
the oracle's every word was true and worthy of the temple,
as he showed when he himself and all his house and issue
were blotted out, along with his kin, however distant.
That was the fate he suffered for even *wishing* to sin;
for the man who silently plans a crime within his heart
bears all the guilt of the deed.   210

                            And suppose he succeeds in his efforts,
his worry is always there; it haunts him even at mealtimes.
His throat is dry, as though with a fever; his food persists
in growing as he tries to chew it. Poor devil, he spits good Setine
out of his mouth; he dislikes the precious age of a mellow
Alban. Show him a choicer vintage still, and a pattern
of creases appears on his forehead as if it were sour Faliscan.
At night, if his trouble by chance allows him a little sleep,
and the body which tossed all over the bed at last lies quiet,
at once he sees the profaned divinity's temple and altar,
and (a sight that weighs above all on his mind, as it sweats with
    terror)   220
he sees *you* in his sleep. Your supernatural image,
larger than life, appals the wretch and makes him confess.
These are the people who blanch and quake at a flash of
    lightning;
in thundery weather they faint at the first premonitory rumble,
as if it were not by chance, or the rage of the winds, but rather
a sign of wrath and vengeance that the fire strikes upon earth.

If *that* storm should pass without harm, the next is awaited
with deeper dread, as though it were just postponed by the calm.
Again, if they start to suffer from pains in the side, with a fever
which will not let them sleep, they believe their bodily ailments 230
are inflicted by a malevolent force. They imagine that these
are the missiles and weapons of god. They are far too frightened
    to offer
a bleating beast at his shrine, or promise a crested cock
to the gods of the hearth. After all, what hope is allowed to the
    guilty
when they fall ill? Their *victims* are more entitled to live.
The nature of wicked men in the main is capricious and shifting.
When they're committing a crime they have plenty of boldness;
    it's only
after the deed is done that they come to acknowledge what's
    right
and wrong. However, their nature, which cannot be changed or
    altered,
reverts to the habits that they have condemned. Who ever
    succeeded 240
in putting an end to his own misconduct? Or ever recovered
his sense of shame when once he had wiped the blush from his
    face?
When did you ever see a man who remained content
with a single outrage? Our fraudulent friend will eventually step
on a trap. He will face the gloomy dungeon and the hangman's
    hook,
or else some crag far out in the Aegean—a rock that is thronged
with important exiles. You will exult in the savage sentence
imposed on the hated figure, and at last acknowledge with joy
that neither a Drusus nor a Tiresias lives on Olympus.

SATIRE 14

The Influence
of Vicious Parents

Many things, Fuscinus, that people rightly condemn,
and that leave a lasting stain on illustrious family records,
are demonstrated by parents themselves and passed to their
    children.
If a father is ruined by gambling, his heir acquires the habit
as a child, and renews the same campaign with his little dice-
    box;
nor, as a lad, will he lead any relation to hope for
better behaviour. Another has learned from the bad example
of his wastrel father, with his gray-haired greed, to enjoy such
    things
as peeled truffles and seasoned mushrooms, and warblers
    steeped
till they drown in the mushrooms' sauce. Although the boy may
    be only   10
seven, and may not as yet have acquired his second teeth,
you may order a thousand bearded teachers to stand on his left
and a thousand on his right, he will still be determined to dine in
    style
and never to fall below his father's culinary standards.
What does the latter convey when he welcomes the clank of
    fetters,   23
and keenly relishes brand-marks, dungeons, and labour
    camps?   24
Does Rutilus foster a gentle temper and a mild reaction   15
to small transgressions, does he teach that the body and soul of
    the slave
are made of the same material as ours and the same ingredients,
or does he impart a cruel streak, when he thrills at the uproar
of a merciless flogging, and prefers the crack of a whip to a Siren?

To his trembling house he becomes Antíphates and
    Polyphemus,   20
only happy when the torturer's called and someone is branded
with red-hot irons for daring to steal a couple of towels.
Are you simple enough to imagine that Larga's daughter is
    faithful
to her man, when however quickly she recites her mother's
    lovers,
reeling off the names, she is forced to stop for breath
more than a score of times? As a girl, she knew all her secrets;
now she writes, at the latter's dictation, her own little notes
and sends them off to her lover by the same degenerate bearers.   30
Such is Nature's law. Examples of vice that are set
within the home corrupt more quickly and easily, in that
they enter our minds on such high authority. Perhaps one or two
of the younger folk may reject such examples—those whose
    souls
were formed by the Titan in kindly mood out of finer clay.
The rest are drawn along in their father's footsteps, and follow
the well-worn path of sin, ignoring previous warnings.

So then, avoid disgraceful conduct—a rule worth keeping
for this if no other reason: it will stop the next generation
from reproducing our crimes. We are all so quick on the uptake   40
when it comes to things that are shameful and crooked. You're
    sure to meet
a second Catiline in any country and any climate;
but you'll never find a man like Brutus, or Brutus' uncle.
No dirty expression or dirty sight should cross the threshold
where there's a family living. Away with the girls provided
by agents; away with the sponger who sings at all-night parties!
A child demands the utmost respect, and so think twice
if you have something nasty in mind. Do not ignore him because
    of
his tender years; why even a cradle should keep you from sin!
For if in future he does something wrong, incurring the censor's   50
anger, and proves not only like you in build and features,
but morally too his father's son, following your footsteps
and guilty in every case of even graver offences,

no doubt you will haul him over the coals, deliver a loud
and bitter lecture, and then arrange to alter your will.
What right, however, have *you* to scowl and scold like a parent,
when you, in later life, are worse; when ages ago
a cupping-glass should have been clapped to your skull—
    vacuum to vacuum?
When a guest is coming, none of your staff is allowed to relax.
'Sweep the marble floor; make sure the columns are gleaming;   60
get down that shrivelled spider and every wisp of its web;
you there, polish the ordinary silver, you the embossed!'
the master bellows, urging them on with cane in hand.
Are you worried, then, poor fellow, in case your friend, when
    he comes,
should be put off at the sight of dog-dirt fouling the hallway,
or of the portico splashed with mud—things that a slave-boy
could put to rights on his own with just a bucket of sawdust—
and yet not take any pains to ensure that the house, which is seen
each day by your son, should be spotlessly clean and above
    reproach?

It's an excellent thing to provide a son for the state and nation,   70
if you see to it that he's an asset to his country, a capable farmer,
capable, too, of discharging the business of peace and war.
For it makes a crucial difference in just what skills he is trained,
and in what habits you bring him up. The mother stork
feeds her young on the snakes and lizards found in the wilds;
they, when their wings are grown, look for the self-same
    creatures.
The vulture hurries home from cattle, dogs, or the gibbet,
carrying bits of the rotting carcase to give to her chicks;
this becomes the food of the full-grown vulture, when he
hunts for himself and makes a nest in a tree of his own.   80
The noble birds that attend on Jupiter scour the glades
searching for hare and hind; that is the prey which is laid
on the edge of the eyrie; and so, when the brood are fully grown
and rise aloft, at the jab of hunger they suddenly swoop
on the very prey that they tasted on first breaking the shell.

Caetronius was a compulsive builder. Now on Caieta's
curving coastline, now on the towering heights of Tibur,

now on Praeneste's hills, he persisted in having constructed
villas with soaring roofs, importing marble from Greece
and abroad. He surpassed both Hercules' temple and that of
    Fortune   90
by as much as Posídes the eunuch surpassed the Capitol's
    glories.
By living like this Caetronius exhausted much of his fortune.
But although his assets diminished, the part remaining was still
substantial. That was frittered away by his crazy son,
who built more villas again, with even costlier marble.

Some by chance were born to a father who observed the
    sabbath.
They worship nothing except the clouds and the holy heavens.
And, since their father abstained from pork, they think it is just
as sacred as human flesh. In time they get rid of their foreskins.
And while they are all brought up to despise the laws of Rome,   100
they carefully learn and keep and revere the Jewish code—
all that Moses handed down in his mystic volume:
never to show the way except to one of the faithful,
never to guide the uncircumcised when they're seeking the
    fountain.
The father's to blame; for he observed the seventh day
as a day of idleness, and kept it apart from normal life.

Young people readily copy most of our vices; meanness
is the only one they're obliged to practise against their will.
That vice is misleading. It wears the form and appearance of
    virtue,
because it's austere in face and bearing, and sober in dress.   110
The miser is certainly praised for being an upright man,
because he's thrifty and watches over his own possessions
with closer attention than the dragons of Pontus or the
    Hesperides
would apply if given the same task. There is also the fact that
the public regards the man I have mentioned as outstandingly
    clever
at making money; for with workers like him, fortunes
    increase.

True, they increase by fair means and foul; but they do grow
  bigger
as the anvil rings and the furnace blazes constantly on.

The father, then, who admires wealth and firmly believes
there is no such thing as a happy pauper, goes on to infer   120
that misers are happy in mind. He therefore urges his sons
to follow that path and become adherents of the same system.
Every vice has certain rudiments. With these he begins
their instruction, insisting they learn the pettiest kinds of
  meanness.
(Later he inculcates an insatiable lust for profits.)
He nips the bellies of his slaves with less than the minimum
  rations;
and he himself goes hungry, for he cannot bear to finish
all the lumps of musty bread that are blue with mould.
Even in mid-September he makes a practice of keeping
a portion of mince from the previous day; yes, and in summer   130
he preserves some beans for tomorrow's dinner, sealed in a jar
along with a piece of mackerel and half a rotten sprat;
he will even count the blades of the leeks as he locks them away!
If invited to such a meal, a wretch from the bridge would refuse
  it.
But what is the point of amassing wealth through these painful
  rigours?
Isn't it utter folly, isn't it obvious madness
to live like a beggar in order to die like a millionaire?
In the mean time, while your satchel bulges, full to the top,
your love of money expands along with the money itself,
and the man who lacks it covets it less. You therefore acquire   140
another mansion when one estate is no longer enough.
Extending your land is a pleasant business; and also, your
  neighbour's
crop appears to be larger and better; so you buy that too,
along with the vineyard and the hill that is grey with many an
  olive.
If the owner refuses to sell his land at any price,
when the corn is green, hungry cattle and half-starved oxen
with weary necks will be driven into his field at night,

and they won't go home till the whole of the crop has vanished
    within
their ravenous bellies. You'd think the job had been done with a
    scythe.
You could scarcely calculate how many folk have suffered like
    this,   150
and how many estates have been put on sale by illegal action.
But what of the talk? What of the horrid blasts of scandal?
'Sticks and stones . . .!' he says. 'Suppose the entire district
sang my praises; it wouldn't amount to a pile of beans
if that meant harvesting low-grade wheat on a tiny croft.'
I suppose you will always be free from sickness and bodily
    ailments,
you will manage to avoid bereavement and worry; and for years
    ahead
you may hope to enjoy a flourishing life and happier days,
provided *you* have as large a holding of arable land
as was ploughed in the time of Tatius by Rome's entire
    population.   160
Later, even the frail old veterans, who had endured
battles with Carthage, or the terrible Pyrrhus' Molossian
    swords,
in the end, for all their grievous wounds received at the most
two acres each. Yet none of them looked on this reward
for his blood and toil as less than his due, or a breach of faith
by a mean ungrateful country. A plot like that was enough
for the father himself and the crowd in the cabin, where his wife
    would be lying
pregnant and four young children playing—one the child
of slaves, and three of them free. But when the grown-up
    brothers
came home from ditch and furrow, they would find a second,
    and bigger,   170
supper prepared, of porridge steaming in large-size pots.
Now such an acreage wouldn't suffice for a kitchen
    garden.

That is the commonest cause of crime. No vice that inhabits
the human heart concocts a greater number of poisons,

or wields the murderer's dagger more often, than the fierce
 desire
for limitless wealth; of course, for whoever is keen to get rich
is keen to do so quickly. But what respect for the laws,
what shame or scruple, is shown by a greedy man in a hurry?
'Remain content, my lads, with those little cabins of yours,
and with those hills,' the Hernican, Vestinian or Marsian father 180
would say in days gone by. 'Let us win our bread by the
 plough—
bread enough for our table. That is the way which pleases
the gods of the country, who gave us the kindly ear of corn,
and helped and encouraged our race to despise the primitive oak.
Sin is spurned by the man who is not ashamed to be seen
in raw-hide knee-boots in frosty weather, who defies the blast
with skins turned inside out. It's that new-fangled foreign
 purple,
or whatever they call it, that is leading our people to crime and
 evil.'
This was the lesson those older men would teach their young
 folk.
But now, when autumn is over, the father rouses his sleeping 190
son with a shout around midnight: 'Get your tablets, my boy;
stay awake, take notes, and prepare your cases; study our elders'
red-lettered laws; or else apply for the centurion's vine-staff.
(But make sure that Laelius takes good note of your uncombed
 mop,
and your hairy nostrils, and also admires the breadth of your
 shoulders.)
Destroy the huts of the Moors and the forts of British tribes,
so that your sixtieth birthday may bring you the coveted eagle
that will make you rich. Or suppose you hate the endless
 exertions
of life in camp, and the frightening sound of bugle and trumpet
moves your bowels, get hold of something you're sure to sell 200
at half as much again; never turn up your nose
at any trade that has to be banished across the Tiber.
You mustn't imagine there's any line to be drawn between
perfumes and hides; for the smell of profit is always good,
whatever it comes from. Here is a saw you should always quote,

a god-like verse that is worthy of even Jupiter's pen:
'Nobody cares where you got it; the vital thing is to have it.'   207
If I heard a father dinning such conduct into his son,   210
this is what I would say: 'Tell me, you silly fellow,
what's the hurry? I guarantee the pupil will come
to excel his teacher. You needn't worry; you'll be outdone,
like Telamon dwarfed by Ajax, and Peleus eclipsed by Achilles.
The young need gentle handling. The poison of adult sin
has not as yet infected their marrow. When the beard grows
     long,
and the lad begins to trim and smooth it with scissors and comb,
then he will bear false witness; he will sell his lies for a trifling
sum, with his hand on Ceres' altar and even her foot.
If his wife brings with her a fatal dowry as she enters your door,   220
consider her dead and buried. Imagine him, closing his fingers
on her throat as she sleeps! For the goods that *you* think ought to
     be gathered
by land and sea will come to *him* by a shorter route.
A major crime involves no effort. Some day you will cry
"I never suggested, much less recommended, an act like that!"
Yet the root and cause of his vicious attitude lie with you.
For whoever instils the desire to own a substantial fortune,
and by his warped advice trains his sons to be greedy,
is also plainly granting them licence to double their assets
by fraudulent means, and is giving the fullest rein to the car.   230
If you call the driver back, he cannot pull up; he ignores you,
and is carried away, leaving the turning-post far behind.
Nobody thinks it enough to do the amount of wrong
that *you* permit. They allow themselves more generous scope.

When you tell your son that only fools make presents to friends
or help to ease the strain on a poverty-stricken relation,
you encourage the lad to rob and swindle and acquire a fortune
by every kind of crooked device. Your love of money
is as great as the love of Rome that burned in the Decii's heart,
as great as Menoeceus' love of Thebes (if Greece can be
     trusted)—   240
the town with the furrows where legions emerge from dragons'
     teeth,

complete with shields, and at once engage in terrible war
all together, as if a bugler had risen beside them.
And so you will see the fire for which *you* supplied the light
burning fiercely and devouring everything far and wide.
Nor will you, poor devil, be spared. With a mighty roar
the pupil-lion in his cage will demolish his trembling trainer.
Your horoscope's known to astrologers. Still, it is tiresome to
    wait
as the spindle slowly unwinds. So before your thread is snapped,
you will die. Already you're in the way; you're delaying the
    dreams   250
of your son; your stag-like longevity is causing him spasms of
    pain.
Send for Archígenes right away, and buy Mithridates'
special compound. If you want to gather a fig next autumn
and to hold another bouquet of roses, you need the drug
which fathers, no less than kings, should take each day before
    dinner.'

I promise an entertainment better than any presented
in race-track or theatre before the munificent praetor's platform,
if you watch how men are prepared to risk their lives to increase
the wealth of their houses, to acquire a brass-bound chest that is
    crammed
with satchels of money, and cash to lodge with the vigilant
    Castor.   260
(His temple's the bank since Mars the Avenger was robbed of his
    helmet
and failed to look after his property.) So, you can give up
    watching
the curtain rise on Flora's and Ceres' and Cybele's shows;
the concerns of human beings provide far greater amusement.
Is any more fun provided by bodies hurled in the air
from a springboard, or by the man who goes in for tightrope
    walking,
than by you? You spend your days on board a Corycian boat,
living there, constantly tossed by winds from east and west.
You are nothing but a reckless small-time trader in smelly sacks,
who enjoys transporting syrupy raisin wine from the coast   270

of ancient Crete in jars that are fellow-townsmen of Jove.
That man, however, who plants his feet with precarious steps,
does it to earn a living; by means of the rope he avoids
cold and hunger. But *you* don't need the number of talents
and villas for which you take such risks. Have a look at the
  harbours
and the ocean covered with bulky ships; most of mankind
is now at sea! Wherever the hope of profit leads,
a fleet will follow, bounding across the Carpathian waves
and Moroccan waters; it will leave Gibraltar far astern,
and hear the hiss of the sun as it sinks in Hercules' main.   280
It's a splendid reward, I'm sure, to arrive back home from such
  places,
proudly carrying a swollen purse and a bulging satchel,
after encountering deep-sea monsters and squadrons of
  mermen.

Madness comes in different guises. One man cowers
in his sister's arms, in dread of the Furies' faces and torches;
as he slaughters an ox, another believes Agamemnon is roaring
or else the Ithacan. Though he may not tear his cloak and tunic,
a man is in need of a minder if he fills his ship to the gunwales
with merchandise, putting a plank between himself and the sea,
when the only reason for facing all this hardship and danger   290
is silver cut into circles, with legends and tiny portraits.
Clouds roll up, with flashes of lightning. 'Cast off!' cries the
  owner,
who has bought a cargo of grain or pepper. 'No need to worry
about that inky sky and the heavy bank of darkness.
It's only summer lightning.' This very night the poor devil
may be pitched overboard as the hull breaks up, and engulfed in
  the waves,
clutching his money-belt tight in his fist or between his teeth.
The man who was not content, in his greed, with all the gold
washed down in the yellow sand of the Tagus or the Pactólus
must now be content with rags to cover his freezing loins,   300
and with scraps of food, while he begs as 'a shipwrecked sailor'
and relies on the storm, now rendered in paint, to keep him
  alive.

Getting your wealth cost trouble. Keeping it means even greater
fear and worry. It's a wretched business protecting a fortune.
The plutocrat Lícinus hands out buckets to his private brigade
and tells them to stay on watch all night. He is rigid with fear
for his pieces of amber, his statues, his columns of Phrygian
    marble,
his ivory, and all that tortoise-shell inlay. The jar of the naked
Cynic is non-combustible; break it, tomorrow another
house will appear, or the same will serve when repaired with
    lead.   310
When he saw that jar with its great inhabitant squatting inside,
Alexander perceived how much more happy was the man who
    desired
nothing at all than the one who claimed the entire world;
for the latter's achievements were bound to be matched by
    enormous perils.
Lady Luck, if the truth were known, you possess no power;
it is we who make you a goddess.

                         However, if anyone asks me
what amount of wealth is enough, here is my answer:
as much as hunger and thirst and the need of warmth require;
as much as Epicurus found sufficient in his little garden;
as much as was stored in days of old in Socrates' larder.   320
Nature never gives one sort of counsel and wisdom another.
Are these examples too harsh? Do I limit you too severely?
Very well, allow for our modern standards; make up the total
required by Otho's law for the fourteen rows at the front.
If this sum, too, produces a frown and a pout of displeasure,
take *two* knights and their money, or a *third* four-hundred
    thousand.
If that doesn't fill your lap, and it keeps on stretching for more,
then neither Croesus' millions, nor all the realms of Persia,
will appease your greedy soul, nor yet the wealth of Narcissus,
the man whom Claudius Caesar presented with all he could ask
    for,   330
the man whose will he obeyed when ordered to kill his wife.

SATIRE 15

A Case of Cannibalism

Volusius, my Bithynian friend, everyone knows
what monsters the mad Egyptians worship. Some of them
    honour
the crocodile, others bow down to the ibis bulging with snakes;
the long-tailed ape is sacred, with its gleaming golden image,
where lyre-strings magically echo from Memnon's mangled
    statue,
and ancient Thebes, with its hundred gates, is a heap of ruins.
In one place cats, in another fresh-water fish, in another
dogs are worshipped by entire towns; Diana by no one.
It's sin and sacrilege to sink your teeth in a leek or an onion
(a holy country indeed where such divinities grow   10
in gardens!); wool-bearing quadrupeds are strictly avoided
by guests at table; it's a sin to slit the throat of a kid.
The consumption of *human* flesh is in order. Ulysses, describing
a crime like that to the astonished Alcinous as they sat over
    dinner,
elicited anger, or in certain quarters possibly laughter,
as a spinner of lying yarns: 'Will nobody throw the fellow
into the sea? He deserves the horror of a real Charybdis—
he and his preposterous Cyclopes and his Laestrygonians!
I'd sooner believe in his Scylla, or those Cyanean rocks
that clash together, and the mighty winds tied up in a wine-skin,   20
or how Elpenor was struck with an elegant tap by Circe,
who packed him off to grunt amongst the swinish oarsmen.
Does he take the folk of Phaeacia for such a witless lot?'
That would have been a fair response from a guest, still sober,
who had drunk no more than a sip of wine from a jar of Corcyra;
for the Ithacan told that tale on his own; there was none to
    confirm it.

I have a story which, strange as it sounds, recently happened
when Iuncus was consul, beyond the town of sweltering
    Coptus.
Mine's a *collective* story; the stage can boast nothing like it.
You may look through all of tragedy's wardrobe from Pyrrha
    on,   30
but you'll find no *people* guilty of outrage. Now hear this
    example
of appalling barbarity, which has come to light in modern times.

Ombi and Téntyra are neighbours; but an old, long-standing
    feud
blazes between them still. It's an open wound and a source
of undying hatred. The madness infecting the two communities
comes from the fact that each detests the other's religion,
convinced, as it is, that the only deities worth the name
are those it worships itself. When one of the towns was holding
a sacred feast, the enemy's chiefs and leaders resolved
to a man that the chance should be seized to prevent the folk
    from enjoying   40
the happy auspicious day; they must not be allowed the pleasure
of a splendid banquet, with tables set at cross-road and temple,
and couches that knew no sleep by night or day and were
    sometimes
found in place by the sun on his seventh circuit (yes, Egypt
to be sure is uncouth; but in self-indulgence its barbarous mob
aspires as high, or so I have found, as scandalous Canopus).
Victory, too, would be easy over a wine-sodden enemy,
slurred in his speech and reeling drunkenly. Here there were
    menfolk
prancing about to a negro piper, complete with perfumes
(such as they were) and flowers and garlands over their
    eyebrows.   50
There stood hunger and hate. It began with noisy insults;
but when tempers are boiling, these are the bugle that starts the
    fray.
Raising a common cry, they charged. In the absence of weapons
bare fists flew; and scarcely a jaw was left unbroken.
From the press of battle few, if any, emerged with a nose

that was not smashed in. Through all the ranks you could see
   men's faces
mangled, with unrecognizable features; cheek-bones poking
through gaping wounds, knuckles covered with blood from
   eyes.
And yet the combatants think it is just a game—like children
playing at soldiers—because no bodies are there to stamp on.   60
What is the point of a host of thousands starting a fight
if no one is killed? And so the attack grows fiercer; they look for
stones on the ground; then, bending their arms, they proceed to
   hurl them—
the type of weapon normally used by rioting crowds,
not great rocks of the size propelled by Turnus and Ajax,
and not so heavy as that with which the son of Tydeus
smashed Aeneas' hip, but such as the hands of today
can manage to throw, hands of a kind so different from theirs.
For the human race was already declining in Homer's time.
Now the earth gives birth to such nasty and puny creatures   70
that any god who observes them is moved to laughter and
   loathing.

After that brief digression our story continues. When one side
was joined by reserves, suddenly swords appeared in their
   hands;
they at once stepped up the attack with showers of deadly
   arrows.
As Ombi advanced, those who reside in the shady palmgrove
of nearby Téntyra turned their backs and fled in disorder.
One, as he ran in mindless panic, happened to trip,
and was seized. He was promptly chopped into countless bits
   and pieces,
so that a single corpse might furnish numerous helpings.
After that, the victorious mob devoured the lot,   80
and picked his bones. They didn't boil him in a seething
   cauldron
or roast him on spits. It seemed too long and too slow a business
to wait for a hearth. They were happy to eat the carcase raw.
One can only be grateful here, that they didn't profane the fire
which you, Prometheus, stole from the highest courts of heaven

and gave to earth. Three cheers for that element! And I imagine
you share my pleasure. But, to the man who chewed the corpse,
that was the most delicious meat he had ever tasted.
Nor, in this horrid act, would I leave you wondering whether
it was only the leader's gullet that experienced pleasure. The
    man   90
who had stood on the edge of the scrimmage, when nothing was
    left of the carcase,
scratched the ground with his nails to obtain a lick of the gore.

The Váscones, so the story goes, turned to such victuals
to prolong their lives. But the case was different; for over there
they had to contend with a hostile fortune, the disasters of war,
desperate conditions, the appalling distress of a lengthy siege.   96
It was when they had eaten every plant and creature and object   99
to which the pangs of a famished stomach drove them, when
    even   100
their enemies pitied their pallor and their wasted skeletal limbs,
that they tore at another's flesh in their hunger; they were ready
    to swallow
even their own. What man or god could withold indulgence
from bellies reduced to such frightful, and such outlandish,
    extremities,
bellies which could be forgiven by the very ghosts of the people
whose bodies they used as food? Now, of course, we know
    better
thanks to the teachings of Zeno, but who would expect a
    Spaniard   107–8
to be a Stoic, at least in the days of old Metellus?
Today the entire world has its Graeco-Roman culture;   110
smooth-tongued Gaul has been coaching British barristers; now
there's talk of hiring a rhetoric-teacher in Timbuctoo!
The community mentioned, however, was noble. It was
    matched by Zacynthus
in valour and loyalty, and indeed outweighed in the scale of
    disaster.
But what excuse does Egypt have for being more savage
than Crimea's altar? (For the Tauric founder of that ghastly rite,
if one accepts the poets' tradition as worthy of credence,

contents herself with human sacrifice. Therefore the victim
has nothing more hideous to fear beyond the knife.) What
    affliction
recently goaded *them*? What ravenous hunger, what army   120
besieging their city walls impelled them to hazard an outrage
so revolting? What more could they do, if the land of Memphis
were parched with drought, to shame the lazy Nile into rising?
Neither the dreaded Cimbrian hordes, nor the barbarous
    Britons,
nor the grim Sarmatians, nor yet the wild Agathyrsi raged
with the utter frenzy displayed by that soft and worthless rabble
who are used to setting their tiny sails on earthenware vessels,
and to bending over their miniature oars in painted potsherds.

You will never match such a crime with punishment, or devise
    retribution
to suit communities such as these; for in *their* way of thinking   130
hunger and anger are one and the same. By giving tears
to the human race Nature revealed she was giving us also
tender hearts; compassion is the finest of all our feelings.
She therefore moves us to pity the accused, as he pleads his case
unkempt in body and dress, or the orphan who brings to court
his swindling guardian, and whose face, streaming with tears,
    and framed
by his girlish hair, invites the question 'Is he a boy?'.
It is Nature who makes us cry when we meet the cortège of a girl
on the eve of marriage, or a little child too small for the pyre
is laid in a grave. For what good man—the sort who deserves   140
the initiate's torch and lives as the priest of Ceres would have
    him—
believes that any woes are remote from *him*? It is this
that marks us off from the brutish herd. Moreover, we only
possess an intellect worthy of homage, have god-like powers,
and are able to learn and practise the arts of civilization,
because we received that gift, sent down from the castle in
    heaven,
which is lacking in four-footed creatures that stare at the
    ground. To them,
when the world began, our common creator granted no more

than the breath of life; to us, a soul as well. He intended
that our fellow-feeling should lead us to ask and offer help;   150
to gather scattered inhabitants into communities, leaving
the ancient woods, and deserting the groves where our ancestors
    lived;
to put up houses, placing another man's dwelling beside
our own abode, ensuring that we all slept safe and sound
in the knowledge that each had a friend next door; to shield with
    our weapons
a fallen comrade or one who reeled from a shocking wound;
to sound the call on a common trumpet; to man the turrets
in joint defence, and fasten the gate with a single key.

But nowadays snakes maintain a greater harmony. Spotted
animals spare their spotted kin; when did a stronger   160
lion tear the life from a weaker? Was there ever a forest
where a boar was killed, gashed by the tusks of a larger boar?
In India, one ferocious tigress lives with another
in constant peace; and savage bears observe an agreement.
To man, however, it is not enough to have forged his deadly
blades on an evil anvil. Early smiths were accustomed
to spend their energies fashioning only hoes and scuffles,
mattocks and ploughshares; they hadn't the skill to produce a
    sword.
But here is a people whose fury is not appeased by an act
of simple murder, who regard trunks, and arms, and faces   170
as a kind of food! What, one asks, would Pythagoras say?
Would he not take flight to no matter where, on witnessing these
enormities—that man who refused all meat, as though it were
    human,
and denied himself even the pleasure of certain vegetable dishes?

SATIRE 16

The Advantages of Army Life

No one, Gallius, can count the rewards of a soldier's life,
when things go well. For if you join a successful unit
   ⟨the profits can be enormous⟩
With luck on my side, I too would become an anxious recruit
and enter the gate of the camp. To be born a favourite of Fortune
is a greater boon than a reference written to Mars by Venus
or by his mother, who takes such pleasure in sandy Samos.

First consider the advantages common to all. Not least
is the fact that no civilian would dare to beat you up;
indeed, if he's beaten himself he will try to keep it dark.
He will never dare to show the judge the gaps in his teeth, 10
the black lumps on his face, the numerous swollen bruises,
and the one eye left, about which the doctor will make no
  promises.
If he seeks redress, a hob-nailed judge is assigned to the case;
brawny calves bedeck a row of enormous benches.
Ancient military law applies, and the rule of Camillus
forbidding a soldier to attend a trial outside the rampart,
away from the standards. A hearing before a centurions' panel
is wholly fair, they tell me; so even I will obtain
redress from a soldier, provided my complaint is soundly based.
The whole of the cohort, however, is hostile; and all the
  detachments 20
combine to ensure that your 'damages' call for medical
  treatment,
and prove to be worse than the initial assault. So in view of the
  fact that
you have only one pair of legs, it would take the declaimer
  Vagellius

with his mulish brain to provoke so many boots,
so many thousands of hobnails. Besides, what witness would
    venture
so far from the city? Who but a Pýlades could be expected
to pass the massive rampart? So come, let's dry our tears,
and let's not pester our friends (they will only make excuses).
When the judge invites you to call your witness, whoever he is,
who saw the attack, just let him dare to say 'I saw it',   30
and I'll swear he's a worthy son of the bearded and hairy Romans
of yore. It's an easier thing to produce a perjured witness
against a civilian than a man who is willing to tell the truth,
when it poses a threat to a soldier's purse or impugns his honour.

Now let us note some other rewards and other incentives
held out by an army career. Suppose a dishonest neighbour
does me out of a valley or field on my family acres,
uprooting the sacred stone from the midst of the boundary strip
(the stone I have honoured every year with cakes and pottage),
or say a debtor will not repay the money I lent him,   40
claiming the signature isn't his and the tablet's invalid,
I shall have to wait for the time of year when the whole
    population
begin their suits; and even then I shall have to put up with
countless delays and frustrations. Often the benches are ready;
the fluent Caedicius is removing his cloak, and Fuscus is having
a last-minute leak; we are all prepared—when the case is
    adjourned.
We troop away. A courtroom combat is always protracted.
But as for those who are girt with a sword and embraced by a
    baldrick—
a time for hearing the case is fixed at *their* convenience,
nor are their means worn down as the case drags on and on.   50

Moreover, a soldier alone has the right of making a will
in his father's lifetime. Monies earned in military service
(so says the law) are deemed not part of the total assets
of which the father has sole control. And therefore Coranus,
because he's on active service, earning a soldier's pay,
is wooed by his father, decrepit as he is. The son is promoted

(fair enough) and receives a reward for his noble efforts.
Indeed it seems to be very much in the general's interest
that whoever is brave should also be seen as the most successful,
that all should have the pleasure of medals and necklets, and all   60
should . . .

Explanatory Notes

The transmission of Juvenal's text is summarized by R. J. Tarrant in
Texts and Transmission, ed. L. D. Reynolds (Oxford, 1983) 200–3.
Over the centuries that text has been corrupted by careless copying,
by deliberate interpolation, and by accidental loss; see the preface to
A. E. Housman's edition (2nd edn., Cambridge, 1931). Whereas
commentators can discuss alternatives and occasionally admit defeat,
the translator must present a façade of omniscience. The notes in
square brackets, however, will indicate some of the problems. The
letter C. refers to Professor Courtney's commentary. Nisbet (i) and
(ii) refer to Professor Nisbet's conjectures in the *Journal of Roman
Studies* 52 (1962) 233–8 and in *Bull. Inst. Class. Stud.* Suppl. 51 (1988)
86–110.

SATIRE 1

1 *a listener only*: Juvenal puts his complaints against the current
literary scene in the context of the public recitations, first organized
in the Augustan age by Asinius Pollio as an easy way for writers
to make their work known. Attendance inevitably became a
tiresome social duty: see Juvenal's facetious comment at 3. 9.
Rich patrons like Fronto (l. 12) lent their premises: compare
7. 39 ff.

6 *the final margin*: the papyrus roll was written in columns and
wound round a roller. Here the margin between the last column
and the roller has been filled up and the writing is continued on the
back of the papyrus.

8 The grove of Mars at Colchis was where the Golden Fleece was
kept. The rocks of Aeolus, the god who controlled the winds, are
the group of volcanic islands to the north-east of Sicily: Vulcan
was supposed to have his forge on one of these.

10 f.   Aeacus was one of the judges of the Underworld. Monychus was a Centaur, half man, half horse. The battle between the Centaurs and the Lapiths at the wedding-feast of Pirithous and Hippodamia, a popular subject in poetry and art, is the occasion referred to here.

    The nameless allusion to Jason and the Golden Fleece is of a kind much used by Juvenal to achieve a wide range of nuances, e.g., here and at 52 f. dismissive, at 20 and 51 entirely respectful.

15 f.   Juvenal means that, after attending the grammar school (see on 7. 215), he underwent the full rhetorical training which was essential to a complete Roman education. This is a rare auto-biographical detail and an intimation of his leaning towards a declamatory tone. The exercises in rhetoric included the *controversia*, the arguing of fanciful legal cases, and the *suasoria* (referred to here), in which the student offered advice to historical characters faced with some moral dilemma, e.g., Shall Caesar cross the Rubicon and plunge the country into Civil War?

20   The mighty son of Aurunca is Gaius Lucilius (Index), the inventor in the second century BC of the branch of satire practised by Horace, Persius, and Juvenal, all of whom appeal to his precedent. He was born in Suessa Aurunca on the edge of Campania.

26   *Crispinus*: see on 4. 1.

33   *informed on a powerful friend*: the literature of the period, especially Juvenal and Tacitus, is full of such cases. Tacitus, *Histories* 1. 2, makes the bitter comment that 'those who had no enemies were destroyed by their friends'. For a case in point see 3. 116. Tacitus, *Annals* 3. 28, refers the rise of this espionage to the provisions of Augustan legislation to check celibacy and encourage procreation, especially the *Lex Papia Poppaea* of AD 9, which granted rewards to informers. Tiberius' revival of the treason law, AD 15, encouraged the practice (Ibid., 1. 72 ff.).

35   *Massa . . . Carus*: these were notorious informers under Domitian. The unnamed one they all fear may be Regulus, the most active and dreaded of them all. See Pliny, *Epistles* 1. 5.

36   *Thymele . . . Latinus*: the informer Latinus, a famous actor of mimes, was an intimate friend of Domitian. The incident in which he seems to have sent his leading-lady Thymele to

appease another informer is not otherwise known. See also
6. 43, 8. 197.

44 *contest at the grim altar of Lyons*: in rhetorical contests instituted
by the emperor Caligula the losers had the option of expunging
their compositions with the tongue as an alternative to a
flogging or a ducking in the river (Suetonius, *Caligula* 20). The
altar, dedicated to Rome and the genius of Augustus by Drusus
in AD 12, stood at the confluence of the Rhone and the
Saône.

49 In AD 100 Marius Priscus, governor of Africa, was banished for
extortion and cruelty. His punishment was relegation, a form of
exile not necessarily involving loss of property or civil rights:
hence Marius' high spirits and his province's dejection. For the
whole subject of provincial exploitation by Roman governors
see 8. 87 ff.

51 *Venusia's lamp*: i.e., satire like that of Horace (65–8 BC), who
was born in Venusia, a Roman garrison town on the borders of
Apulia and Lucania. Juvenal's satire is however much more
astringent than that of the mild and genial Horace. The image of
the lamp is probably chosen to indicate Horace's painstaking
craftsmanship.

52 ff. See Index under Hercules, Diomedes and Daedalus ('the
flying joiner'). Three crisp phrases dispose of the venerable
legend of Daedalus: as at lines 10 f. anonymity underlines
contempt.

60 *Automedon*: the name of Achilles' charioteer in the *Iliad* is often
used facetiously for any fast driver. This man has the effrontery
to aspire to an equestrian career (the first step was command of a
cohort) though his extravagance has made him ineligible: see on
l. 106 below.

66 *Maecenas*: Horace and Virgil naturally give no hint of the
decadence and effeminacy of their great patron. Post-Augustan
writers, e.g. Seneca, *Epistles* 114, are much less inhibited.

71 *Lucusta*: a poisoner. Her services were much in demand in
imperial circles of the first century AD. Her clients included
Agrippina and Nero, her victims the emperor Claudius and his
son Britannicus.

80 *like mine or like Cluvienus'*: Juvenal, with considerable mock modesty, couples the efforts of a totally unknown writer of (presumably) satire with his own. Horace similarly with tongue in cheek, in telling why he opted for satire, declares it was just something he could do better than Varro of Atax, a recent failure at the genre, 'and certain others' (*Satires* 1. 10. 46).

84 *displayed her naked girls*: again a compendious account of an old story (Ovid, *Metamorphoses* 1. 313 ff., etc.) ends in bathos. Pyrrha emerges as the madam in a brothel showing off her girls.

86 *my volume's hotch-potch*: Juvenal's word is *farrago*, literally a mixed crop sown for animal fodder. Roman grammarians connected the etymology of *satura* ('satire') with the idea of fullness and mixture, e.g., a dish of first-fruits, sausage-meat, etc. Sir Richard Steele adapted these words as the motto of *The Tatler*. A similar adaptation served as the motto of the *Boy's Own Paper* until well into this century.

95 *little 'basket'*: the Latin word is *sportula*, a wicker basket used in distributing meat to the poor after sacrifices or for handing food around at large dinner-parties; it could also mean a scratch meal (Suetonius, *Claudius* 21. 4). It had come to mean the hand-out a client could expect from his patron, originally a meal, then, when feeding large numbers of clients on a regular basis became a nuisance, a basket of food left in the porch for the clients to collect. Finally the food was commuted for money, the famous 100 *quadrantes* (= 25 *asses*) of l. 121 below and Martial 1. 59. 1. Martial calls it 'starvation' but it must have been an important source of income to many, given the strength and extent of the patron–client relationship in Roman society.

100 *Trojan families*: the 'best' Roman families claimed descent from Aeneas and his companions who reputedly settled in Italy after the fall of Troy. The aristocracy in the dole-queue stretches our credulity.

106 *four hundred thousand*: 400,000 sesterces was the property qualification for admission to the equestrian order, the knights, the second order of the Roman people, below the Senate and above the plebs. They supplied officers for the army and administrators for the provinces and were identified with the financial and commercial interests of Rome as well as the municipal aristocracy.

Their distinctive dress included a tunic with a narrow purple stripe (angusticlave). Senators wore a broad purple stripe (laticlave, 'the broader purple') on the tunic.

107 *Corvinus is tending the flocks*: Corvinus is a representative of an old senatorial family now fallen on hard times. He has leased a flock of sheep and is working it on a share-cropping basis with the owner; for the practice see Cato, *Agric.* 150.

109 *Pallas . . . Licinus*: freedmen who to Juvenal's disgust had become fabulously rich: see Index. In this respect they resemble the speaker here. The phenomenon was not a new one: Horace (*Epodes* 4) rails at just such another *nouveau riche* freedman more than a century before this.

the tribunes: originally the champions of the plebeians against patrician oppression, now, with the real tribunician power vested in the emperor, of much less importance but still respected. Their persons were sacrosanct, hence 'sacred office'.

111 *whitened feet*: the slave-dealers whitened the feet of imported slaves with chalk to distinguish them in the slave-market from those bred at home.

116 *replies with a clatter*: the storks nesting on the temple roof clattered their bills whenever people called a greeting to the temple or its divinity in passing.

128 *Apollo the lawyer*: Apollo, whose ivory statue stood near the law-courts in the Roman Forum, has become a legal expert by constant listening to the cases.

129 *the generals' statues*: in the colonnades flanking the temple of Mars the Avenger Augustus had placed statues of victorious generals.

Egyptian wallah: a high-ranking customs official; Juvenal's word is *Arabarches*, literally 'Lord of the Arabs', 'Sheikh'. He is identified as Tiberius Julius Alexander, an Egyptian Jew who became prefect of Egypt, AD 66–70. The statue was probably awarded for his part in Titus' war against the Jews, AD 70.

[132 Juvenal's abrupt passage from the events of the morning to supper-time makes it highly probable that something has dropped out of his account of the daily routine after l. 131. So Housman.]

144 A line of some difficulty. The literal translation is 'hence sudden
     deaths and intestate old age'. But why 'intestate' necessarily
     where a man has lived long enough to make a will? Yet the
     friends are angry because the deceased has clearly failed to make
     some testamentary provision for them, which he might have
     done had he lived. For *intestata* of the manuscripts, *intemptata* has
     been proposed: this implies that old age is unsampled by the
     dead glutton, i.e. effectively cancelled.

153 f. These two questions are clearly meant to be the comment
     of Lucilius. He never shrank from naming those whom he
     satirized, to the amazement of Roman critics of all periods, for
     taking liberties with a man's name was offensive and even
     actionable. All subsequent satirists mention this Lucilian trait of
     outspokenness with respect and indeed envy. The freedom he
     enjoyed did not long survive the collapse of the old Republic.

155 *Tigellinus*: a curious example for the interlocutor to use in
     cautioning the budding satirist and an interesting specimen of
     Juvenal's satiric technique. Tigellinus, Nero's infamous praetorian
     prefect, had been dead since AD 69, over thirty years before.
     See on ll. 170 f. below.

[157 *a vivid pathway of light*: an alternative translation ('tracing a
     broad furrow in the middle of the sand') envisages the burnt-out
     corpses being dragged across the sand of the arena by an
     attendant with a hook. This is Housman's explanation (adopted
     by C.) but it assumes the loss of a line after 156.]

162–4 The interlocutor suggests epic subjects, free from the dangers
     of satire. The Rutulian is Turnus, king of that tribe and the rival
     of Aeneas. Achilles' wounding at the Scaean Gate by Paris and
     Apollo does not actually occur in the *Iliad*. Hylas belongs to the
     story of the Argonauts. After his abduction by the nymphs of
     the well where he was drawing water, he was sought in vain by
     his distraught lover Hercules. Juvenal deftly contrives again to
     take the bloom off a charming story beloved by artists.

170 f. Juvenal declares his intention of playing safe by targeting the
     dead in his satire. Where he does not, he selects for his *exempla*
     people of no significance (e.g. Cordus, Cluvienus), people
     fallen from grace (like the condemned Marius Priscus), or who

have lost their influence (like Crispinus, once a favourite of Domitian), or else he conceals their identity under a fictitious name, (e.g. Automedon).

The Twelve Tables of the Law forbade burial and cremation within the City, so the cemeteries were to be found alongside the main roads out of Rome, like the Via Flaminia going north (cf. line 61 above) or the Via Latina to the south-east. This is why grave-stone inscriptions are addressed to travellers and horsemen.

SATIRE 2

1 *Sarmatia*: the Sarmatians (Sarmatae, Sauromatae), a nomadic people from east of the Don, had pushed steadily westwards and at this time occupied the area between the middle Danube and the Theiss. The name probably had the same bleak associations as the modern Siberia.

3 *The Curii's style*: *the Curii* is a generalizing plural for men like M'. Curius Dentatus, representatives of the best type of Roman manhood in the old Republic. The Bacchic orgies or Bacchanalia were so uninhibited in character and gave rise to so much public disorder that the Senate was obliged to repress them by a decree in 186 BC.

4 ff. With the exception of Pittacus, one of the Seven Sages of Greece, the names are those of distinguished heads of schools of Greek philosophy.

10 *Socratic fairies*: Socrates' predilection for good-looking young men and his association with them, however innocent it may have been, made him and his followers very vulnerable to this kind of innuendo: see, for example, Plato, *Symposium* 215 ff., especially 219B, for Alcibiades' relationship with Socrates.

12 '*a soul of adamant*': Horace had thus described the soul of the Stoic Cato (*Odes* 2. 1. 24).

20 *in Hercules' style*: Hercules was celebrated for his early choice of virtue and the rejection of vice in the well-known story of Prodicus told by Xenophon *Memorabilia* 2. 1. 21 ff.: cf. Juvenal 10. 360 ff., where his labours and suffering in the service of mankind are held to be preferable to self-indulgence.

24 ff. These are all examples of what we might call Satan reproving sin.

28   *Sulla's trio of pupils*: the members of the triumvirate, Octavian (the future emperor Augustus), Mark Antony and Lepidus, appointed in 43 BC by a law of the people for a five-year term in which to put the affairs of Rome on a sound footing after the murder of Julius Caesar. Like Sulla (see 1. 16) they had recourse to proscription in order to liquidate their enemies. This involved publishing the names of persons placed outside the protection of the law and whose property was confiscated. One of their victims was Cicero: see 10. 120.

29 ff. The emperor Domitian became *censor perpetuus* in AD 85 and revived and enforced the laws against vice and immorality. His own licentious habits fell a long way short of the standards he set for others and earned him a reputation for hypocrisy. The incident referred to here, in which his niece Julia became pregnant by him and died as a result of the abortifacient he compelled her to take (Suetonius, *Domitian* 22, Pliny, *Epistles* 4. 11. 6), is a case in point. In spite of legislation passed in AD 49 to enable the emperor Claudius to marry his niece Agrippina, by Roman standards this was incest. The most famous tragedy concerned with incest was Sophocles' *Oedipus Rex*.

Mars and Venus: one of the laws Domitian enforced was Augustus' Julian Law to curb adultery of 18 BC, hence the panic of these divinities. Venus was unfaithful to her husband both with Mars (*Odyssey* 8. 266 ff., Lucretius 1. 31 ff.) and Anchises: by the latter she became the mother of Aeneas and the parent of the Roman people.

35   *bogus Scauri*: in spite of the generalizing plural, one member of the family, the censor of 109 BC, stands out above the rest.

36   *O Julian law*: see l. 30 above and note.

37   Laronia is a respectable name like Creticus and Gracchus below. A historical Laronius (consul 33 BC) commanded in the war against Sextus Pompeius in 36, and Martial 2. 32 has a rich old widow called Laronia. Juvenal's Laronia may possibly have fallen foul of the Julian laws and hence her bitterness. More probably, she is just meant to be some honest whore, no better

than she should be, but 'straight' and incensed at the perversions and hypocrisy of the 'gays'.

40 *a third Cato*: the earlier Catos are (1) M. Porcius Cato, the censor of 184 BC, and (2) his great-grandson, M. Porcius Cato, called Uticensis, the great Stoic hero.

44 *the Scantinian*: i.e. law, first mentioned by Cicero's correspondent, M. Caelius Rufus, in 50 BC (*Epistles to Friends* 8. 12. 3), but obviously earlier. It was directed against sodomy and rigorously enforced by Domitian.

51 ff. Laronia's loyalty to her sex outruns her accuracy. Women did plead in the courts (Valerius Maximus 8. 3) and engage in manly sports (e.g. Maevia in 1. 22 f.; cf. Martial, *Spect.* 6b); for a different view of women, see Satire 6 *passim*.

53 *fighters'*: i.e. gladiators'.

56 f. The stories of Penelope and Arachne revolve around weaving and spinning.

[The translation follows those editors, e.g. Housman, who see here one of Juvenal's nameless references to the story, elsewhere referred to in Satire (Lucilius 599 f. Marx, Persius 1. 78), of Antiopa in servitude to Dirce, her husband's second wife: it would be very much in Juvenal's manner. C. suspects the loss of a line between 56 and 57.]

66 Creticus is a name borne by the Caecilii Metelli (see 8. 38), a great family once but extinct in Juvenal's day. This man is an advocate called Iulius Creticus, according to the scholiast.

68 ff. These are evidently meant to be women arraigned for adultery as part of the Domitian campaign for purity. Wives divorced on the grounds of adultery lost the right to wear the matronly *stola* (Martial 2. 39) and assumed the toga: hence *togata* came to mean adulteress or prostitute (Martial, 6. 64. 4, Horace, *Satires* 1. 2. 63).

81 Juvenal here subtly adapts a proverbial saying recorded by the scholiast, *uua uuam uidendo uaria fit* ('grape changes colour on seeing grape', i.e. rots).

86 ff. The Good Goddess (*Bona Dea*) was a Roman divinity, worshipped exclusively by women. Men were excluded from her festivals, and pictures of male animals covered up. See further

6. 336 ff. and notes for the notorious occasion when Clodius invaded the festival disguised as a female musician: this is the allusion in line 90.

91 f. Cotyto was a Thracian divinity whose worship spread to Athens (Cecrops' city) and Corinth. Her rites were orgiastic and involved a purification ceremony: hence her worshippers were called Dippers (*Baptae*), the title of a play of the Old Comedy by Eupolis (5th century BC).

98 *swears by his master's Juno*: this brands both master and man as effeminates, since women swore by Juno, men by their Genius.

99 Mirrors were strictly for women. There is a fable of Phaedrus (3. 8) where a girl tells on her little brother for looking in one; certainly not a thing for a soldier in the field.

Otho the pathic was, like Galba, one of the contenders for empire in succession to Nero in AD 69, 'the year of the four emperors'. Suetonius (*Otho* 12. 2) mentions his feminine style of grooming and his depilated body.

100 *taken off the Auruncan Actor*: the words are actually Virgil's, *Aeneid* 12. 94, where Turnus boasts of having captured Actor's lance. Otho's prize is a mirror: the inference is obvious. Some see a punning reference to Nero in 'the Auruncan Actor', since Nero was an actor and came from Antium, which was not far from the ancient territory of the Aurunci.

103 *the recent annals and history*: this is thought to be a reference to the *Histories* of Tacitus, which were begun under Trajan (i.e. after AD 98) and still in progress in 106 and later (Tacitus, *Histories*, 1. 1, Pliny *Epistles* 6. 16, 20, and 7. 33). Book 1 deals with Otho's campaign of 69, but does not mention his mirror, though other articles of luxury in his baggage are spoken of (1. 88). Since the earlier books may have been published separately as completed, or their contents made known at readings, this is hardly firm enough evidence for assuming a date between 107 and 110 for the publication of Juvenal's first book.

107 Suetonius (*Otho* 12) says that his use of a facial-pack or poultice was to stop him from ever having a beard.

108 *the quivered Semiramis*: the Assyrian queen, builder of Babylon,

was renowned for her exploits in battle and in the bedroom (Ovid, *Amores* 1. 5. 11).

109 Cleopatra's courageous bearing at the naval battle of Actium, 31 BC, in which she and Mark Antony were finally defeated, was in marked contrast to that of her own men (Horace, *Odes* 1. 37).

[The translation renders C.'s conjecture *saeua* for the inappropriate *maesta* = 'sad'.]

111 *Cybele's crew*: the Galli or priests of the Phrygian Mother Goddess, Cybele, were eunuchs: see line 115 below and 3. 137 f.

[*turpis* ('disgraceful') has not been convincingly explained. The translation gives the general sense.]

115 *the Phrygian mode*: see on line 111 above.

117 Gracchus obviously belonged to a branch of the great family, the *gens Sempronia*, of which the most distinguished members were the reforming tribunes Tiberius Sempronius Gracchus and his brother Gaius. The priesthood he held (l. 125 and note) confirms his high birth. The dowry he gave his 'bridegroom' (enough to qualify him as a knight; see on 1. 106) marks him as a very rich man. For his gladiatorial exploits see also 8. 199 ff. The emperor Nero more than once went through similar forms of 'marriage', both as bride and bridegroom (Suetonius, *Nero* 28, 29, Tacitus, *Annals* 15. 37) and similarly shocked Roman sentiment by appearing on the public stage.

121 *censor . . . or an augur?* Domitian took the office of censor for life (see on l. 30 above), the first of the emperors to do so.

augur: Juvenal's word is *haruspex*, one of an official order of soothsayers who interpreted portents (*monstra*), like those described, for their future significance: but there was also a College of Augurs, who interpreted other signs (*auguria*) as intimations of divine approval or disapproval of a proposed action.

125 The original shield of Mars (*ancile*) fell from heaven in the reign of Numa (715–673 BC), and its existence was thought to guarantee the safety of Rome. To prevent theft, copies were made of the original and regularly paraded through Rome by the Salii (dancing priests), of whom there were two companies, one

connected with Romulus (Quirinus), 'father of our city' (l. 126), the other with Mars (l. 128). Membership was restricted to men of the highest birth, like Gracchus.

132 *great Park*: the Campus Martius or Field of Mars at Rome, much used for military exercises and civilian sports.

133 *Quirinus' valley*: the situation is uncertain (the Roman Forum? below the Quirinal Hill?) but the inference is clear. Quirinus is Romulus, heroic founder of Rome and representative of early manliness in contrast to latter-day decadence.

141 Lyde (a 'literary' name, found in Horace and Martial) is here the name of some back-street quack.

142 On 14 February in each year the Luperci, priests of Lupercus, i.e. Faunus, an Italian fertility God, ran through the streets naked except for a loin-girth of goatskin, wielding strips of hide. Infertile women put themselves in their way to be beaten as a cure for their infertility. See the opening scenes of Shakespeare's *Julius Caesar*.

143 ff. The enormity of Gracchus' appearance in the arena lies in the fact that (1) gladiators were slaves, prisoners of war, or condemned criminals, and they and their occupation were regarded as the lowest of the low; (2) even among gladiators, the *retiarius* (see on 8. 201 ff.) was looked down on; (3) it is an indication of the depths to which he has sunk from the standards expected from one of his birth. The families mentioned, by contrast, all figure in the history of the Roman Republic as shining examples of virtue.

148 *the man who provided the show*: if the emperor is meant (after Domitian, games at Rome could only be given by the emperor), then it must be Nero, a Julio-Claudian, and therefore impeccable in point of family background if nothing else, and not Domitian, a Flavian, descended from tax-farmers and centurions: otherwise the comparison loses point.

149 ff. Juvenal's sceptical account of the nether regions, with the rivers of Hades and the ferryman Charon punting the dead across, carries many suggestions of the famous Virgilian descriptions of the descent to the underworld, *Georgics* 4. 467 ff.

and *Aeneid* 6. 295 ff. For similar views see Lucretius 3. 978 ff. (Epicurean) and Ovid, *Metamorphoses* 15. 153 ff. (Pythagorean).

153 f. These were great warriors of the Republican period, men of legendary fame.

155 *Cremera's legion*: the *gens Fabia*, an ancient patrician family, undertook the conduct of a war against the Etruscan city of Veii. The entire family, it was said, with the exception of one boy, 306 in all, perished at the battle of the River Cremera on 13 February 477 BC.

Cannae: the village in south-east Italy where Hannibal in the Second Punic War inflicted a swingeing defeat on the Romans with enormous casualties, 216 BC.

158 *laurel-twig*: here used for ritual aspersion as part of a purification rite, in contrast to the sulphur and torches, which suggest actual fumigation.

159 *process in disgrace*: like captives led in the triumphal procession of a conqueror.

160 f. A reference to Agricola and his exploits by land and sea during his governorship of Britain, AD 78–84, described by Tacitus in *Agricola*, written AD 97–98. The invasion of Ireland was contemplated in 82 but not carried out.

[167 The translation follows Clausen's *indulget* for the manuscripts' *indulsit*. C. prefers to assume, with Leo, the loss of the equivalent of a line.]

170 Artaxata, the capital of Armenia, had been destroyed by Corbulo in AD 58, but was rebuilt by Tiridates.

SATIRE 3

3 *the Sibyl*: the seer who centuries before had sold her prophetic books to King Tarquinius Priscus (616–579 BC). Her abode was at Cumae, the oldest Greek colony in Italy, now in decline, situated on the neck of the peninsula on which stood the ever popular resort of Baiae, north of the Bay of Naples.

5 *Prochyta*: a barren island off the same peninsula.

Subura: a district of Rome and also a bustling and disreputable street leading eastwards out of the City. Juvenal, according to

Martial 12. 18 and on his own evidence (10. 156, 11. 51, 141) was well acquainted with it.

11 *the Porta Capena*: a gate in the Servian Wall, south-west of Rome, giving onto the south-bound Appian Way. It was crossed by an aqueduct, the Aqua Marcia, the water of which used to percolate through the stone. The van stood here, outside the city wall, because with few exceptions, e.g. builders' drays (see lines 236 ff. below), chariots in a triumphal procession, etc., vehicular traffic was forbidden in Rome during the hours of daylight.

12 *Numa*: King of Rome (715–673 BC). He claimed to have been instructed in the ordinances of the Roman religion by the nymph Egeria, whom he met at night in the grove of the Camenae, near the Porta Camena. Livy 1. 21. 3 calls her Numa's *coniunx* ('wife' or 'mate'), but Juvenal casts doubt on the seriousness of the king's motives.

14 *Jews*: expulsion of the Jews from Rome had taken place from time to time and as recently as the reign of Claudius (AD 41–54), but Judaeism remained a tolerated religion (*religio licita*) and their numbers at Rome had been swollen by the dispersal of the Jews following the destruction of Jerusalem by Titus in AD 70.

a hay-lined chest: the most plausible explanation is that they prepared food in advance, warmed it and placed it in an airtight box packed with straw to continue cooking for the Sabbath when such work was forbidden. Similarly at 6.542.

25 *Daedalus . . . wings*: i.e. Cumae, where, according to one version of the story, Daedalus (see 1. 54 and Index) landed after his flight from Crete.

27 *Lachesis*: see on 9. 135 f.

33 i.e. who sell up in a fraudulent bankruptcy. A spear (called 'the owner's' because the sale conferred ownership) was set up to indicate that an auction was in progress, a relic of the days when the spoils of war were sold thus. The line should be understood as a sale of the debtor's goods, not the sale of an individual.

34 ff. From providing a musical accompaniment for the gladiatorial contests in country towns, these people are now putting up the

money for shows of their own, at which they preside, like Roman magistrates or even emperors.

44 f. *never studied the innards of frogs*: the wording suggests some form of divination (cf. 6. 550 f.) rather than the preparation of poison as at 1. 70, 6. 659.

53 Verres is the stereotype of the guilty provincial governor in dread of prosecution. Cicero's successful conduct of the case against Verres for extortion in his province of Sicily put him in the front rank of his profession, 70 BC.

54 *the sand of shady Tagus*: the Tagus, one of the chief rivers of the Iberian peninsula, entering the sea at Lisbon, was famous in antiquity for its gold-bearing sand.

61 Juvenal means more particularly a Rome full of Greeks. Achaea was the Roman province of that name, i.e. the Peloponnese and part of central mainland Greece—Greece properly so-called as it were, as opposed to other parts of the eastern Mediterranean which Alexander the Great had made Greek.

68 *Grecian smudge*: the smudge came from the surface of the wrestling-ring; cf. 6. 246. Conservative Romans disapproved of the wrestling-school, a Greek institution, as encouraging homosexuality.

69 f. Of the places mentioned only two (Amydon in Macedonia, Sicyon of Argolis) are on the Greek mainland; see on l. 61 above. Andros and Samos are Aegean islands; Tralles and Alabanda were in Caria in Asia Minor.

71 *Willows' hill*: (like the Esquiline, one of the seven hills of Rome. Its real name, Viminal, did not fit the metre: hence the descriptive allusion.

74 *Isaeus*: a Syrian rhetorician whose skill and fluency created a great impression when he performed at Rome in AD 97.

85 *Aventine air . . . Sabine berry*: i.e. I am a pure-bred Roman. (In this respect Umbricius is unlike Juvenal.) The Aventine is one of the Seven Hills. The Sabine berry is the olive, home-produce unlike figs and damsons.

89 Antaeus, the giant wrestler of Libya, who drew his strength from his mother earth, could only be beaten by Hercules lifting

him off it and squeezing the life out of him: the contest was a
favourite subject with sculptors.

94 *Thaïs . . . the wife . . . Doris*: these are stock characters in plays of
the Greek New Comedy type and their Roman adaptations
(*palliatae*). Thaïs is a prostitute as in Terence's *The Eunuch*; the
wife is the respectable matron; Doris is the maidservant.

98 f. These were Greek comic actors working at Rome. Stratocles
and Demetrius are praised by Quintilian (11. 3. 178 ff.) for their
versatility in a wide range of New Comedy roles, the latter
particularly for his matrons and old women.

108 A line of impenetrable difficulty. The translation envisages
some form of commode or chamber-pot with a false inner
bottom that flipped over into place after use. Others think of a
drinking-glass that gurgled when emptied.

112 In these times a friend would stop at nothing. Thus Piso (see 5.
109) had made off with a friend's wife (Tacitus, *Annals* 15. 59),
who had nothing whatever to commend her except her looks.

[113 Recent editors follow Housman in regarding this line as spurious.
It says 'they wish to know the household's secrets and, for that
reason, to be feared.']

114 The gymnasia were among the haunts of homosexuals.

116 The Stoic philosopher P. Egnatius Celer in AD 66 gave evidence
against his patron and pupil Marcius Barea Soranus, who was
prosecuted for association with Rubellius Plautus (see on 8. 39–
40) and plotting revolt (Tacitus, *Annals* 16. 30–2, *Histories*
4. 10). Egnatius was born in Berytus (Beirut) but evidently
educated in Tarsus on the banks of the river Cydnus, where a
feather (Greek *tarsos*) of the winged horse Pegasus is supposed
to have fallen. Pegasus sprang from the blood of the Gorgon
Medusa when she was beheaded.

120 The typical Greek names are intended to convey contempt.

129 The lictors were the official public attendants of the Roman
magistrates. For legacy-hunting and the significance of being
childless see line 221 below, 5. 136 ff., 6. 38 ff., 12. 93 ff. The
frequent references to legacy-hunting indicate the continuing
failure of Augustus' legislation of 18 BC to encourage marriage
and child-bearing.

130 Albina and Modia are the childless women referred to in the previous line, evidently considered important enough to receive the morning salutation described in Satire 1.

131 In Horace's satire on legacy-hunting (2. 5. 16 ff.), the penniless Ulysses is affronted when recommended to walk on the outside of a rich ex-slave.

133 Calvina and Catiena are evidently women of aristocratic birth. The name Calvina recalls a famous sex scandal of the year AD 49 (Tacitus, *Annals* 12. 4).

135 Chione (from the Greek *chion*, 'snow') is the name of a prostitute in several of Martial's epigrams.

137 In 204 BC P. Cornelius Scipio Nasica was adjudged the best citizen of Rome and was therefore sent to Ostia to escort to the City the image of the Idaean Mother Goddess Cybele, which had been brought from Asia Minor as a means of driving out Hannibal.

138 *Numa*: see on line 12 above.

139 *frightened Minerva*: In 241 BC L. Caecilius Metellus lost his sight in rescuing the statue of Minerva from the burning temple of Vesta. The suggestion of human frailty in the mighty daughter of Jupiter is Juvenal's own idea.

144 f. *the altars of Samothrace*: the Cabiri, divinities worshipped in the islands of the north Aegean, especially Samothrace, punished people guilty of perjury.

154 f. By the *Lex Roscia theatralis*, passed in 67 BC by the tribune L. Roscius Otho (l. 159 below), the first fourteen rows of seats in the theatre behind the orchestra (where the senators sat) were reserved for the knights, a wealthy order (see 1. 106 and note). The law had recently been revived by Domitian as censor, and is often referred to by writers of the period, e.g. by Martial in his fifth book.

158 *a fighter's*: i.e. a gladiator's.

159 *brainless Otho*: see on 154 f. His discriminatory law occasioned serious disorders in the theatre in 63 BC, and it required all Cicero's tact as consul to calm the rioters in a speech now lost.

162 *aediles*: they were magistrates whose responsibilities included
    public order, traffic, weights and measures, and (before Augustus)
    the games. They had jurisdiction in the lower courts but,
    relatively unimportant as they were, they never, says Juvenal,
    invited poor men to sit with them as assessors on the bench.

169 The Marsi and the Sabelli (Samnites) were hardy and warlike
    peoples of central Italy. This is one of Juvenal's many echoes of
    Virgil (*Georgics* 2. 167).

176 *gaping mouth . . . whitened mask*: the actors' masks were often
    coloured or (as here) whitened to help identify the characters
    portrayed.

185 Veiento, who is coupled with the deadly Catullus at 4. 113, was
    a dangerous informer (Aurelius Victor *Epitome* 12. 5). This
    Cossus was presumably no different: the Scholiast merely calls
    him 'a haughty noble of that period'.

186 The first clipping of the beard, like the cutting of the long locks
    of boyhood, was something of a *rite de passage* and celebrated
    accordingly.

188 The client hands over the money, but tells the slave what he can
    do with his cake.

191 These country-towns were all in Latium, except Volsinii, which
    was in Etruria. Horace (*Epistles* 1. 11. 7) and Juvenal (10. 100)
    speak of Gabii as a place that had seen better days.

198 *Ucalegon*: another Virgilian echo, from *Aeneid* 2. 312, where the
    neighbour Ucalegon's house burns down during the sack of
    Troy.

203 Cordus, in spite of his love of books, is not necessarily the poet
    of 1. 2. Procula (the name of an adulteress at 2. 68) was evidently
    shorter than average.

205 The sideboard is supported on the figure of the Centaur Chiron,
    done in marble, which is merely the local stone of much of Italy,
    therefore a poor man's possession.

212 Asturicus is a well-to-do senator (Scholiast), otherwise unknown:
    see below on l. 221.

217 f. Euphranor was a celebrated Greek sculptor and painter of the fourth century BC: Polyclitus, also a sculptor of great influence and fame, was of the fifth century.

221 If Persicus and Asturicus (l. 212) do not denote the same person, i.e. Persicus Asturicus (or vice versa), and logically they should, then Persicus' house may have been called 'Asturicus' mansion' from a previous owner.

224 These are another group of country towns in Latium.

229 The Pythagoreans followed a vegetarian diet: cf. 15. 171 ff.

236 f. This problem was partly solved by restricting vehicular traffic to building-contractors' drays during daylight hours. See l. 10 and note above. Nero's rebuilding after the great fire of AD 64 had also effected some improvement in the layout of the streets.

238 Seals according to Pliny (*Nat. Hist.* 9. 42) are heavy sleepers. The emperor Claudius (Tiberius Claudius Drusus Caesar) slept so badly at night that he often dozed off while presiding at the law-courts next day (Suetonius, *Claudius* 33. 2).

240 *Liburnian galley*: the litter or palanquin resembled a four-poster bed with carrying-handles for as many as eight bearers. Juvenal compares this one to a type of battleship.

251 Gnaeus Domitius Corbulo, a distinguished Roman general under Claudius and Nero, was renowned both for his huge size and the respect accorded him by his enemies (Tacitus, *Annals* 13. 8 f.).

265 f. The frightful ferryman is Charon who ferried the souls of the dead across the river Styx (see on 2. 149 ff.), but only those who had been prepared for burial in due form and had a coin in the mouth to pay for their passage: so the hero of this little story waits in vain.

279 f. *Achilles . . . mourning his friend*: the night of grief of Achilles mourning for Patroclus, killed in action against the Trojans, is described by Homer, *Iliad* 24. 10 f.: he wept 'now lying on his side, now on his back, now on his face and finally standing up'.

[281 This line, which says 'therefore he will not be able to sleep in any other way; for some people . . .', is almost certainly an

explanatory comment or gloss, which a copyist has turned into
a hexameter.]

296 The thug finally pretends to identify his victim as a beggar
and a Jew, the latter especially offensive given the attitude of
Umbricius and his sort to the immigrant communities of
Rome. See on l. 14 above and ll. 62 ff.

306 The Pontine Marshes were a large tract of marshland, about 300
miles square, on the coast of Latium between Circeii and
Terracina, traversed by the Appian Way and a navigable canal.
They were successfully drained by Mussolini only in the 1930s.
The Gallinarian forest was an extensive pinewood near Cumae
in Campania. Both places were the haunts of robbers.

313 *kings and tribunes*: Rome was governed first by kings (753–510
BC), then in the Republican period by two annual consuls and
the senate, but in some years between 444 and 367 BC the regular
consuls were replaced by military tribunes with consular power.
It is these probably, and not the tribunes of the people (see 1. 109
and note), that Juvenal has in mind here.

321 *Helvius' Ceres and your Diana*: these would have been temples.

SATIRE 4

1 It is not clear why Juvenal says 'again'. Does it refer back to lines
26–9 of Satire 1 (which is often thought to have been written
later as an introduction), or to some satire which has not been
preserved, or (least likely of all) to the Crispinus of Horace,
Satires 1. 1, 3, 4, and 2. 7? At any rate Juvenal did not in fact
'often bring Crispinus on to the stage'.

9 Vestal virgins who broke their vows by unchastity were buried
alive or, more precisely, entombed or immured. There were
several such trials in Domitian's reign, not all of which ended in
the death sentence. Some see here a reference to the case of
Cornelia, who suffered this fate in AD 93, but there is no hard
evidence that Crispinus was involved in it. Juvenal may just be
retailing gossip.

23 *Apicius*: a celebrated gourmet under Augustus and Tiberius;
cf. 11. 3. He was only 'modest and frugal' in comparison with
Crispinus.

29 *The emperor himself*: i.e. Domitian. Juvenal's language here is archaic and elevated, partly from metrical necessity, partly to heighten the enormity.

31 *'purple-clad clown'*: the description of Crispinus in 1. 26–9 also emphasizes his ostentatious dress sense. The indiscriminate wearing of purple was not encouraged (Suetonius, *Nero* 32). Juvenal's word for 'clown' (*scurra*) means anything from well-dressed man-about-town to tiresome buffoon.

33 Canopus, slightly to the east of Alexandria, is where Crispinus hailed from (1. 26). According to Juvenal's account, which is doubtless a travesty, he was a hawker of imported, therefore salted, fish, i.e. *salsamentarius*, a common term of abuse (Suetonius, *Horace* 1).

34 ff. Calliope is one of the Muses, the maidens of Pieria, near Mount Olympus. She is to sit: there is no need for singing, which was usually done standing, because Juvenal's present theme is not the stuff of elevated poetry, but something (he claims) that actually happened. The flippancy is characteristic of later attitudes to the Muses and their inspiration; compare Ovid, *Ars Amatoria* 1. 25–30, Persius, *Prologue*.

37 The last of the Flavian dynasty, which gave Rome three emperors between AD 69 and 96, was Domitian (81–96), 'the bald-headed Nero'. The comparison between Domitian and the earlier despot is often made, and Suetonius (*Domitian* 18) confirms this detail of his baldness.

39 Ancona in Picenum was an important Adriatic seaport, founded by Dorian Greeks from Syracuse in the early fourth century BC. It was famous for the worship of Venus.

42 f. Maeotis is the Sea of Azov, where fish wintered in large numbers, making their way into the Black Sea (Pontus) and Bosporus after the thaw.

46 *the highest priest*: i.e. Domitian himself. As a 'monster', the fish has to be interpreted by the chief religious authority.

48 Sea-weed was proverbially worthless. This is Juvenal's exaggerated way of conveying the relentless official scrutiny that even the most insignificant aspects of life are subjected to under a tyranny.

53 Palfurius (?Sura, Suetonius, *Domitian* 13) and Armillatus are said to be the names of people influential with Domitian and ingeniously anxious to widen the scope of the emperor's pretensions.

55 ff. *to prevent it going to waste*: i.e. to turn the lucky catch to good account. Autumn with its deadly south wind, the Sirocco, was the time when food went off, diseases occurred and undertakers prospered (Horace, *Satires* 2. 6. 18 ff.) But winter was coming on and with luck one's ailment would prove to be no more than the rarely fatal quartan fever, a mosquito-borne disease in which the attacks occurred at intervals of 72 hours, i.e. every fourth day.

59 *southerly breeze*: see on 55 ff.

60 f. Alba Longa, the oldest town in Latium, was founded by Ascanius, the son of Aeneas. It housed the sacred flame of Vesta, brought from Troy, even after the town had been destroyed by King Tullus Hostilius (673–642 BC) and the flame had been kindled in a new shrine at Rome. It was near the Alban Lake and Lake Nemi, and Domitian's favourite residence was in the neighbourhood.

65 Domitian is called Atreides, i.e. Agamemnon, son of Atreus (Homer calls him 'King of men', *Iliad* 1. 172): a highly satirical affectation of the heroic style. The Picene is the fisherman: see on l. 39 above.

73 f. The fact that the emperor's council (the *Concilium Principis*) was a panel of personal advisers known as the Friends of Caesar (*amici Caesaris*) helps to explain the bitter intensity of this comment. The failure and the denaturing of friendship, both at the personal level and as a traditionally potent force in Roman public life, is something that the moralists and historians of the period found particularly disturbing.

75 ff. Liburnus, i.e. 'the Illyrian', is here an usher. Cf. 6. 477.
    The names of the members of Domitian's council are Pegasus (76), Crispus (81), the Acilii, father (94) and son (95), Rubrius (105), Montanus (107), Crispinus (108), Pompeius (109), Veiento (113), Catullus (113). 'Here are jurists, soldiers, diplomats, aged and venerable counsellors—a most respectable and capable body

once we have penetrated behind the screen of prejudice with which their careers have been overlaid' (J. A. Crook, *Consilium Principis*, Cambridge, 1955, p. 51).

76 *Pegasus*: Plotius Pegasus, a very learned jurist and sometime City Prefect.

77 Under Domitian, so Juvenal alleges, the exalted office of City Prefect (*praefectus Urbi*) was reduced to something resembling the job of a farm-manager.

81 *Crispus*: see Index.

94 f. *Acilii*: see Index.

98 A 'son of the soil' is proverbial in Roman literature for a person of unknown family or origin, and the Giants who stormed Heaven were the sons of Earth. The play on the two ideas is underscored by the contrast in 'little brother' and 'towering'.

100 f. *the Alban arena*: Domitian's palace at Alba included an amphi-theatre, where Acilius took part in *venationes*, i.e. the pitting of men against wild beasts. Domitian himself had a passion for slaughtering animals (Suetonius, *Dom.* 19).

103 L. Junius Brutus (the name Brutus means 'stupid'), who roused the Romans to expel the kings, feigned idiocy in order to escape the fate of his brother, who was murdered by their uncle, Tarquinius Superbus, last king of Rome (535–510 BC), in whose day beards were generally worn. See Livy 1. 56. 7. We are to understand that Acilius Glabrio could feign subservience to Domitian by demeaning himself in the arena, but Domitian was not so easily fooled as Tarquinius Superbus.

105 *Rubrius*: Rubrius Gallus, who held military commands under Nero and succeeding emperors, was adept at switching loyalty. His offence was the seduction of the empress Domitia, according to the Scholiast.

107 *Montanus*: possibly the father who successfully petitioned Nero for the pardon of his son, Curtius Montanus, when the latter was condemned for defamation of the emperor in AD 66 (Tacitus, *Annals* 16. 28, 33).

the Stomach: referring to his gastronomic expertise; cf. lines 139–43 below.

108 *Crispinus*: see on l. 1 above. Perfume was only used by men when the day's business was done. At funerals it was used to kill the smells of putrescence and cremation.

109 *Pompeius*: identification is difficult, but obviously an informer.

111 Cornelius Fuscus, then prefect of the praetorian guard, had in fact a considerable reputation as a soldier under Nero and Vespasian. Tacitus, *Histories* 2. 86. 3, says 'he had less joy in the rewards of his perils than in the perils themselves'. He was killed probably in an unsuccessful battle against the Dacians in AD 86.

113 *Veiento*: Fabricius Veiento (Index). L. Valerius Catullus Messalinus, consul AD 79 and 85, the blind informer, whose name is here and elsewhere coupled with that of Veiento.

[116 This line ('a sightless sycophant, a sinister courtier from the bridge') is bracketed by C. as spurious.]

118 The steep hill on the Appian Way leading down to Aricia, in the neighbourhood of Domitian's Alban villa, caused carriages to slow down when ascending and to brake when descending: hence it was a good stand for a beggar.

122 *Cilix*: the Cilician, a gladiator called after his country of origin; compare Thracian and Syrian in Horace, *Satires* 2. 6. 44.

   the awning: in the theatre, that is, where boy actors played flying Cupids and the like.

123 Bellona, the Roman goddess of war, was originally identified with Ma, a Cappadocian deity, whose frenzied priests indulged in self-wounding and prophesy: cf. 6. 512 ff.

126 Arviragus is otherwise unknown in classical literature but occurs in Geoffrey of Monmouth (4. 16), the ultimate source of Shakespeare's play, as one of the sons of Cymbeline.

129 *Fabricius*: i.e. Veiento of line 113.

133 Prometheus fashioned men out of clay (cf. Horace, *Odes* 1. 16. 13 ff.), therefore a potter was called a Prometheus by the Athenians (Lucian, *Prometheus* 12).

138 *Falernian*: a highly prized wine from Campania.

141 Circeii, on the coast of Latium near the Pontine Marshes (3. 307), like the Lucrine Lake near Baiae (3. 4) and Richborough (Rutupiae) in Kent, was famous for its oysters.

148 The Chatti and Sygambri were tribes inhabiting Germany. There was an inconclusive campaign against the Chatti by Domitian in AD 83, for which he celebrated a triumph. The Sygambri posed no threat at this time.

153 f. The Lamiae are mentioned as representative of Rome's most ancient families. One of them, Aelius Lamia, lost his wife to Domitian and was later put to death for making jokes about the matter (Suetonius, *Domitian* 10).

the workers' fears: the men who conspired to murder Domitian belonged to the lower orders of Roman society, non-commissioned officers, freedmen, gladiators and the like.

SATIRE 5

3 f. Sarmentus was a freedman or slave of M. Favonius (a political opportunist executed after Philippi, 42 BC), prosecuted for passing himself off as a knight, but acquitted on declaring that Maecenas had secured his freedom. Gabba also belonged to the circle of Maecenas and Augustus: his wit was highly spoken of. Like Sarmentus (see Horace, *Satires* 1. 5. 52 ff.) he was a *scurra* (see on 4. 31) and a parasite of Augustus, the Caesar of l. 4.

8 f. Suitable pitches for setting up as a professional beggar.

22 *great friendship*: see on 1. 33 and 4. 73 f.

22 The 'frosty waggon' is the constellation of the Great Bear, also called the Plough or Charles's Wain. The 'sluggish' herdsman is Bootes, the Drover. Being at the North Pole, the movement of this constellation is minimal: hence the epithet.

27 Saguntum, near the west coast of Spain, was famous for its pottery.

30 He means wine of great age, bottled in the far off days before shaving the beard and cutting the hair became common. The consuls gave their names to the year, and when wine was bottled the seals of the jars were impressed with the consuls' names.

31 The War with the Allies or Social War (91–88 BC) broke out when the Italians could not wrest the franchise from Rome by peaceful means.

33 f. The Alban and Setine Hills in Latium produced wines of outstanding quality.

36 Thrasea Paetus and his son-in-law Helvidius Priscus were prominent members of the aristocratic Stoic opposition under Nero. Thrasea was put to death by Nero in AD 66, Helvidius Priscus by Vespasian. They demonstrated their conservative Republicanism by celebrating the birthdays of the Liberators, Marcus Brutus, Decimus Brutus and Cassius, the assassins of Julius Caesar in 44 BC.

38 *Helios' daughters*: i.e. amber. When Phaethon, the son of Helios the Sun God, was struck by Jove's lightning and hurled into the Eridanus (Po) to end his disastrous attempt to drive his father's horses, his sisters were turned into poplars and their tears into amber. For the story see Ovid, *Metamorphoses* 2. 1 ff.

44 f. The youth preferred to Iarbas, King of the Gaetulians, was Aeneas; the object of their passion, Dido of Carthage. See Virgil, *Aeneid* 4. 36 ff., 196 ff.

47 Vatinius was an ex-cobbler, deformed and disreputable, who attracted Nero's attention (Tacitus, *Annals* 15. 34). The cup evidently had four nozzles, recalling Vatinius' own long nose (Martial 14. 96).

48 Hawkers used to take broken glass in exchange for sulphur matches (Martial 1. 41. 4 ff.). The Latin could also mean 'demanding sulphur for its broken glass', in which case the reference is to the use of sulphur as a cement: so the Scholiast.

50 The invention of iced-water, first boiled, then cooled in snow, was claimed for Nero (Pliny, *Nat. Hist.* 36. 199).

56 f. An attractive page-boy: 'flower' in Latin often carries suggestions of homosexual charm. Tullus Hostilius (673–642 BC) and Ancus (642–617 BC) were early kings of Rome. Juvenal may be thinking of *Tullus diues et Ancus* ('rich Tullus and Ancus') in Horace, *Odes* 4. 7. 15.

59 *African Ganymede*: the original Ganymede, fairest of all mortal youths, was carried up to heaven by the Gods to be Jupiter's cupbearer (so Homer, *Iliad* 20. 230 ff.) or by Jupiter himself in the guise of an eagle (Ovid, *Metamorphoses* 10. 155 ff.).

75 *the colour of your bread*: i.e. black, in contrast to that served to Virro, which is 'snowy-white' (l. 70).

76 ff. These are Trebius' words.

85 *fit for a ghost*: like the offerings of eggs, lentils, and salt brought to the graves of the recently deceased, the simplest of fare—'the dead ask for little' (Ovid, *Fasti* 2. 535).

86 The olive-oil of Venafrum on the borders of Samnium and Latium was the very best.

89 Micipsa was a king of Numidia in the second century BC. This is Juvenal's contemptuous way of saying 'imported from Africa'.

90 The name Boccar has a decidedly African ring to it, but does not denote any particular individual.

93 Tauromenium was on the east coast of Sicily.

96 The fish of the local waters, i.e. the Tyrrhenian or Tuscan Sea, off the west coast of Italy.

98 This mercenary couple are otherwise unknown. The point is that he plies her with gifts of fish, which she regularly sells off.

101 Aeolus, the lord of the winds, was supposed to keep them imprisoned in a cave when they were not in action (Virgil, *Aeneid* 1. 52 ff.).

102 *Charybdis*: see on 15. 17.

[104 The translation is based on Campbell's conjecture *glutto* for the manuscripts' *glacie* ('with ice').]

106 *Subura*: see on 3. 5.

109 *Seneca . . . Piso . . . Cotta*: see Index.

116 Meleager was a prince of Calydon in Aetolia. He slew the great boar sent by Diana to ravage the country when his father Oeneus had neglected her sacrifices. See Ovid, *Metamorphoses* 8. 273 ff.

118 Rome was heavily dependent on north Africa for her supplies of corn. Alledius is an otherwise unknown gastronome.

120 ff. Cf. 11. 136 and note for the teaching of carving meat etc.

125 ff. A free-born Roman had three names, *praenomen*, *nomen*, and *cognomen*; e.g. Marcus Tullius Cicero.

127 Cacus was a giant who inhabited a cave on the Aventine Hill, one of the seven hills of Rome. When Hercules came to Italy with the oxen taken from the three-headed Spanish monster Geryon (one of the Labours of Hercules) he slew Cacus with his club for stealing some of the cattle, and in Virgil's words 'dragged out his shapeless carcase by the feet' (Virgil, *Aeneid* 8. 264).

132 *four hundred*: i.e. the 400,000 sesterces necessary for the status of a knight.

138 *no tiny Aeneas*: i.e. no son and heir. Juvenal closely adapts some words of Dido, 'Had I only some tiny Aeneas playing within my halls!' (*Aeneid* 4. 328 f.).

141 ff. The sequence of thought is puzzling. We might expect: 'If you were rich and childless, Virro would shower you with attentions and choice gifts. But since you are poor, the size of your family is irrelevant, and Virro treats you with contempt.' Instead, Juvenal seems to be saying: 'But since you are poor, if your wife has children Virro will ingratiate himself with them by cheap little gifts, with the intention of training up a new generation of parasites.' The difficulty is not reduced by ignoring the reference to a wife in line 77 and assuming that Mycale is a concubine. Jenkyns, p. 196: 'To the end we are left uncertain whether Virro's indulgence to them (i.e. Trebius' hypothetical children) constitutes his one redeeming feature or his most sinister baseness . . . Commonly, the kindness of adults to children is like their kindness to pets, at once affectionate and ruthlessly self-gratifying.'

143 *racing green*: i.e. in the colour of the 'Greens', one of the most fanatically supported teams of chariot-drivers. Compare 7. 114 and 11. 198.

145 *infant parasite*: the parasite or regular dinner-guest was well known in Roman society and a stock character in the plays of the New Comedy. Originally the word had been fairly neutral but eventually came to mean 'free-loader'.

147 f. The emperor Claudius, having appointed his stepson Nero as his successor in preference to his own son, is said to have been given poison by his wife Agrippina in a dish of mushrooms (Suetonius, *Claudius* 44). Cf. 6. 620 f.

151 *Phaeacia's endless autumns*: in the *Odyssey* 7. 117 ff. the fruits of this island (Corcyra, Corfu) were said to observe no season but ripened all the year round.

152 One of Hercules' labours was to steal the golden apples guarded by the Hesperides. One tradition placed their orchard at Mount Atlas in Africa. The apples were Earth's gift to Juno on her marriage with Jupiter.

153 f. The rotten apple is the reward for a performing monkey sitting like a cavalry-man on the back of a goat. The Embankment is the earthwork built in the days of the kings to protect the City on the East; in later times it was a popular place for walks.

164 f. These are emblems of free birth. As a charm against ill-luck children wore a locket (*bulla*) of gold if their parents were freeborn, or a knot of leather if they were the children of freedmen. This custom, like so many other Roman institutions and practices, especially in the areas of religion and superstition, was evidently regarded as Etruscan in origin.

172 In the slapstick comedy of the mime there was much noisy smacking of bald or shaven heads, a type of humour by no means obsolete.

SATIRE 6

1 Saturn, the ancient Italian god of sowing, later identified with Kronos, chief of gods, was dethroned by his son Zeus (Jupiter), exiled from heaven, and obliged to find refuge on earth. That was the Golden Age, the age of man's innocence. Cf. 13. 38–40.

7 Cynthia was the mistress of Propertius and the subject of much of his elegiac love-poetry. The 'other lady' is Lesbia, the notorious Clodia, immortalized in the poems of Catullus: Juvenal is here referring more particularly to Catullus' third poem. They belong to the first century BC. Both ladies were sensual and sophisticated, in complete contrast to Juvenal's blameless cavewoman.

10 *acorn-belching*: the discovery of corn came much later.

12 Men were said to have been fashioned from clay by Prometheus
    (see on 4. 133): another account says they were born from rocks
    and oaks (Virgil, *Aeneid* 8. 314 f.).

15 f. Jupiter succeeded Saturn, and under his rule the Golden Age
    gave way to the Silver Age. Bronze and Iron Ages followed,
    each successively worse: compare Ovid, *Metamorphoses* 1). Hesiod
    makes the fourth age an Age of Heroes (*Works and Days* 156).

17 Juvenal's hatred of the Greeks (see 3. 57 ff.) surfaces again.
    People swore by the head, i.e. life: to swear falsely by another
    man's head meant that divine vengeance would fall on the
    innocent, not on the perjured. Compare 13. 84 f.

19 Justice or Astraea, the star-bright goddess, was the last of the
    immortals to withdraw from earth in the Age of Iron (Ovid,
    Metamorphoses 1. 149). She became the constellation Virgo.

21 Nothing is known of Postumus, the apparent addressee of this
    satire. Ursidius (38 and 42) is also credited with matrimonial
    intentions.

23 See on l. 15 above.

38 See on l. 21. The Julian Laws of 18 BC (see on 2. 29 ff.) were
    intended to promote matrimony and the procreation of children.

40 For the attentions paid to the childless by legacy-hunters, see on
    3. 129.

43 He means that Ursidius often had to hide in a chest to elude the
    husbands he was cuckolding, like the actor Latinus (see 1. 36
    and note) in some well-known farce.

46 The doctor is to bleed Ursidius for madness, thought to be
    caused by a plethora of blood.

48 f. The Tarpeian shrine on the Capitoline Hill was the temple of
    Jupiter and of Juno, the goddess of marriage.

56 Gabii and Fidenae were in Latium. Both are spoken of by
    Horace (*Epistles* 1. 11. 7 f.) as run-down country towns; but
    even here, according to Juvenal, temptation lurks.

63 Bathyllus, a favourite of Maecenas, famous for his balletic
    performances (Tacitus, *Annals* 1. 54). The name may have been
    assumed by some contemporary dancer, a common practice in
    theatrical circles then, but no Bathyllus is known at this time:

more probably Juvenal uses the name loosely to denote a dancer.

[65 *sicut in amplexu subito et miserabile longum*, 'suddenly emits a long, pitiful squeal, as though in a lover's embrace'. This line, with its awkward word order, is bracketed by C. as a gloss on the word *gannit*.]

66 The celebrated actress of 1. 36 is just a learner, devoid of urbanity, compared with this Bathyllus.

69 The People's Games (*Ludi Plebeii*) were held in November (4–18); the *Ludi Megalenses* in honour of Cybele were held in April (4–10). Theatrical and other entertainments were given at these times of public holiday: they were not available all the year round like our own.

71 f. The Atellane farces, so called from the Oscan town of Atella in Campania, were knock-about country comedies, often used to provide light relief after a tragedy. They relied on their own stock characters; so the lady Autonoë, who belongs to high tragedy, would be out of place unless introduced for purposes of farce. With her sisters Agave and Ino she dismembered Pentheus in a Bacchic frenzy.

73 The 'pin' (*fibula*) was a surgical clasp for closing wounds, or a contrivance worn by males, especially singers and actors, to prevent sexual intercourse, which was thought to be bad for the voice.

75 Quintilian, Rome's most distinguished teacher of rhetoric (see Index): here probably mentioned as the boring old husband of a wife much younger than himself. She died in her nineteenth year. See also 6. 280, 7. 186 ff.

80 The father is a member of the aristocratic *gens Cornelia*. The baby he is presented with is ambivalent in looks, resembling the tragic young Trojan hero of *Aeneid* 9 perhaps, but unmistakably declaring his real father, a gladiator.

83 *Pharos*: the island off the port of Alexandria. Its lighthouse was famous.

Lagus' notorious city: Alexandria. The Macedonian Lagus was the reputed father of Ptolemy I, founder of the Greek dynasty of

Egypt. Canopus, a city on the Nile Delta, east of Alexandria, was known for its luxury.

87 There were pantomime actors of this name in the reign of Nero and later under Domitian. The later Paris was executed in AD 83. He is involved in the stories of Juvenal's alleged exile: cf. 7. 87.

92 The Tyrrhenian or Etruscan Sea was that part of the Mediterranean to the west of Italy. The Ionian Sea lay between Sicily and the 'heel' of Italy and mainland Greece.

[107 'weal' translates *sulcus*, a conjecture by Nisbet (i) for the manuscripts' *sicut*.]

110 *Adonis*: a youth handsome enough to be loved by Venus herself. This better-known name has been substituted for Juvenal's Hyacinthus.

113 A gladiator on retirement was presented with a wooden practice sword. Veiento is presumably Eppia's senator husband, possibly the Veiento of 3. 185. Once Sergius loses the glamour of the arena he will be as boring as the husband.

115 The emperors had for some time now been arrogating divine honours to themselves and, when at death the process of deification (*apotheosis*) was complete, they were accorded the title 'Divine' (*Divus*). The emperor Claudius (AD 41–54) in spite of his literary and intellectual pretensions was notoriously at the mercy of his designing freedmen and imposed on by his wives, Messalina and Agrippina. The latter eventually poisoned him. The 'imperial harlot' here is Messalina, a woman of quite exceptional depravity.

[120 Before 120 Courtney postulates the loss of a line with the meaning 'did not blush'.]

124 Britannicus was the son of Claudius by Messalina. He was passed over for the succession in favour of Nero, the son of Agrippina, Claudius' next wife, and murdered in AD 55.

[125 This line (*excepit blanda intrantis atque aera poposcit*) has been inadvertently omitted from C.'s text.]

[126 *ac resupina iacens multorum absorbuit ictus*, 'and, lying back, took in the thrusts of many'. This line (sometimes beginning *continueque*) is not found in the oldest MSS.]

[135 This translates *minimumque*, which C. obelizes, i.e. puts between daggers as unintelligible.]

136 The Caesennii were a prominent family but the lady in question is not otherwise known. Her dowry is princely, sufficient to enable her husband to enter the senate if otherwise eligible. Compare Gracchus' dowry at 2. 117 ff. and Messalina's at 10. 336.

[138 The line is regarded by C. as spurious.]

150 Canusium was in Apulia, famous for its flocks. The Falernian wine from Campania was justly famous.

153 During the midwinter festival of the Saturnalia (17-19 December) there was a street-market called Sigillaria from the sale of figurines (*sigilla*). This was held in the Campus Martius (2. 132 and note), and the canvas booths erected to accommodate the stalls hid from view the mural paintings of Jason and the Argonauts that decorated the Arcade of Agrippa (*Porticus Agrippae*). Jason is downgraded to a mere trader, a class despised by the ancient moralists as daring all merely for greed, e.g. Horace, *Satires* 1. 4. 29 ff. and Juvenal 14. 267 ff.

157 *Queen Berenice . . . Agrippa*: this is Agrippa II, King of Chalcis, a descendant of Herod the Great. His sister Berenice, on the death of her husband, took up residence with him: hence the suggestion of incest. Paul made his defence before the pair at Caesarea (*Acts* 25: 23).

159 A characteristically Juvenalian way of referring to Judaea and the dietary laws of the Jewish religion. Cf. 14. 98.

163 *ancient ancestors*: i.e. statues or perhaps *imagines* (see on 8. 2). One's nobility was measured by the number of these.

164 The Sabine women, abducted by the Romans in the days of Romulus, averted a war by interposing themselves between their Roman husbands and their Sabine kinsmen. As a race the Sabines were characterized by bravery, endurance, and chastity.

167 *Cornelia*: see Index. Her father, P. Cornelius Scipio Africanus Maior, defeated Syphax, a Numidian prince, and burned his camp in 203 BC during the Second Punic War, defeating Hannibal himself at the battle of Zama, the following year.

172 ff. Niobe, the wife of Amphion, King of Thebes, offended
Latona by boasting of her seven sons and seven daughters.
Latona therefore sent her two children, Apollo (Paean, the
Healer) and Diana, to kill Niobe's children with their arrows.
Amphion committed suicide and Niobe was turned into a rock
which forever drips with her tears (Ovid, *Metamorphoses* 6.
146 ff.).

177   The white sow with its litter of thirty had an honoured place in
Roman tradition, though Juvenal's allusion to it here is as coarse
as it sounds. It identified for the Trojans the place where Alba
Longa was to be founded, and the thirty piglets represented the
thirty cities of the Latin League (Virgil, *Aeneid* 3. 389 ff.,
8. 42 ff.). See also 12. 70 ff.

187   Sulmo, a town in the Sabine country, was the birthplace of the
poet Ovid. Cecrops in myth was the first king of Athens.

[188   'Though it is more shameful for our women to be ignorant of
Latin'—a flat-footed comment which has found its way into the
text.]

195   Literally 'Life and Soul'. The expression in itself is not especially
lascivious. It is the affected use of Greek that could make it
titillating (for a similar point see Martial 10. 68); but not when it
comes from an 85-year-old woman.

[The translation follows *loquendis*, the suggestion of Nisbet (ii)
for the transmitted *relictis*.]

198   Haemus and Carpophorus are evidently actors: for the former
see 3. 99.

205   The emperor Trajan (AD 98–117) took the title Germanicus in
AD 97 after the war with the Suebi, and Dacicus in AD 102 after
the Dacian War. These titles are found on his coins. The verse
cannot therefore have been written before 102.

225   She goes through so many marriage ceremonies that her wedding-
veil is worn out.

230   There was no suggestion that a Roman marriage was intended
to be for life, though it was accounted a great merit in a woman
to have been the wife of only one husband, and the fact was
often recorded on their tombstones.

236 A distinguished Syrian doctor of the reign of Trajan, referred to
again at 13. 98 and 14. 252. The daughter's adultery takes place
at her mother's house.

244 They are not only well versed in the niceties of the law but
confident enough to instruct an experienced advocate how best
to put their case. Celsus is probably the distinguished rhetorician,
A. Cornelius Celsus, frequently referred to by Quintilian.
Compare Laronia's denial at 2. 51 f.

250 The Floralia, the games in honour of Flora, the goddess of
flowers, were held from 28 April to 3 May and were marked by
great licentiousness. For female athleticism see Laronia again at
2. 53 ff. and note.

254 Tiresias, who had been both a man and a woman, pronounced
that women got more pleasure out of sex than men (Ovid,
Metamorphoses 3. 320–33).

257 i.e., if she fights as a Thraex or Thracian, in which case she will
have protective covering for both legs, unlike the so-called
Samnite type of gladiator, whose armour (described in lines
256 f.) provided covering for one leg only.

265 f. These are representatives of the most distinguished and ancient
Roman families: see Index.

267 Asylus is evidently a gladiator. The gasping is caused by the
exertion of sparring with a tree-stump: cf. ll. 247 f. above.

280 Quintilian (see Index), though chiefly celebrated as a teacher of
rhetoric, also practised at the bar with considerable success.

290 f. During the Second Punic War Hannibal in 211 BC threw
Rome into a state of terror by his sudden appearance under its
walls. The Roman army was encamped between the Colline
Gate and the Esquiline Gate (Livy 26. 10). Heavy rain held off a
battle: see 7. 163 f.

296 f. These are all Greek cities, of which Sybaris and Tarentum
were Greek colonies in the south of Italy. Garlands and drinking
naturally go together, but there may be a reference to an
occasion in 281 BC at the start of the war with Pyrrhus, when the
Tarentines, garlanded and *en fête*, insulted a Roman envoy.

[307 is bracketed by C. If genuine, it is better taken after 308: 'what Tullia, the foster-sister of the notorious Maura, says'.]

314 The Good Goddess (*Bona Dea*) was a Roman fertility goddess who responded only to the solicitations of women. The ceremonies attached to her festivals in May and December, the latter at the house of a chief magistrate, were conducted by the Vestal Virgins. Chastity and sobriety (the wine used in the rituals was re-christened 'milk') and, above all, the total absence of the male sex, human or animal, were the order of the day on these occasions.

315 Priapus, son of Dionysus (Bacchus), was a fertility god who presided over gardens. He is always depicted as having a huge erection. The Maenads were the frenzied devotees of Bacchus.

320 Saufeia appears again at 9. 117 as a heavy drinker. The name suggests another of Juvenal's women of good family letting her class down: similarly Medullina at line 322.

326 Priam and Nestor (see Index and on 10. 246, 258) are legendary examples of men who lived to a great age.

337 Juvenal refers to the scandal created in December 62 BC, when P. Clodius Pulcher profaned the mysteries of the Good Goddess, which were being celebrated at the house of Julius Caesar as Chief Pontiff, by his intrusion in the guise of a female musician. At his trial the following year he avoided condemnation by extensive bribery.

338 M. Porcius Cato, called Uticensis, i.e. of Utica, where in 46 BC he committed suicide after the collapse of the Republican cause, had strongly opposed Caesar in the Civil War. After his death he was praised effusively in Cicero's *Cato*, to which Caesar replied with a first and second *Anti-Cato*.

343 Numa is the legendary second king of Rome (see on 3. 12) and author of the national forms of worship. The cult-vessels of his day were of cheap earthenware, like that produced on the Vatican Hill, whereas later ages preferred gold and silver.

345 *Clodius*: see on l. 337 above.

[346–8 'I hear what you, my old friends, have long advised—"bolt the door and lock her in". But who will guard the guards themselves? The wife is careful, and begins her intrigues with them.' These lines are much the same as verses 30–4 of the Oxford fragment, for which see below after 365. The theory is that when the first 29 lines of the fragment had been lost, the remaining five were rewritten thus by a scribe.]

360 Classical moralists are fond of telling their readers to 'go to the ant', a model of industry and providence. An early example in satire is Lucilius 561–2 Marx, followed by Horace, *Satires* 1. 1. 31 ff.

[The lines designated as O1–O34 occur only in a manuscript of about AD 1100, written at Monte Cassino and now in Oxford. Their genuineness is disputed by some; but they are accepted by C. and others (see *Bulletin of Classical Studies* 14, 1967, 38–50). Some editors place them after line 345.]

O9 f. The distinction is possibly between gladiators, in particular those who fought with the net (*retiarii*) and amateurs, i.e. citizens who disgraced themselves by engaging in this most despised of activities. They wore the tunic, unlike the professionals, who fought naked except for a loin-girth: cf. the tunic-clad Gracchus at 2. 143. So Courtney, following Colin. Since the distinction Juvenal is making in this whole passage is between the sexually normal and the pervert, a distinction which, he maintains, is observed even in the wrestling-school, one might reasonably suppose with Housman that 'the tunics that signal disgrace' have more to do with sexual perversions than with amateur status. But the problem then is to see why tunics should have had these associations.

[O11 The translation renders Leo's *pulsatoremque* for the manuscripts' *pulsatamque arma*, obelized by C.]

[O18 The translation renders the conjecture *releuant* or *soluunt* for the transmitted *seruant*, obelized by C.]

O26 In bed with a woman the creature is unmasked as his true sex asserts itself. The farce is over. This is neither woman nor homosexual but a lusty, well-endowed (*tri-phallus*) male of normal instincts. There may be an allusion here to a situation of this kind in some balletic mime. Thais was the most famous of Greek courtesans, the mistress of Alexander the Great.

373 *Heliodorus*: a surgeon, Greek, as members of this profession usually were. The barber loses because the castrated boys will grow their hair long.

376 *guardian of vine and plot*: Priapus. See l. 315 above and note.

378 Bromius is evidently a pretty boy called after the youthful god Bacchus, beloved by Postumus. Such a boy will be injured by the priapic eunuch just described.

379 f. Singers will cease to take precautions (on the 'pin' see l. 73 above and note) to protect their voice. The praetor is the magistrate who commissioned the pieces to be performed and engaged the performers for the entertainments given at the regular festivals.

383 *Hedymeles*: i.e. 'melody sweet', an apt name for a singer and possibly Juvenal's invention.

385 This lady is descended on one side from the Aelii Lamiae, on the other from the Claudii, two of Rome's very best families.

387 *Pollio*: a celebrated harpist and singer of the day, mentioned again at 7. 176. The 'Capitol crown' (of oak leaves) was the prize in the musical section of the contests instituted by Domitian in honour of Capitoline Jupiter (Suetonius, *Domitian* 4).

397 *augur*: see note on 2. 121. He is constantly on his feet as he does his work.

407 f. Comets were thought to presage the fall of princes and change the fortunes of nations. The one this busybody is supposed to have seen was visible in Rome in AD 115, and Trajan, having defeated the Armenian king in 114, was conducting a campaign against the Parthians in 115: a useful piece of hard evidence for dating the poem.

410 f. The Niphates is actually a mountain in Armenia, not a river, but she is not alone in this error. Poets of the first century AD share her confusion. There was, however, an earthquake at Antioch in December 115, which has a bearing on the second part of l. 411.

[414 'with a curse' renders Martyn's *exsecrata*, instead of the transmitted *exorata*, obelized by C.]

423 Seneca, living over the baths, claimed he could tell from the sound whether the masseur's hand was cupped or open as he slapped his customers' bare bodies! (*Epistles* 56. 1)

428 Martial's Philaenis (7. 67. 9 f.), another athletic woman, follows the same revolting practice. Seneca (*Epistles* 122. 6) denounces drinking on an empty stomach as something contrary to nature.

431 *Falernian*: one of the strongest of wines, produced in Campania. There is obviously a reference here to some fable about a serpent in a wine-vat. The fondness of serpents for wine is mentioned by more than one writer of antiquity.

435 *Elissa*: i.e. Dido, queen of Carthage in Virgil's *Aeneid*.

437 *Maro*: Virgil's cognomen (Publius Vergilius Maro).

443 Eclipses of the moon were thought to be caused by magical influences, which could be stopped by creating a din.

446 i.e. she should leave off the matron's *stola* and assume male attire, the *tunica*, which did not cover the knees. Sacrificing to Silvanus, the husbandman's god, was a male prerogative. Men were admitted to the baths for a *quadrans*, literally 'a quarter', the smallest coin in use: it follows that women must have paid more than men.

452 Q. Remmius Palaemon was a distinguished, if thoroughly disreputable, schoolmaster of the first century AD and the author of a famous grammar.

[460a Following Teuffel, C. assumes the loss of some lines after 460 which would give sense to 'meanwhile' (461).]

462 *layers of bread*: the bread, soaked in hot water, is made into a facial-pack and serves as a beauty treatment by drawing out impurities in the skin. Cf. 2. 107.

Poppaean ointments: i.e. as used by Poppaea, Nero's beautiful but licentious second wife, whom the woman may be taking as a model; see further on line 468.

468 ff. Like Poppaea, who used to bathe in asses' milk and took a train of five hundred she-asses about with her to ensure a good supply (Pliny, *Nat. Hist.* 11. 238). The Hyperboreans were a fabulous people who lived beyond the North Wind.

477 *stripped*: i.e. for a thrashing.

Liburnian chair-man: Liburnian (Dalmatian) and Moesian slaves (9. 143) seem to have been employed to carry the litter: see on 3. 240.

486 The Sicilian tyrants, like Phalaris of Agrigentum (6th cent. BC) and Dionysius I (5th–4th. cent. BC) of Syracuse, became pro-verbial for cruelty.

489 The temple of Isis in the Campus Martius was considered a good place for sexual encounters: cf. 9. 22.

503 Andromache, wife of Hector, was a woman of heroic stature. According to Ovid *Ars Amatoria* 2. 645 f., she was even con-sidered over-large, except by her husband.

512 ff. *Bellona and the Mother of the gods*: they are virtually one and the same. For Bellona, see 4. 123 f. and note; for Cybele, the great mother goddess and her eunuch priests, see 2. 111, 3. 137 and 9. 62.

525 i.e. the Campus Martius (see on 2. 132) which was said to have belonged originally to the Tarquins. Tarquin the Proud (Tarquinius Superbus) was the last king of Rome. When he was expelled in 510 BC the Campus was dedicated to Mars.

526 Io, beloved of Jupiter, was turned into a white cow to avoid the jealousy of his consort, Juno. Her subsequent adventures took her to Egypt, in consequence of which she tended to be confused with the goddess Isis, who also had horns. For a general account of Isis, with numerous illustrations, see R. E. Witt, *Isis in the Graeco-Roman World*, London, 1971. [C. puts the semi-colon after the if-clause.]

529 The worship of Isis was not permitted in the City and her temple was therefore set in the Campus Martius (2. 132 and l. 525 above). By the 'ancient sheepfold', Juvenal means the pens (*saepta*) in which the voters were placed in their 'centuries' (divisions of the people) during elections.

534 The cult of Isis included a re-enactment of her grief at the murder of her consort, Osiris. In the procession the priest representing the dog-headed god Anubis, guardian and attendant of Isis, laughs to himself at the credulity of her devotees.

538 *silver serpent*: the symbol of divine majesty and royal power, best known to western readers as Cleopatra's asp. The nodding

of disapproval mentioned here would have been due to super-stitious hallucination or priestly fraud.

540 *Osiris*: see on l. 534 above.

545 A puzzling description. It is simplest to suppose that Juvenal is referring to the itinerant, open-air life of the Jews at Rome, and that the fortune-teller pursues her occupation under a tree: compare 3. 12 ff. Possibly stylized representations of the seven-branched candlestick as seen on the Arch of Titus may have been mistaken for trees: so D. S. Wiesen, *Classical Journal* 76, 1980, p. 14.

552 For the activities of informers see on 1. 33, 35, 3. 116.

553 The Chaldaeans (or Babylonians) worshipped the heavenly bodies, and their priests developed skills in astronomy and astrology, for which latter especially they were much in demand far beyond their own shores, so that *Chaldaeus* became syn-onomous with fortune-teller. This method of divination was not incompatible with current Stoic thinking and, though regularly expelled from Rome (see ll. 557 ff. below), the Chald-aeans were consulted even by the emperors.

555 *the fountain of Ammon*: there was a celebrated oracle of Jupiter Ammon at the oasis of Ammonium (Siwa) in north Africa.

The famous Greek oracle of Apollo at Delphi in Phocis, like the other great oracles of Dodona and Ammon, had by this time fallen into neglect, largely as a result of the spread of Roman domination and the indifference and scepticism of the Romans in religious matters. The oracles enjoyed a temporary revival under the emperor Julian the Apostate in the fourth century AD.

557 ff. Juvenal refers to the frequent decrees made to expel the Chaldaeans from Rome in attempts to destroy the influence they wielded at the highest levels: see on l. 553 above. Tacitus' accounts mention also the death-penalty (*Annals* 2. 32).

[558-9 'Through whose friendship and whose horoscope, prepared for money, the great citizen (i.e. Galba), who was feared by Otho, died'. These lines have poor manuscript authority and interrupt the sense. They are therefore bracketed by C.]

564 The place of banishment for state criminals was often a tiny island like Seriphos, one of the Cyclades.

565 The original Tanaquil was the wife of the legendary fifth king of Rome, Tarquinius Priscus (616–579 BC). She was skilled in divination and foresaw the future greatness of her handmaiden's son, Servius Tullius, who succeeded Tarquinius: hence Juvenal's use of the name for a clairvoyant wife.

569 f. The planet Saturn was supposed to have an evil influence: Venus and Jupiter brought good fortune and happiness.

573 Women carried balls of amber for the scent it produced in the warm hands.

576 Thrasyllus was the name of an astrologer favoured by the emperor Tiberius (AD 14–37). The 'sums' are the intricate calculations involved in drawing horoscopes, which earned the Chaldaeans the name *mathematici*.

581 Petosiris was an Egyptian priest of the second century BC, one of the reputed founders of astrology. Pliny the elder quotes from books purporting to be by him. The name here denotes a type.

582 *pillars at the racetrack*: the *metae*, three conical pillars on a plinth at either end of the racetrack, marked the turning-points for the chariots. The Circus Maximus, where these races took place, was the haunt of fortune-tellers; thus Horace calls it the 'deceitful Circus' (*Satires* 1. 6. 113).

584 *popping her lips*: evidently as part of the ceremony and to help the magic along.

[After 585 a line with the sense indicated is thought to have fallen out. The crocus grew in Cilicia and the Cilicians are said to have specialized in augury.]

587 A 'greybeard' (i.e. a priest) would see to it that charred remains were buried and that the site was walled off.

588 *the rampart*: see on 5. 154 f.

590 The towers were probably movable and used in mock-battles. On the *spina*, a low wall running the length of the Circus between the *metae* (see on l. 582), were seven columns supporting dolphins. The number of dolphins visible indicated the number of laps completed.

603 ff. *filthy latrines*: where unwanted children were left immediately after birth. (Others however take the place to be the public

tank from which domestic water supplies were drawn.) These children were often taken home and reared as their own by those who badly wanted a child. So they could be adopted by great families like the Scauri and later hold priestly offices for which none but the highly born were eligible: see on 2. 125.

[614abc 'If only you do not continually carry water to a cracked vat, shouldering a burden, with the jars themselves leaking, as a result of which you become mad, turning from our monarch into a Phalaris'. These awkward lines, describing a man who is maddened by an aphrodisiac and cannot satisfy his lust, are insecurely supported in the manuscript tradition and are bracketed in modern editions.]

616 The emperor Caligula (AD 37–41), 'Nero's famous uncle', is said to have gone mad after taking an aphrodisiac administered by his wife Caesonia (Suetonius, *Caligula* 50). The membrane (*hippomanes*) on the forehead of a newly born foal was supposed to have aphrodisiac properties.

620 *Agrippina's mushroom*: see on 5. 147 f.

[622 C., with most editors, keeps the oxymoron *in caelum descendere*, 'to go down to heaven'. The translation renders the conjecture of Nisbet (ii) *decedere*.]

628 Juvenal does not mean that the law actually allows the murder of stepchildren but simply that the lax morality of the day would tend to condone it. The cruel stepmother was of course a stock character in plays and a commonplace in rhetoric.

631 *blackening cakes*: the poison they contain turns the body blackish. Cf. 1. 72.

634 *theatrical boots*: i.e. the buskin (*cothurnus*), the high boot worn by actors in tragedy.

636 Sophocles, fifth century BC, is selected as a representative of high tragedy in the grand style.

638 There is a Pontia mentioned as a poisoner by Martial (4. 43 and 6. 75). The Scholiast asserts that she was the daughter of a Petronius: if true, this is almost certainly not the Petronius Arbiter who wrote the *Satyricon*.

643 f. Procne killed and served up her own son to her husband
Tereus, king of Thrace, to avenge her sister Philomela, whom
he had raped.

The 'woman of Colchis' is Medea, who, when she ran off
with Jason, killed her little brother and strewed his limbs on the
sea to hold up her father's pursuit. When Jason proved unfaithful,
she also killed the two children she bore him.

These stories featured in tragedies by Sophocles and Euripides
respectively.

652 Apollo prevailed on the fates to save Admetus, king of Thessaly,
from death if father, mother or wife would die in his stead. His
wife Alcestis took his place but was afterwards returned from
the lower world by Hercules. This is the subject of a play by
Euripides.

655 Eriphyle was the wife of Amphiaraus, one of the 'Seven against
Thebes', who was persuaded by her to join the expedition
though he was aware of its fatal consequences. Eriphyle did this
in return for the bribe of a necklace.

656 The fifty daughters of Danaus, all except one, murdered their
husbands as they slept on their wedding-night, for which they
were condemned in the afterlife for ever to pour water into
leaky vessels.

Clytemnestra, daughter of Tyndareus and wife of Aga-
memnon, son of Atreus, lived in adultery with Aegisthus while
her husband was engaged in the Trojan War. On his return to
Mycenae she slew him with the help of her lover. Her son
Orestes killed her to avenge his father.

660 Juvenal means, of course, the husband *you* want to get rid of.

661 The 'thrice-defeated monarch' is Mithridates VI, king of Pontus
(120–63 BC), against whom Rome led no fewer than three
expeditions between 88 and 63 BC before he was eventually
defeated by Pompey. He took his life rather than be taken
captive. Pontic drugs were legendary. Pontus included Colchis,
the birthplace of Medea (see on l. 643 above). Mithridates
himself was said to have made himself immune to poison by
daily doses of a drug of his own concocting: Martial 5. 76,
Juvenal 14. 252.

SATIRE 7

The identity of the Caesar referred to as the only source of literary patronage is much disputed. (1) Possibly no emperor in particular, merely 'the emperor'. Against this lines 20–1 suggest a particular individual and a contemporary. (2) The literary scene described suggests to some critics the reign of Domitian (even 'bad' emperors supported the arts: see Suetonius, *Domitian* 4); but Juvenal's satiric technique relied heavily on conferring contemporary relevance on situations from the past. (3) The Satires appear to follow a chronological order in which the earliest possible date for Satire 6 would be 116. Satire 7, therefore, would fit a point soon after the accession of Hadrian in 117.

6 f. Clio is one of the nine Muses (later the Muse of history), whose haunts included Mount Helicon in Boeotia with its fountains Aganippe and Hippocrene. They were born at Pieria (l. 8) at the foot of Mount Olympus.

12 Paccius and Faustus are otherwise unknown.

[15 'and although the knights of Cappadocia and Bithynia do it'. The prosody of *Bithyni* with first syllable short is unexampled, and the line interrupts the sense. Therefore it is bracketed by modern editors.]

16 i.e., the weals left by the fetters they wore when they first came to Rome as slaves. Now they are freedmen and Roman knights. For perjury as a characteristic of foreigners, see 6. 16.

18 Apollo's priestess at the Delphic oracle was said to get her inspiration from laurel, and these poets get their inspiration the same way. Apollo was the god of poets (l. 37).

25 Venus' husband is Vulcan, god of fire.

32 Juno's bird is the peacock.

39 One school of Roman literary criticism held that the ancients were necessarily better than the moderns: see Horace *Epistles* 2. 1. 18 ff.

[42 The translation follows the conjecture *porcas* (Jessen) for the manuscripts' *portas*, 'gates'.]

[50–1 The text is corrupt. The translation assumes that l. 51 (*consuetudo mali, tenet insanabile multos*) is spurious, and that l. 50 ends with *ambitiosum*. But there are other possibilities.]

60 The *thyrsus* was an ivy-wreathed staff tipped with a pine-cone, carried by the Bacchants, a symbol of Bacchic inspiration.

62 Bacchus too was a source of poetic inspiration and as such is hailed by Horace in *Odes* 2. 19; compare also *Odes* 3. 25.

64 f. The lords of Cirrha and Nysa are Apollo and Bacchus respectively. Cirrha was on the sea-coast near Apollo's shrine at Delphi. The mountainous Nysa was the scene of Bacchus' childhood, a name loosely given to more than one place connected with him.

68 The allusions here are to the *Aeneid* of Virgil and in particular to *Aeneid* 7. 445 ff., where Juno sent the Fury Allecto to arouse the jealousy of Turnus, king of the Rutuli, against his rival Aeneas.

72 Rubrenus Lappa, another unknown, has to pawn some of his things to support him while writing his *Atreus*. The buskin usually implies tragedy; see on 6. 634.

79 M. Annaeus Lucanus (AD 39–65), a member of the wealthy Spanish family that included Seneca. The author of an epic on the Civil War between Caesar and Pompey, as well as other compositions now lost, he was a victim of the purge that followed Piso's conspiracy against Nero in AD 65.

80 f. Saleius Bassus and Serranus were epic poets of the first century AD, who died young. Bassus is mentioned in Tacitus' *Dialogus* 9. 2 (dramatic date *c.* AD 74) where he is said to have received a substantial gift from the emperor Vespasian. Both are mentioned by Quintilian 10. 1. 89 f.

82 P. Papinius Statius (*c.* AD 45–96) wrote, principally, a *Thebaid* in twelve books and five books of *Silvae*, occasional poems containing much fulsome praise of Domitian. He was a successful professional poet and Juvenal probably exaggerates his poverty. The day fixed is for a public reading of his poem.

87 His 'virgin Agave' means a hitherto unperformed pantomime on the tragedy of Agave and her Bacchanalian exploits, but Juvenal makes Statius sound like a pimp. Compare his 'darling

Thebaid' above. There is no other evidence that Statius wrote for the stage. Paris was a famous pantomime actor executed by Domitian in AD 83 on suspicion of an affair with the empress.

88 Officers (*tribuni*) of the legion automatically qualified for eques-trian status (see on 1. 60), the insignia of which included a gold ring. At this time the military service was in many cases a mere formality (Pliny the younger spent his six months auditing, *Epistles* 7. 31) and a pretext for the advancement of all sorts of people.

91 A Barea was put to death by Nero: see 3. 116. The Camerini belonged to the *gens Sulpicia*: see 8. 38.

92 *Pelopea . . . Philomela*: the names of pantomimes in which Paris might have danced the title-roles. Lines 90–3 are reputed to have been responsible for Juvenal's alleged banishment. Pelopea was the daughter of Thyestes and by him (incestuously) mother of Aegisthus; for Philomela see on 6. 643 f.

[93 This line, retained in the translation, is bracketed by C. as spurious.]

94 Maecenas, patron of Virgil and Horace and other leading writers of the age of Augustus. His name became synonymous with literary patronage. C. Proculeius, his relation by marriage, divided his property among members of his family who had lost their own in the Civil War (Horace, *Odes* 2. 2. 5 ff.). Fabius and Cotta were friends of the poet Ovid. Lentulus cannot be identified among the many who bear this name. Presumably, like the others, he was one of the munificent Augustans whose disappearance Juvenal so deplores.

104 The slave who read out the *acta diurna*, an official gazette, would not be paid at all.

110 The lawyer's big talk is stimulated by the prospect of getting the brief.

114 The name Lizard (*Lacerta*) occurs again in the illustration of a charioteer on a lamp. The Reds were another of the racing factions: see on 5. 143 and 11. 198.

115 The line opens with a parody of Ovid's account of the dispute between Ajax and Ulysses over the armour of Achilles (*Meta-morphoses* 13. 1 ff.): see also 8. 269, 10. 84, 11. 30.

118 The street-doors of advocates were decorated with palms when they had a success in court. This man's palm has to be placed on his staircase, because, living in a tenement, he has no front-door of his own.

121 The best wines were imported and therefore came from *down-river.*

Though Cincius' Law of 204 BC placed certain restrictions on the remuneration of advocates, the practice of making gifts in kind had set in at an early date and persisted. A 'maximum fee' (cf. l. 124) of 10,000 sesterces had been fixed by Claudius (Tacitus, *Annals* 11. 7).

129 f. These are less successful members of the bar who ruin themselves by aping the life-style of their richer brethren. Matho was one of Juvenal's earlier targets: see 1. 32.

[134 has been transposed to follow 137, as C. suggests in his commentary.]

151 The 'Cruel Tyrant' was one of the most hackneyed themes in the school of rhetoric. The tyrant (e.g. Phalaris of Agrigentum, 8. 81) figured more largely in Greek history than in Roman, but the topic was a sensitive one with emperors e.g. Caligula: see on Carrinas Secundus, l. 204 below.

159 Arcadia was a backward region of Greece, famous for its asses. Cf. Persius 3. 6.

161 'Hannibal the Terrible' was another common subject for exercises in declamation: cf. 10. 166 f. Juvenal is here thinking of the *suasoria*: see on 1. 15. For the events described see on 10. 160 ff. and 6. 290 f.

168 ff. These are the titles of subjects in the other great exercise of the school of rhetoric, the *controversia*, the arguing of the legal questions attaching to often very contrived situations involving, e.g. rape, poisoning, mistaken identity, kidnap and surprising turns of fortune. Here Juvenal seems to refer to a theoretical case where a wife mixed poison, which miraculously restored her husband's sight. If he then divorced her, would he be open to the charge of ingratitude?

175 *a corn coupon*: entitling the holder to share in the corn-doles. Cf. 10. 81.

176 These musicians have appeared in 6. 74, 387.

177 Theodorus of Gadara was the rhetoric master of the emperor Tiberius. The textbook mentioned is not known.

183 Grand houses might have more than one dining-room. The one described here is given a southern aspect to catch the winter sun. The use of imported red and yellow marble from the great quarry of Simitthu (Chemtou) in north Africa was very much in vogue at this period.

187 M. Fabius Quintilianus, the most famous of the Roman rhetoricians. See Index.

190 Juvenal facetiously distorts a Stoic theory regarding the self-sufficiency of the wise man, as Horace had done before him, even down to the detail about the cold (*Epistles* 1. 1. 108). For wise man Juvenal substitutes lucky man.

[191–2 The translation omits the words *sapiens et nobilis et generosus / adpositam*. See C.]

192 The crescent on the shoe denoted that the wearer was a senator or a member of a patrician family.

[194 The translation reads *nisi* for the manuscripts' *si*. See C.]

197 Domitian had conferred on Quintilian the title and insignia of consul.

199 P. Ventidius Bassus, consul of 43 BC, came to Rome as a captive in the procession of a triumphant general (l. 201).

  Tullius is Servius Tullius, legendary sixth king of Rome (578–535 BC). He was the son of Ocrisia, a captive taken in war, who became slave to Tanaquil, wife of Tarquinius Priscus: see on 6. 565 and 8. 259.

  Ventidius and Tullius are referred to, in reverse order, in l. 201.

204 Thrasymachus, a teacher of rhetoric, is said by the Scholiast to have died by hanging. The story is not supported elsewhere. Carrinas Secundus was banished by Caligula for teaching the declamations against tyrants: see on l. 151 above. He evidently poisoned himself.

212 Achilles was taught by the centaur Chiron, half-man, half-horse.

214 This is puzzling. The Gauls had a high reputation for oratory (see on 1. 44 and l. 148 above), but clearly the members of Rufus' unruly class do not intend a compliment. Rufus is not otherwise known.

215 These men were *grammatici*, teachers of the 'secondary' stage of education, mainly language and poetry, before the third stage, the school of rhetoric, was reached. Celadus is not known. Q. Remmius Palaemon, ex-slave and weaver, flourished under Tiberius and Claudius and was famous as the teacher of Quintilian and Persius. He was the author of a well known *Grammar* (6. 452) and a highly successful teacher, but thoroughly immoral and extravagant.

226 f. As the *grammaticus* taught poetry, his school-room was adorned with busts of the major poets. Flaccus is Horace (Quintus Horatius Flaccus). Maro is Virgil (Publius Vergilius Maro). It is possible however that Juvenal refers to *texts* of these poets becoming soot-blackened. Classes started before dawn; so the pupils carried lamps; hence the soot.

233 Phoebus' establishment: a private bath-house, run by someone called Phoebus.

234 f. The questions all refer to characters in the *Aeneid* but Virgil does not supply the answers. Tiberius and Hadrian loved to put this sort of question to the *grammatici*. (1) Anchises' nurse: the Scholiast says Tisiphone, a name borne by one of the Furies. (2) Anchemolus had incestuous relations with his stepmother (*Aeneid* 10. 389). Servius says she was called Casperia. (3) The age of Acestes and the quantity of wine he gave to the Trojans (*Aeneid* 1. 195, 5. 73) are not recorded.

242 *he says*: i.e., a parent engaging a schoolmaster.

243 *fighter*: i.e. a gladiator. Ferguson sees the victor as a charioteer.

SATIRE 8

Note: This Satire abounds in the names of families and individuals famous in Roman history, who can be recognized as such from the context. To avoid repetition, details are often confined to the Index of Names. In general it may be noted that personal names derived from the name of a place (e.g., Ponticus, Creticus) suggest that some ancestor had waged a successful campaign in that place, and that family names in *-anus* (e.g., Aemilianus) mean that the holder of the name or a forebear had been adopted into another family.

1 f. It was the custom to deck the entrance-halls of Roman houses with wax-masks (*imagines*, l. 19) of ancestors who had held one or other of the magistracies which ennobled the holder, e.g. the consulate. These masks were paraded at family funerals. There were also family-trees (*stemmata*), consisting of miniature portraits and names connected up in 'lines' and 'branches'.

Ponticus, the person harangued in this Satire, cannot be identified but has obviously patrician or noble pretensions. He was possibly aiming at the consulship (l. 23) and the governorship of a province that regularly followed.

[6–8, bracketed by C., are retained here, with *pontifices posse ac* for the manuscripts' *Coruinum posthac*. This is the solution proposed by Housman.]

8 At times of national emergency, the usual magistrates were suspended and temporarily replaced by a dictator (the word had honourable associations), who was assisted by an official called the master of the horse.

11 The title Numantinus was conferred on Scipio Aemilianus after his capture of Numantia in 133 BC.

13 f. The Fabii were reputedly so old a family as to be descended from Hercules, the Stoic model of virtue (10. 360 f.), and the daughter of King Evander. The Great Altar of Hercules in the cattle-market at Rome recalled how Hercules slew the monster Cacus who stole his cattle. A Fabius assumed the title Allobrogicus, after defeating the Gallic tribe, the Allobroges, in 121 BC. His son was a noted degenerate: so was the consul Fabius Persicus of AD 34 who is pilloried by Seneca.

15 The sheep of the Euganei, a people originally inhabiting Venetia but subsequently driven westwards, were highly prized for their wool.

16 Catina or Catana, in Sicily, was near Mount Etna, therefore a source of the volcanic rock, pumice, much used for depilation.

21 L. Aemilius Paulus Macedonicus defeated Perseus of Macedon at the battle of Pydna, 168 BC. Gnaeus Cornelius Lentulus Cossus (consul I BC) received the title Gaetulicus for defeating the Gaetuli of North Africa in AD 6. Nero Claudius Drusus (died 9 BC during a campaign in Germany) was the brother of the emperor Tiberius.

26 *Gaetulicus*: see on l. 21 above.

Silanus: the Iunii Silani were an illustrious family, conspicuous in the early Empire (Tacitus, *Annals* 3. 24).

29 f. The worship of Isis (see 6. 529 ff. and notes) included re-enactment of the search for her murdered consort Osiris. His discovery and resurrection were greeted with shouts of 'We have found him, we rejoice!' (Seneca, *Apocolocyntosis* 13. 4).

33 f. Atlas was the giant who carried the heavens on his shoulders; he gave his name to the Atlas mountains. Europa's beauty captivated Jupiter, who assumed the shape of a bull and bore her off to Crete.

38 One of the Metelli (see on 3. 139), the consul of 69 BC, was given the name Creticus for his conquest of Crete.

Camerinus: i.e. a member of the ancient *gens Sulpicia*, a family prominent in both the early Republic and the early Empire.

39 f. A man of this name married Julia, grand-daughter of Tiberius. Their son Rubellius Plautus was executed by Nero in AD 62. Juvenal's Rubellius Blandus may have been another son of the same marriage; his mother will have been the daughter of Drusus Caesar, son of Tiberius.

42 Julia (see on ll. 39 f. above) could, through Augustus, claim membership of the Julian clan, reputedly descended from Iulus, son of Aeneas.

43 *embankment*: see 5. 154 and note.

46 Cecrops was said to have been the first king of Athens and indigenous to the land of Attica. The 'bravo' is ironical: Juvenal's views on the Greeks were made abundantly clear in Satire 3.

51 f. i.e., a soldier who defends the Empire from East (Euphrates) to West. A revolt of the Batavi, a people of the Low Countries on

the Rhine, was crushed in AD 69. The eagles are, of course, the standards of the legions stationed there.

limbless Herm: Hermes (Mercury), amongst his many other functions, was god of roads and boundaries, where busts of him, called Herms, were placed. The bust and its base, square and plain except for a phallus, were all of one piece.

62 Coryphaeus and Hirpinus would have been familiar to students of the turf as the names of well known horses. The latter is also known from Martial (3. 63).

72 Nero was great-grandson of Drusus, the brother of Tiberius. See on l. 39 above.

81 Phalaris, tyrant of Agrigentum in Sicily (6th century BC), used to roast his victims in a brazen bull.

86 Gauran oysters are those of the Lucrine Lake, below Mount Gaurus in Campania: cf. 4. 141.

Cosmus is an appropriately named manufacturer of cosmetics, well known to Martial.

93 *Tutor and Capito, Cilicia's pirates*: corrupt governors of the province of Cilicia. Tutor is not otherwise known, but Cossutianus Capito was successfully prosecuted for extortion in AD 57 (Tacitus, *Annals* 13. 33). Juvenal's ironic point is that they turned the tables on Cilicia, itself a hotbed of piracy until Pompey stamped it out in 67 BC.

95 ff. Chaerippus, a Cilician, has to sell off the little he is left with by two other corrupt governors, Pansa and Natta (the names seem to be fictitious) in order to raise the money he will need for his fare, if he takes his case to the Senate at Rome.

102 ff. These are the names of Greek artists of the very top rank. Phidias, Myron, and Polyclitus were pre-eminent as sculptors in the fifth century. Phidias was the sculptor of the Parthenon frieze. By his 'ivories' Juvenal means magnificent statues of gold and ivory. Parrhasius, who flourished about 400 BC, was a painter, and Mentor, fourth century, was a silversmith.

105 It is not clear which Dolabella is intended. Three people of the name are known to have been guilty of the offence. Cn. Cornelius Dolabella, consul 81 BC, was prosecuted by Julius

Caesar for extortion in his province of Macedonia in 77; another of the same name was accused in 78 of the same offence in Cilicia; the consul of 44 BC, P. Cornelius Dolabella, plundered the cities of Greece and Asia on his way to take up the governorship of Syria and was actually declared a public enemy.

Antonius is C. Antonius Hybrida, Cicero's colleague in the consulship in 63 BC and uncle of Mark Antony. He too was prosecuted for plundering Macedonia when governor in 62 and was exiled in 59.

['Greedy' translates the conjecture *rapax* (Nisbet ii) for the transmitted *hinc*, which is obelized by C.]

106 C. Verres (see on 3. 53) is the infamous propraetor of Sicily, prosecuted for extortion by Cicero in 70 BC. His depredations in that province include temple-robbing: hence 'unholy'.

111 The Lares were the guardian deities of hearth and home. Their images were kept in a cupboard, the Lararium. The typical image was of a youth in a short tunic wearing a garland and carrying a drinking-horn. Juvenal here transfers a Roman institution to a foreign province.

[111 This translates C.'s tentative conjecture *haec retinentes* for the transmitted *haec etenim sunt*. Certainly some textual surgery is needed to produce a coherent sequence of thought.]

113 For Rhodes as a source of Greek decadence, see 6. 296. Corinth, destroyed by the Romans in 146 BC but rebuilt and colonized by Julius Caesar in 46 BC, had regained its former prosperity and licentiousness.

117 The reapers who feed the capital are African (l. 120). Rome relied heavily on North Africa and Sicily for its supplies of grain.

120 Marius is Marius Priscus, the corrupt governor of Africa, whose prosecution is referred to in 1. 49.

126 The Sibyl of Cumae (see on 3. 3) is supposed to have delivered her oracular responses on palm-leaves.

130 Celaeno is the name of one of the Harpies ('snatchers'), foul, winged creatures with the faces of women, always pale, and long talons. In Virgil's *Aeneid* 3. 209 ff. they torment the

Trojans, newly landed in the Strophades islands, by carrying off or befouling their food.

131 The woodpecker king was Picus, son of Saturn, grandfather of Latinus and king of Laurentum; consequently in legend an early forebear of the Romans. This bird (Latin, *picus*) was sacred to Mars and credited with magical powers.

133 The Titans, the sons of Earth, Ge, were the older race of gods, displaced by Jupiter and the other Olympian gods. Prometheus (see on 4. 133) was one of them.

[134 'Select a great-grandfather from whatever book of myths you please' is bracketed by C. and others as an explanatory gloss on ll. 131–3.]

146 *Lateranus*: two identifications have been proposed: (1) Plautius Lateranus, who was consul *designate* in AD 65 when he was executed by Nero; (2) T. Sextius Lateranus, consul under Domitian in 94. There are difficulties with both suggestions. See further on Nero (170).

past his family's ashes: see on 1. 171.

156 *Numa*: see on 3. 12.

157 *Epona*: goddess of muleteers, whose picture was found in stables (Apuleius, *Metamorphoses* 3. 27). She is of Gallic origin like so much else connected with transport.

159 Syrians are regularly associated with inn-keeping: compare Virgil's Copa Surisca. The Palestine Gate may possibly be used derisively of the Porta Capena district, where numbers of Jews were found: see on 3. 10.

169 f. These rivers denote the natural frontiers of the Roman empire at this date.

170 f. If Nero is specifically the emperor Nero, that causes difficulties with both identifications of Lateranus (146). But if he is not specifically Nero, one would expect some indication of this (as in 4. 38); and the references to Armenia, Syria, the Rhine, and the Danube (169–70) lose force, since all were trouble-spots under Nero. See also the 'Neronian' references in the notes on 185, 186, 198, and 212 below.

182 Brutus and Volesus are not the original holders of these honoured
    names but their unsatisfactory descendants.

185 Damasippus cannot be identified. Tacitus tells how Nero induced
    certain noblemen in reduced circumstances to throw family
    honour to the winds and appear on the public stage (*Annals*
    14. 14).

186 Catullus (cf. 13. 111) was a writer of mimes under Claudius and
    Nero. Plays about ghosts had been a popular part of the New
    Comedy repertoire and were now evidently a subject for mime.

187 Lentulus would be a member of the *gens Cornelia* but otherwise
    unidentifiable. A well-known melodrama, also by Catullus,
    showed the crucifixion of a bandit, Laureolus. On at least one
    occasion it was performed with a condemned criminal playing
    the part and actually being fixed to a 'proper cross' and mangled
    by a bear (Martial, *Spectac.* 7).

193 *no Nero compels*: see on l. 185 above.

197 Thymele: see on 1. 36. Corinthus is an unknown actor of
    mimes.

198 *emperor plays the harp*: a reference to Nero (Suetonius, *Nero* 20).

200   For Gracchus see 2. 117 ff., 143 ff.

201 ff. *'fishman's' gear*: the fishman or *murmillo* was heavily armed
    and wore a fish on his helmet. He was usually pitted against a
    net-man or *retiarius*, lightly clad and armed with a trident and a
    net. For most of the time the *retiarius* would have his face hidden
    by the net poised for a throw. However Gracchus' conical hat
    (l. 208 below), if correctly taken as part of the official outfit of
    the Salian priests (see on 2. 125), would have given him away in
    any case.

[202–3 The words *sed damnat et odit, nec galea faciem abscondit*, 'yes, he
    rejects and hates them; nor does he cover his face with a helmet',
    are bracketed by C. and other editors.]

209 *'the chaser'*: the *murmillo* (see on 201 ff. above), a slave following
    the despised occupation of gladiator, is ashamed to be matched
    with one who has sunk so low.

212 L. Annaeus Seneca, Stoic philosopher, dramatist, and letter-
    writer, a member of a rich and famous Spanish family, was

mentor to the young Nero in the early part of his reign and, though a good influence in other respects, abetted him in murdering his mother Agrippina. His influence waned as the vicious side of Nero's nature asserted itself. Seneca went into retirement, but was implicated in the conspiracy of Piso to kill Nero in 65, which, it was said, had the further aim of killing Piso himself and making Seneca emperor (Tacitus, *Annals* 15. 65). He was obliged to commit suicide.

213 f. The punishment for a parricide like Nero (see on l. 215 ff. below) was to be placed in a sack with an ape, a dog, a snake, and a cock and thrown into water.

215 ff. Orestes, the son of Agamemnon, killed his mother Clytemnestra: but she was killed out of the dutiful desire of a son to avenge the husband she had wronged and murdered. Orestes stopped there: he had no designs on his loyal sister Electra or on his wife Hermione, the daughter of Menelaus of Sparta. Nero murdered, as well as his mother Agrippina, his first wife Octavia, his second wife Poppaea, his step-brother Britannicus and his step-sister Antonia. See on Lucusta, 1. 71.

221 Nero wrote an epic on Troy.

222 Julius Vindex, legate of Gallia Lugdunensis, rebelled against Nero with a view to making Galba emperor in AD 68. The revolt was crushed by Verginius Rufus, legate of Upper Germany, one of the best men of the age, who however later supported Galba's election as emperor, having declined the office himself.

225 f. In AD 67–8 Nero did the rounds of the festivals of Greece, taking every prize for singing and actually introducing a music contest into the previously all-athletic Olympic Games. The parsley wreath was the prize at the Nemean and Isthmian Games.

228 By Domitius Juvenal means the image of one of Nero's most distant ancestors. Before his adoption into the imperial family Nero was L. Domitius Ahenobarbus. His own father Gnaeus, a despicable rogue whom nothing could demean (Suetonius *Nero* 5), is hardly meant. Evidently Nero had performed in the tragedies named.

[229 The translation adopts C.'s suggested text *syrma aut Antigones personam uel Melanippes*.]

230 Suetonius (*Nero* 12) records that Nero ordered a wreath won for harpistry to be placed on Augustus' statue. There was no *marble* statue of Nero, though he had erected one of brass, 120 feet high, in the vestibule of his Golden House.

231 f. Catiline and Cethegus (see on 10. 287 f.) were of good patrician stock. Their plans were said to include the burning of Rome and a massacre of the principal citizens.

234 An attempt was made by the Catilinarian conspirators to enlist the help of a Gallic tribe, the Allobroges. Narbonese Gaul was called *Gallia Bracata* ('trousered') from the dress of the inhabitants.

    The Senones, originally a Gallic tribe of northern France (cf. Sens, Seine), had long been settled on the Adriatic coast of Italy, between Rimini and Ancona. They captured Rome in the Gallic Wars, 390 BC.

235 The 'shirt of discomfort', first used on the Christians accused of causing the great fire of Rome in AD 64, was soaked in pitch. The wearers were tied to a stake and the garment ignited. See 1. 155 ff.

236 Cicero alerted a somewhat incredulous Rome to the dangers he feared from Catiline and his followers in 63 BC, and the measures he took as consul effectively led to their isolation and defeat. He was from an equestrian family of the Latian town of Arpinum, the first of his family to hold the consulate, a magistracy which conferred nobility, i.e. what the Romans snobbishly dubbed 'a new man'.

240 f. Juvenal is undoubtedly thinking of a well-known scrap of Ciceronian verse relating to his consulship 'Let arms give way to the toga'. The toga was the symbol of civil, as opposed to military, authority and status.

241 Leucas was near the scene of the great sea-battle of Actium, 31 BC, against the fleet of Antony and Cleopatra, a victory which made Octavian, later Augustus, undisputed master of the Roman world.

    ['Off Leucas' gives the sense intended; but the *in* before *Leucade* is corrupt.]

242 Juvenal means the battle of Philippi in 42 BC, in which Octavian and Antony defeated Brutus and Cassius. It was actually in Macedonia, not Thessaly, which was the scene of the battle between Caesar and Pompey at Pharsalus in 48.

245 This is C. Marius, the great soldier and democrat of 10. 276. In 102 BC he defeated the Teutones at Aquae Sextiae (Aix-en-Provence), and in the following year he defeated the Cimbri, a Celtic tribe, near Verona. These northern tribes caused great alarm by migrating into southern France and northern Italy in vast numbers. The great size of the inhabitants of northern Europe is often remarked on, e.g. Tacitus, *Germania* 20.

253 Marius' noble colleague was Q. Catulus, member of the distinguished *gens Lutatia*. He had not shared in the victory over the Teutones at Aquae Sextiae, therefore his triumph was overshadowed by that of Marius.

254 As consul in 340 BC in the Latin War P. Decius Mus, a plebeian, 'devoted' himself (i.e. rushed into certain death after committing himself and the enemy to the infernal gods), thus turning the tide of battle in favour of the Romans. In the Samnite Wars his son repeated his father's sacrifice at Sentinum, 295 BC.

[258 'For the Decii are worth more than what is saved by them' is an intrusive gloss.]

259 This is Servius Tullius (578–535 BC) the legendary sixth king of Rome, the son of a slave: see on 7. 199. He was murdered after a mainly peaceful reign by the wicked Tarquinius Superbus, whose expulsion in 510 brought the monarchy to an end. Quirinus is the name given to Romulus, founder of the city of Rome, after his ascent to heaven and apotheosis.

261 The first consul of the newly established Roman Republic was Brutus; he presided over the execution of his own sons and their accomplices, who had conspired to bring back the Tarquins.

264 f. In the early days of the emergent Republic these three performed actions of great heroism during the struggle against Lars Porsenna of Clusium and his attempts to restore the kings. Mucius Scaevola held his hand in the fire to demonstrate the unflinching determination of the Romans. Horatius Cocles stopped Porsenna's men from crossing the bridge until it could

be destroyed. Cloelia was a Roman hostage who escaped from Porsenna and swam home across the Tiber.

266 The slave who disclosed the treachery of the sons of Brutus (see on l. 261 above) was named Vindicius, from *vindex*, 'liberator'. The matrons of Rome observed a year's mourning for Brutus, who had secured the exile of Tarquin in punishment for the rape of Lucretia.

269 Thersites was the meanest and most despicable of the Greeks before Troy in Homer's *Iliad*. Achilles, son of Peleus, grandson of Aeacus, ruler of the Myrmidons, was the bravest and most dazzling of the Greeks. When his friend Patroclus, wearing his arms, was killed and stripped by the Trojans, Hephaestus (Vulcan) made Achilles a new set.

273 Romulus (see on Quirinus, l. 259 above), to increase the population of Rome, made a sanctuary or asylum for runaway slaves, criminals, and others desiring refuge, on the Capitoline Hill (Livy 1. 8).

SATIRE 9

2 Marsyas was a satyr who challenged Apollo to a contest of musical skill, the condition being that the winner should do what he liked with the loser. Apollo won and bound Marsyas to a tree and flayed him alive. Marsyas' expression would be well known from his statue in the Forum.

14 Pitch, prepared from the resin of the pine-trees of Bruttium, the toe of Italy, was used (like pumice, see l. 95 below) as a depilatory by effeminates.

22 The temple of Isis in the Campus Martius was regarded as a likely place for picking up a woman: see on 6. 489.

23 *Peace's Ganymede*: evidently a statue of Ganymede in the temple of Peace built by Vespasian. See l. 47 below.

Immigrant mother: the shrine of the Great Mother, whose worship, essentially a female cult, was introduced to Rome in 204 BC, was on the Palatine Hill. See on 2. 111 and 3. 137.

24 The temple of Ceres was important both in the Roman religion and in public life: senatorial decrees were deposited there for

inspection. Her August festival, the Cerealia, was celebrated only by women, and abstinence from sex was required of the participants.

37 Homer actually said 'It's the steel itself that draws a man on' (*Odyssey* 16. 294, 19. 13).

47 *a butler in Heaven*: i.e. another Ganymede.

53 *Ladies' Day*: i.e. the Matronalia, the feast of Juno, the protectress of women, celebrated on 1st March.

55 *those kites . . . pastures*: the area covered by these large birds of prey in their flight is often used to indicate the vast extent of someone's estates. Cf. Persius 4. 26.

56 f. The Trifoline Land would have been near Trifolium in the neighbourhood of Naples. For Cumae see 3. 3 and for Gaurus (Monte Barbaro), a range of volcanic mountains between Cumae and Naples, see 8. 86.

62 The patron's cymbal-playing friend is obviously meant to be a Gallus, one of the castrated priests of Cybele, therefore of dubious sexuality. See 2. 110, 6. 512 ff., 8. 176.

64 Polyphemus the Cyclops, so called from having only one round eye in the middle of his forehead, was blinded by Ulysses when he was asleep. Ulysses thus escaped and avoided the fate of some of his comrades whom Polyphemus devoured alive (Homer *Odyssey* 9).

86 ff. Under the Julian Laws (see on 2. 29 ff., 6. 38) and the Lex Papia Poppaea of AD 9, parenthood was rewarded and celibacy and childlessness penalized, particularly in the matter of inheritance. Thus a childless heir could not take more than half of what he was willed (l. 88): the other half fell to any parent named in the same will, or lapsed to the treasury.

90 The father of three legitimate children enjoyed special privileges in regard to taxation, magistracies, etc.

101 The highest judicial assembly of the Athenians, called the Areopagus because it met on the Hill of Mars, in Greek Ares, was noted for the secrecy in which its business was conducted.

102 *Corydon, Corydon, alas!*: a quotation from Virgil's *Eclogues* 2. 69, in which the shepherd Corydon reproaches himself for fretting over his unrequited love for the handsome boy Alexis.

112 *the straps*: used to punish slaves.

117 *Saufeia*: see 6. 320 and note. There, as here, she appears as a totally unworthy celebrant of the rites of the Good Goddess (Bona Dea).

[119 'that you may be able to ignore a slave's tongue' is bracketed as spurious by C.]

[122–3 'The man who will never be free, however, is in a worse plight than those whose lives he maintains with his bread and money.' These lines are marked as spurious by C.]

133 Scratching the head with one finger is said to be the gesture of an effeminate who does not wish to disarrange an elaborate hair-style by scratching with more.

[134 C. suggests that some lines with the sense indicated in the parenthesis have fallen out.]

134A The salad plant called 'rocket' was supposedly an aphrodisiac.

135 f. Clotho and Lachesis (see on 3. 26) are two of the three spinning-women by whom the inexorable Fates were repre-sented. Clotho held the distaff, Lachesis drew out the length of thread representing man's life-span. A third, Atropos, cut the thread at his death.

142 The censor of 275 BC, C. Fabricius Luscinus (2. 154, 11. 91) expelled from the Senate the ex-consul P. Cornelius Rufinus for possessing more than the permitted amount of silver plate, about ten pounds.

143 The Moesi lived in the area south of the Danube.

146 It is not at all clear why Naevolus should want so many portraits—for purely decorative purposes? with a view to going into business and selling them? to create a set of 'ancestors' (see 8. 1 f. and notes)? None of these suggestions is entirely convincing.

149 f. Ulysses stopped the ears of his comrades with wax as they sailed past Sicily, so that there would be no possibility of hearing and yielding to the songs of the Sirens (Homer, *Odyssey* 12).

SATIRE 10

10 Milo of Croton, champion wrestler at both the Olympic and
Pythian games, attempted to open further a tree-trunk partly
split by wood-cutters. The wood sprang back, trapping his
hands and, unable to free himself, he became a prey to wolves.

16 f. These men all suffered in the wake of C. Calpurnius Piso's
unsuccessful conspiracy against Nero in AD 65. C. Cassius
Longinus was banished to Sardinia, ostensibly for possessing a
likeness of Cassius, one of Julius Caesar's assassins. For Seneca
and Lateranus see on 8. 212 and 8. 146(1).

21 The reeds and the barge-pole suggest a journey along the
Appian Way, which involved a boat-trip through the Pontine
Marsh (cf. Horace in *Satires* 1.5), a danger-spot for travellers.
See on 3. 306.

27 *Setine*: i.e. wine. See on 5. 33 f.

28 *the two philosophers*: Democritus and Heraclitus. Democritus
(born *c*.460 BC in Abdera in Thrace), the 'laughing philosopher',
was a founder of the atomic theory in physics. In ethics he
stressed the ideal of peace of mind through the cultivation of
virtue, and laid the foundations of the great Hellenistic system
of philosophy developed by Epicurus. His importance to this
satire is explained by Juvenal's preoccupation with the more
ridiculous aspects of human aspiration and his contention that
the highest goal, viz. tranquillity of life, can only be reached by
the path of goodness (l. 363 f.). He was the author of a treatise
'On Cheerfulness'. Heraclitus of Ephesus (6th century BC), not
here mentioned by name, was more melancholy in disposition
than Democritus and more obscure in expression. His theory
involved the view that everything was in a state of change
between two conditions, e.g. hot~cold, wet~dry etc. The
characterization of this pair of philosophers as 'laughing' and
'weeping' was popularized by Seneca.

38 ff. Magistrates presiding at the games and generals celebrating a
triumph, wore the palm-embroidered tunic and gold-encrusted
toga and carried the sceptre of Capitoline Jupiter, borrowed

from his temple for the occasion: hence the warning against hybris (l. 42).

[42 *official*: Juvenal's word is *consul*, which can hardly be right and is obelized by C.]

50 This is Abdera in Thrace, the birthplace of Democritus, Protagoras, and other men of high intelligence, in spite of which it had become a byword for the alleged stupidity of its people. The connection between disposition and climate is made in the Hippocratic *Airs, Waters, and Places*; cf. what Horace says of Boeotia in *Epistles* 2. 1. 244.

55 Petitions written on wax-coated tablets were placed on the knees of gods.

62 L. Aelius Sejanus, prefect of the praetorian guard, wormed his way into the confidence of Tiberius and wielded immense influence, particularly after the emperor took up residence in Capri. His efforts to secure the succession for himself eventually aroused Tiberius to express his fears to the senate (l. 71). He was executed on 18 October, AD 31, and his body was dragged about the streets in the manner described.

72 In AD 27 Tiberius retired to the island of Capri, where he spent the last part of his reign festering with suspicion and allegedly indulging his depraved sexual appetites.

74 Nortia was the Etruscan goddess of fortune: Sejanus was a native of Volsinii, her cult-centre.

77 Juvenal means that, when the old republican constitution became defunct with the supremacy of Augustus after the Battle of Actium in 31 BC, the people lost their sovereign power. The election of magistrates and the appointment of commanders were transferred from the people to the Senate by Tiberius in the first year of his reign, AD 14. The 'rods' are, of course, the insignia of office.

83 The purport of this and the next two lines is far from clear. One Bruttidius Niger in AD 22 took part in the prosecution of C. Silanus in circumstances that may have given rise to the suspicion that he was serving the ends of Sejanus by helping to remove his opponents.

84 Ajax, mad for revenge when the arms of Achilles were awarded to his rival Ulysses, ran amok and slaughtered a flock of sheep instead of the umpires. The explanation adopted here is that the speaker, afraid in this crisis to be heard using real names, means by Ajax the unbalanced Tiberius, now possibly about to institute a purge of the Senate for its neglect of his interests. Some prefer to equate Ajax with the dead Sejanus, and to interpret *ut male defensus* as 'for being ill-advisedly supported'.

93 Tiberius on Capri (the name is derived from the word for roedeer, *caprea*) is seen as (a) one in need of care and protection, (b) a herdsman looking not after his flock but his Chaldaeans.

94 *Chaldaeans*: see on 6. 553. Tiberius was much impressed by one in particular, Thrasyllus (Tacitus, *Annals* 6. 20–2: cf. 6. 576).

100 ff. Fidenae, Gabii, and Ulubrae are all towns in Latium, now suffering from the general depopulation of Italy. Horace speaks of them in similar terms. The aedile here is simply a country magistrate charged with responsibility for weights and measures.

108 f. He means the members of the so-called First Triumvirate of 60 BC. The unnamed member is Julius Caesar who later became sole ruler. It was an informal coalition against the Senate of the two most politically ambitious men of the day, Cn. Pompeius Magnus and Caesar, with M. Licinius Crassus representing the financial interests of the equestrian order. All three died violent deaths: Crassus following his defeat at Carrhae, 53 BC; Pompey as he landed in Egypt after his defeat at Pharsalus, 48 BC; Caesar by assassination in 44 BC.

112 Ceres' son-in-law is Pluto, lord of the underworld, who abducted her daughter Proserpine.

114 Demosthenes (385–322 BC), foremost of the Athenian orators, in a series of speeches called *Philippics*, strove unsuccessfully to alert his countrymen to the designs of Philip of Macedon on Greece. For his end see lines 126 ff. below and note.

M. Tullius Cicero (106–43 BC), orator, statesman, and philosopher, was the first of his family to reach senatorial rank, becoming consul in 63 BC. Cf. 8. 236. His political goal was the harmony of the orders (senate, knights, and people). After Caesar's assassination in 44 BC he opposed Mark Antony in a series of *Philippics* (the name is borrowed from Demosthenes) of such power that he was proscribed and killed in 43. See on l. 120 below.

115 *Minerva's vacation*: i.e. 19–23 March. It was called *Quinquatrus* because it began on the fifth day (by inclusive reckoning) after the Ides (15 March), and was of special interest to schoolboys. Minerva being the goddess of wisdom and of arts and crafts, her festival was also a school-holiday. She is called 'thrifty' because she makes do with the schoolboy's modest offering.

120 Those responsible for Cicero's death cut off his head and hands and brought them to Mark Antony: see on l. 114 above. They were then fixed to the *rostra* in the Forum, from where Cicero had so often addressed the people.

122 Cicero's consulship was in 63 BC, the year of Catiline's conspiracy. Cicero's handling of the crisis was celebrated *ad nauseam* in his own writings, not least in the poem on his consulship, from which this verse is taken. The pomposity of the line and its rhyming word-endings laid it open to ridicule.

125 The second of Cicero's series of fourteen speeches against Antony (see on l. 114 above), a brilliant piece of invective and widely admired, purports to be a speech delivered in Antony's hearing in the Senate, but it was never actually delivered. It was circulated privately before being released to a wider public.

126 In the war to recover their independence from Macedonia, the Greeks were defeated at Crannon in 322 BC. To avoid capture Demosthenes took poison in the temple of Poseidon on the island of Calauria.

130 Juvenal belittles Demosthenes' father who was not a mere blacksmith but a wealthy manufacturer of armaments. He died when Demosthenes was 7, leaving him to the care of guardians who squandered the property.

150 *different elephants*: i.e. different from the Indian.

153 Livy 21. 37 records how Hannibal split the rocks in his passage over the Alps by first heating them with fires, then dousing them with vinegar.

156 The Subura (see on 3. 5) was actually Rome's red-light district; so this is an example of Juvenalian bathos.

158 Livy 22. 2. 10 describes how in the spring of 217 BC Hannibal crossed the Apennines into Etruria on his one remaining elephant, losing an eye from ophthalmia.

Gaetulian: North African.

160 ff. After his defeat at Zama in 202 BC Hannibal's standing at Carthage became so low that he took service with Antiochus, king of Syria. When the Romans defeated Antiochus in 190, they demanded Hannibal as a prisoner. He fled for refuge to king Prusias of Bithynia; but, when Rome sent an envoy to seek him out, he took the poison he carried in a signet-ring and died (183 BC). The build-up to the final words 'a ring' is noteworthy. Rome's vengeance on Hannibal lay in a ring: the messenger who brought to Carthage the news of Rome's defeat at Cannae in 216 showed as confirmation a bushel of gold rings taken from the Roman dead.

167 For Hannibal as the subject of rhetorical exercises, see 7. 161 and notes.

168 Pella was the capital of Macedonia and the birthplace of Alexander the Great (356–323 BC). Juvenal exclaims at the effrontery of this small-town boy fretting because one whole world was not enough for him.

170 Gyara or Gyarus and Seriphos were small islands used as places of banishment. See 1. 74 and 6. 564.

171 The walls of Babylon were constructed of bricks by its foundress, Semiramis. The point here is that it had been foretold to Alexander that it was at Babylon that he would meet his death, as in fact he did.

174 ff. In 480 BC Xerxes, king of Persia, led an expedition against Greece, crossing the Hellespont by a bridge of boats. His troops are said by Herodotus to have numbered over two and a half million. His fleet, to avoid the repetition of a shipwreck that overtook a previous Persian fleet in 492, sailed through a canal, previously dug across the Isthmus of Athos, of which traces are still visible (Herodotus 7. 21, 33 ff.).

[The translation adopts Kidd's conjecture *aequor* for the transmitted *isdem*.]

175 Herodotus (5th century BC), the authority for the Persian Wars, had a fondness for picturesque detail and a tendency to repeat travellers' tales. Otherwise he is a more accurate historian than Juvenal gives him credit for, particularly where he relies on his own observations. Tacitus shares Juvenal's view of Greek credulity (*Annals* 5. 10): cf. also 14. 240.

178 *Sostratus*: no poet of the name can be confidently identified. The soaking pinions could be wet with wine and hence unable to soar. The Latin could also mean 'with sweaty armpits'.

179 *Salamis*: an island off the coast of Attica, where Themistocles in 480 BC in a great sea-battle smashed Xerxes' fleet.

180 *Corus . . . Eurus*: the north-west and south-east winds. Herodotus 7. 35 tells how Xerxes whipped the Hellespont, not the winds.

181 *Aeolus' cave*: Aeolus kept the winds under control in a cave. See on 5. 101.

182 Xerxes ordered fetters to be thrown into the Hellespont when his first bridge of boats was broken up (Herodotus 7. 35). The earth-shaking god is Poseidon (Neptune).

184 Another of Herodotus' reports. Branding the sea with a red-hot iron is, of course, the idea of a lunatic. All the punishments described are of a sort commonly inflicted on slaves.

In Greek mythology Neptune had served Laomedon and Apollo Admetus.

[194 For *iam mater*, obelized by C., Ferguson suggested *Garamantis*, i.e. African. Nisbet (ii) proposes *iam marcens* 'now withered'.]

195 *Thabraca* (Tabarka): a sea-port on the coast of Numidia in North Africa. Herodotus 4. 194 speaks of the number of apes in the area.

209 Juvenal refers presumably to the fact that sexual activity in the old is widely felt to be unnatural and disgusting. Some epigrams of Martial, cited by C., accuse those impotent through age of oral sex.

211 Seleucus is otherwise unknown. The name has an eastern ring to it: the Seleucids were the ruling dynasty of Syria.

215 f. Time-measuring devices, water-clocks, graduated candles, sundials, etc., were not as common as clocks are now. In large houses slaves announced the time every so often.

221 Juvenal has possibly borrowed the name Themison from an eminent physician of the late first century BC.

222 Basilus is a businessman: hardly the lawyer of 7. 145.

223 Hirrus is a guardian who appropriates the property in trust for his wards; he is not otherwise known.

224 The name Maura means 'Moorish': perhaps the Maura of 6. 306 ff. who showed such contempt for the altar of Chastity.

Hamillus: boys were often introduced to vice by those responsible for their education, a risk that Horace's father took pains to avoid (*Satires* 1. 6. 81 ff.). Q. Remmius Palaemon of 6. 452 was notorious in this respect. Hamillus is not otherwise known.

246 Nestor, king of Pylos, ruled over three generations of men. He took part in the Greek expedition against Troy in spite of his age, but returned safely to Pylos. The crow was said to live for nine generations.

249 Units and tens were counted on the fingers of the left hand, hundreds and upwards on the right.

253 Antilochus accompanied his father Nestor to Troy and was killed by Memnon the Ethiopian. His beard marks his youth: he has not yet begun to shave.

256 Peleus was king of the Myrmidons in Thessaly and father of Achilles by Thetis.

257 This is Laertes, king of Ithaca, the aged father of Ulysses, here described as the 'Ithacan swimmer'. He did in fact swim ashore at Phaeacia when swept off his raft in a storm.

258 Priam was too old to take part in the fighting when the Greeks landed on his shores. Assaracus was the son of Tros, founder of Troy, great-uncle of Priam.

Cassandra and Polyxena were daughters of Priam by Hecuba. Cassandra fell to Agamemnon as his share of the spoils. Polyxena was sacrificed to the shade of Achilles.

260 Hector, one of Priam's fifty sons, was killed by Achilles.

263 It was Paris, Priam's second son, who started the Trojan War, when he sailed to Sparta and abducted Helen, the wife of Menelaus. She had been promised him by Venus for awarding her the golden apple inscribed 'for the fairest' in preference to Juno and Minerva—the famous Judgement of Paris.

267 f. Cf. Virgil's account of Priam's death in *Aeneid* 2. 506–58.

272 Hecuba, the wife of Priam, was taken prisoner by the victorious Greeks. She was later metamorphosed into a dog and leapt into the sea at Cynossema ('Dog's grave').

274 For Mithridates, king of Pontus, see on 6. 661.

   Croesus (6th century BC), the last king of Lydia, a ruler of legendary power and wealth was told by Solon, the great Athenian law-giver, to call no man happy before the end of his life (Herodotus 1. 32).

276 C. Marius (157–86 BC), soldier and democrat, after serving six consulships, in 88 won a vote of the people transferring to him the command in the first war against Mithridates, which the Senate had conferred on Sulla. When Sulla marched against him, Marius hid from his pursuit in the marshes of Minturnae (Latium). Then, narrowly escaping capture and death, he fled to Carthage. Juvenal omits to mention that he lived to take up a seventh consulship in 86. See further on 8. 245.

282 *Teutonic car*: for Marius' victories over the Teutones and the Cimbri see note on 8. 245.

283 f. Pompey (see on l. 108 above) survived a serious illness at Naples in Campania in 50 BC, only to be treacherously killed and to have his head cut off as he landed in Egypt after his defeat at Pharsalus in 48 BC. Death in 50 would have spared him this fate: therefore the illness was desirable.

287 Lentulus and Cethegus were two of Catiline's principal henchmen. They were put to death by garotting in the Tullianum prison on 5 December, 63 BC, but at all events they were not mutilated like Pompey. See on 8. 231.

288 Catiline himself died the honourable death of a soldier in the thick of his opponents at the battle of Pistoia in 62 BC.

292 Latona (Leto) was the mother of Apollo and Diana, both very beautiful. The father was Jupiter, disguised as a swan.

293 Lucretia, the wife of L. Tarquinius Collatinus, killed herself, when she was raped by Sextus, the son of Tarquinius Superbus. The incident led to the expulsion of the kings and the establishment of the Republic in 510 BC (Livy 1. 57 f.).

294 Verginia was killed by her father to prevent her falling into the hands of Appius Claudius (5th century BC), a Roman magistrate who coveted the girl (Livy 3. 44 ff.). Rutila is not otherwise known.

306 Nero is said to have attempted to turn his male 'bride' Sporus into a girl by means of castration (Suetonius, *Nero* 28; see on 2. 117).

314 Mars, when committing adultery with Venus, was trapped in a net by her husband Vulcan.

317 *a mullet*: an unofficial punishment for adultery was for the offended party to insert this fish with its sharp spines into the adulterer's rectum.

318 *Endymion*: Juvenal gives his youthful gigolo the name of the youth, famed for his looks, who, as he lay in perpetual sleep on Mount Latmus in Caria, was visited by Selene (the moon), who embraced him and slept by his side.

319 Servilia was the name of an aristocratic clan.

322 *Oppia*: the name of a nymphomaniac at line 220 above, possibly taken from an unchaste Vestal Virgin condemned in 483 BC (Livy 2. 42).

Catulla: the name is found again at 2. 49. The Catulla of Martial 8. 53 is beautiful but a slut.

325 f. Hippolytus, son of Theseus, resisted the efforts of his stepmother Phaedra to seduce him. In revenge she falsely accused him to his father, who cursed him so that Poseidon sent a bull from the sea which made the horses of Hippolytus' chariot bolt and drag him to his death.

Bellerophon was the victim of a similar accusation by his hostess Sthenoboea, wife of Proteus, king of Argos.

[After 325 C. marks a lacuna, which would have contained a line alluding to Phaedra and Sthenoboea, e.g. 'when hostess and stepmother attempted seduction . . .']

327 The woman of Crete is Phaedra: she was the daughter of Minos, king of that island. See on l. 325 above.

329 In AD 48 Messalina, wife of the emperor Claudius, became infatuated with the consul-designate, the handsome C. Silius, obliged him to get rid of his wife, and finally went through a regular form of marriage with him in front of witnesses (Tacitus, *Annals* 11. 26–38). Juvenal here explores the dilemma of Silius ('He was fully aware of the peril, but to refuse her meant certain death' Tacitus, *Annals* 11. 12), as if it were the theme of a *suasoria*: see on 1. 15 ff.

341 Claudius was absent in Ostia and so in ignorance of these events. They were disclosed to him by two of his mistresses at the instigation of his freedman Narcissus, who hurried on the execution before he could relent.

356 *mens sana in corpore sano*: there can be few more famous phrases in Latin literature.

357 ff. We are to strive to attain the Stoic ideal of *apatheia*, i.e. freedom from the emotions he describes. Though the labours of Hercules were undertaken at the bidding of Eurystheus of Tiryns in expiation of a previous crime, they were later seen as services to all mankind, and Hercules himself was regarded as the embodiment of the true Stoic virtue.

362 Sardanapallus, last king of the Assyrian empire of Nineveh, was a byword for luxury and licentiousness and the very antithesis of Hercules.

363 Epicurus had said, 'It is pointless to ask the gods for what one is capable of providing for oneself' (fragment 65 Bailey), an idea taken over by Seneca, *Epistles* 41. 1.

SATIRE 11

1 f. *Atticus*: Tiberius Claudius Atticus Herodes. His vast fortune was founded on a treasure discovered on his estate in Attica. He was twice consul, and a provincial governor.

3 *Apicius*: see on 4. 23.

7 i.e., he is about to enter a gladiatorial school to train for the arena. The oath of service to the trainer (*lanista*) was very harsh:

a man made himself over 'body and soul' (Petronius, *Satyricon* 117).

8 A free man embarking on such a course was required to notify one of the tribunes of the people. The tribunes had no powers of compulsion in the matter: they were, after all, guarantors of popular freedom. Juvenal implies perhaps that some nobles *had* been compelled to degrade themselves in this way, e.g. by Nero: see on 8. 185, 193.

20 Having sold off the family silver (l. 18), the gourmet eats supper off earthenware plates: the next meal is eaten in the mess of the gladiatorial school.

27 Juvenal quotes the maxim 'Know thyself' in Greek (*gnothi seauton*) as it was inscribed on the temple of Apollo at Delphi. The maxim is attributed sometimes to Apollo himself, sometimes to one of the Seven Sages. Juvenal (35 ff.) gives the words a satirical twist recalling Horace's 'You are what you have' (*Satires* 1. 1. 62).

30 The arms of Achilles were claimed by Ajax and Ulysses: see on 7. 115. Thersites (8. 269 ff.) was not a contestant. The episode in which Ulysses disgraced himself is not recorded.

34 Matho occurs again at 1. 32 and 7. 129: Curtius must also be an advocate but is otherwise unknown.

43 The ring was an important badge of membership of the equestrian order: see on 7. 88. Membership would be forfeited if a knight ceased to satisfy the property qualification of the order. Pollio is perhaps the Crepereius Pollio who was looking about for a loan in 9. 6 ff.

49 *Baiae's oysters*: i.e. those of the Lucrine Lake. See on 4. 141.

51 On the disreputable district of the Subura see 3. 5, 5. 106, 10. 156. The Esquiline Hill (where Virro lived, 5. 77) was evidently a 'good address' as well as being cool and healthy (cf. Horace, *Satires* 1. 8. 14) in comparison with the close and crowded Subura.

56 *Persicus*: all we have is the name. If it belongs to a real acquaintance of Juvenal, we have to take into account the outrageous banter of 186 ff. If it belongs to an imaginary figure, it might have been

suggested by the opening line of a Horatian ode on simplicity: *Persicos odi, puer, apparatus*, 'I have no use for Persian elaboration' (*Odes* 1. 38. 1).

61 Evander before the Trojan War led a colony of his native Arcadians from Greece to Italy, where they settled on the future site of Rome. The eighth book of Virgil's *Aeneid* tells how this peaceful ruler gave hospitality both to Hercules (born or brought up at Tiryns in the Argolid according to some accounts) and to Aeneas (the lesser guest) and his Trojans. Hercules was raised to heaven from his funeral-pyre on Mount Oeta by his father Jupiter. Aeneas was drowned in the river Numicius.

73 f. The pears of Signia (Segni) in Latium and of Tarentum (a Syrian variety) are highly spoken of by writers on husbandry. Horace's 'expert' on good food, Catius, rates the apples of Picenum in the north east of Italy above those of Tivoli (*Satires* 2. 4. 70).

78 M'. Curius Dentatus, four times consul between 290 and 274 BC, and conqueror of Pyrrhus, king of Epirus, who invaded Italy, was preparing his own vegetables for the pot when approached by a Samnite delegation (Seneca, *Cons. Helv.* 10. 8).

90 *Fabii*: see on 2. 155, 8. 13 f. Scaurus: 2. 35, 6. 604. Fabricius: 2. 154, 9. 142. These were all families of the highest standing in the Republican period: many of them held the office of censor. M. Porcius Cato, the great censor of 184 BC, became a legend because of his austerity and his disapproval of the inroads being made by Greek culture. The censors reviewed the senators and knights, expelling those deemed unworthy of membership. The censors of the year 204 BC, C. Claudius Nero and M. Livius Salinator, used their censorial powers against each other to pay off old grudges (Livy 29. 37).

95 The ends of the couches, on which the diners lay propped up, were inlaid with tortoise-shell.

Trojan elite: the oldest Roman families liked to think they 'came over' with Aeneas after the fall of Troy.

[99 'So their house and furniture were as simple as their food' is bracketed by C.]

106 The helmet shows the familiar device of Romulus and Remus, the twin sons of Mars and Rhea Silvia, being suckled by the she-wolf. Quirinus is another name for Romulus: hence both twins are loosely called 'Quirini', just as the wolf is described as 'Romulus' beast'.

112 This incident preceded the sack of Rome by the Gauls in 390 BC. One M. Caedicius, a plebeian, heard a voice 'louder than human' telling him to warn the authorities that the Gauls were coming (Livy 5. 32). The reference to Ocean is a rhetorical flourish: the invasion came by land.

124 *Syene's gate*: Aswan on the Nile had long been the furthest outpost of the Roman empire, which now extended to the Red Sea (Tacitus, *Annals* 2. 61).

126 The Nabateans (capital Petra) were a people of Arabia, not itself a source of ivory but on the trade-route to India which was. Elephants do not discard their tusks.

129 *iron ring*: i.e., as worn by plebeians. Senators and knights wore gold rings.

136 The art of carving was taught by Dainty (Trypherus, a Greek as one would expect for this kind of thing), using wooden models to demonstrate the technique. Cf. 5. 120 ff., 9. 109.

155 Free-born youths, like those the slave-lad resembles, during boyhood wore the *toga praetexta*, i.e. having a broad purple or crimson stripe.

157 When seen in the baths without his clothes he is manifestly a normal, clean-living lad, just coming up to the age of puberty and devoid of sexual precocity.

[161 'Wine and server come from the same district.' The Latin verse has five elisions; elsewhere Juvenal has no more than three. It is best seen as a gloss on ll. 159–60.]

[165–6 'Married women watch this with their husbands reclining beside them—a sight which one would be ashamed to describe in their presence.' These lines form an awkward parenthesis, and *ipsis* has to be emended to *illis*. C. and others cut them out.]

[168–9 The translation follows the Oxford text, which brackets 'yet that particular pleasure is greater in the other sex (i.e. women)'.

The last two interpolations can be seen as coming from some-
one who wished to attribute to women rather than men the
reaction described by Juvenal. C. adopts the more drastic
solution of bracketing the whole passage 165–70.]

175 This refers to the Greek custom of tasting wine and spitting it
out again, as professional wine-tasters still do.

180 *Maro's poem*: the *Aeneid* of Virgil (P. Vergilius Maro).

193 f. The Megalesian Games are now in progress. This dates
Juvenal's dinner-party to somewhere between the 4th and the
10th of April. The games were in honour of Cybele, the Great
(in Greek *Megale*) Mother. For the importation of her rites see
on 3. 137. The napkin was used as a starting signal.

194 f. The praetor was the magistrate who presided at the games.
Juvenal's account of the ceremonial on these occasions (10.
36 ff.) is the fullest extant.

201 Hannibal's crushing defeat of the Romans at Cannae is recalled
again at 2. 155, 7. 163, 10. 165. The dust of Cannae, raised by
the Sirocco, is mentioned in Livy's account of the battle, 22. 46.
9.

SATIRE 12

3 ff. Each of the three great Capitoline deities is to have an offering:
lambs for Juno and Minerva, a calf for Jupiter. Juno, consort of
Jupiter, king of the gods, was worshipped under the cult-title of
Queen (*Regina*).

4 Minerva carried on her aegis (shield) the head of the Gorgon
Medusa, which Perseus slew in Mauretania.

5 *Tarpeian*: i.e. Capitoline. The Tarpeian rock was at the southern
extremity of the Capitol: cf. 6. 48.

11 Hispulla is probably the stage-struck woman of 6. 74, 'a familiar
figure in the streets of Rome' (Duff).

13 The Clitumnus was a small river in Umbria, very famous in
literature for its rich pastures and the white cattle which made
the most acceptable sacrificial victims: cf. the white lamb in l. 3.

28 Isis was the goddess who protected mariners in time of danger. Those saved by her aid employed artists to paint the scene on votive tablets for the temples (l. 27) and also on boards to display when begging (14. 301 f.).

36 The beaver reputedly bit off its own testicles and left them for its hunters in order to avoid capture. They secreted a drug (*castoreum*), whose heavy odour had a narcotic effect (Lucretius 6. 794).

39 *soft Maecenas*: for the degenerate nature of the great Augustan patron see 1. 66 and note.

40 Baetica was a region of southern Spain, taking its name from the river Baetis (Guadalquivir). Martial, himself a Spaniard, boasts of the sheep of this area, whose fleece, unlike the Tyrian, needed no dyeing. The colour was believed to come in part from the gold-bearing waters of the river (Martial 9. 61, 14. 133).

44 Parthenius is possibly the chamberlain of Domitian. The value of works of art is enhanced if they have belonged to some notable: cf. 45 and on l. 47 below.

45 Pholus was a centaur who hurled a huge mixing-bowl in the fight between the Centaurs and Lapiths. He also entertained Hercules with a similar vessel.

Fuscus' wife: another bibulous wife, otherwise unknown.

47 The royal purchaser of the Greek city of Olynthus in Chalcidice was Philip II of Macedon, who took it in 348 BC by bribing two of its citizens: see on 10. 114.

[50–1 'Some men do not make fortunes for the sake of living, but, blinded by their vice, live for the sake of their fortunes.' These lines are bracketed as an interpolation by C. and others.]

63 *the Parcae*: see 3. 27, 9. 135 f. and note.

71 f. Iulus or Ascanius, the son of Aeneas, left the city of Lavinium founded by his father and called after his stepmother Lavinia, when the population increased. He built his new city on the Alban Mount, the 'lofty peak', and called it Alba ('white') after the white sow which prophecy said would be found where Iulus was to build his city (Virgil, *Aeneid* 8. 42 ff.). See on 4. 60 f. and 6. 177.

75 ff. These lines give a fair description of the Portus Augusti, which the emperor Claudius built two miles to the north of Ostia, the old port of Rome at the mouth of the Tiber, now silted up. Suetonius (*Claudius* 20) also mentions the two enclosing walls of the harbour, the mole off the entrance and the lighthouse, called 'Tuscan' because the new works were on the right or Etruscan bank of the Tiber.

80 An inner hexagonal basin had been added by Trajan, whose calm waters could happily have been used by the light pleasure-boats of Baiae.

81 The shaving of the head is presumably to honour a vow made when the danger was at its height: cf. Petronius 103.

92 The passages cited by Mayor suggest that lanterns in daytime were a sign of rejoicing.

93 i.e., I am no legacy-hunter. The practice has been mentioned often in previous satires, e.g. 1. 37 ff., 3. 129, 4. 18 ff. For the significance of the 'three little heirs' see on 9. 90.

97 'Sterile', in spite of his three children, because any legacy-hunter would simply be wasting his time on a man with live issue.

98 ff. Here votive tablets for the recovery of these rich and childless individuals are plastered over the walls of the temple-porches by the legacy-hunters: see 10. 55.

105 The emperor's elephants were housed in Latium at Laurentum, which was near Ardea, the capital of Turnus and his Rutulians: see 1. 162 ff.

106 *the dark man's land*: a Juvenalian periphrasis for Ethiopia, literally 'the land of the sun-tanned faces'.

107 f. Elephants were used in battle most famously by Hannibal of Tyre (i.e. Carthage, which was colonized from Tyre) but before him by Pyrrhus, king of Epirus (the Molossians were one of his peoples), who invaded Lucania in 280 BC with his 'Lucanian cows' (*Lucae boves*) as the Romans called them. The Romans first used elephants in the war against Philip of Macedon in 200 BC (Livy 31. 36. 4).

111 ff. Pacuvius Hister and Novius are uninhibited legacy-hunters, otherwise unknown.

118 Iphigenia, is the name of the daughter of Agamemnon, king of Mycenae, who was prepared to sacrifice her to Diana in order to obtain a wind to carry the Greek fleet to the Trojan War. According to one version, represented by Euripides, she was spared by the goddess and a deer was sacrificed in her place.

121 *my fellow Roman*: i.e. Pacuvius.

122 *a thousand ships*: i.e. the Greek fleet. See on l. 118 above.

123 The goddess of death was Libitina; the undertakers stored their equipment in her temple.

trapped in the creel: a lobster-pot from which there is no escape.

127 *a maid of Mycenae*: i.e. an Iphigenia. See on l. 118 above.

128 For the longevity of Nestor, king of Pylos, see on 10. 246.

SATIRE 13

4 The praetor was one of the great Roman law-officers. The urn was used in selecting the names of the panel of judges and also for collecting their votes. Possibilities for cheating existed at both stages. At an earlier stage the urn was used to draw lots determining the order in which cases were to be heard.

6 Calvinus had evidently deposited 10,000 sesterces (l. 71) with a friend for safe-keeping, a common enough practice in an age when banking services were rudimentary. The friend subsequently denied that he had ever received it.

17 A line of limited usefulness for the dating of the satire. Consuls of this name are recorded for AD 58, 59, and 67, which would make the earliest possible date either 118–19 or 127: the latter is generally favoured. See C. p. 2.

27 Thebes in Boeotia had seven gates (cf. Aeschylus' *Seven against Thebes*: each champion takes on one gate) and the Nile ('wealthy', because its waters enrich the land of Egypt) had seven mouths. Some equate Juvenal's seven good men with the Seven Sages of antiquity.

28 Juvenal is either extending the Hesiodic idea of five ages of man, each, except the fourth (the Age of Heroes), denoted by a metal (see on 6. 1 and 15); or (less likely) he means that the ninth century from the foundation of the City in 753 BC, which prophecy said would be Rome's last, is now in progress. M. J. McGann (*Hermes* 96, 1968, 509 ff.) discusses the problem in terms of the Judaeo-Christian *Sibylline Oracles* and their description of a ninth age, near the end of time and full of horrors, to be succeeded by a tenth age ushered in by a series of even more dreadful happenings.

32 Faesidius is otherwise unknown.

33 i.e. his clients, the people who receive the *sportula* from him: see on 1. 95 ff.

39 *Saturn*: see on 6. 1. When he was banished from heaven he took refuge in Latium and turned its rude inhabitants away from a life which knew nothing of farming (Virgil, *Aeneid* 8. 314 ff.).

41 Mount Ida in Crete was the scene of Jupiter's childhood (cf. 14. 271): at this time he had not succeeded his father Saturn.

43 f. The Trojan boy is Ganymede, Jupiter's cupbearer: see on 5. 59, 9. 23. Hebe, daughter of Jupiter and Juno and wife of Hercules after his deification, had the task of filling the cups of the gods with nectar.

44 f. Vulcan, the Italian god of fire, inherited the attributes of his Greek counterpart Hephaestus, and so is represented as a blacksmith and armourer. His forge was supposed to be in the volcanic Lipari islands, to the north east of Sicily.

46 f. The inhabitants of heaven are increased in number by the deification of the emperors after death and the importation to Rome of foreign gods and goddesses, e.g. Isis.

48 Atlas supported the heavens on his shoulders: see on 8. 33.

50 In the division of the world by lot among the sons of Cronus, Jupiter won the heavens and the upper earth, Neptune the sea and Pluto the nether regions. Pluto's bride was Proserpine, the daughter of Ceres the corn-goddess, whom he abducted from Sicily.

51 These are the tortures of the damned in classical mythology: Ixion on his wheel, for making advances to Juno; Sisyphus pushing a rock, for disclosing the secrets of the gods; Tityos with vultures preying on his liver, for his attempt on Diana. The Furies punish mortals for the sins they have committed in life.

57 *wild strawberries . . . acorns*: this is the age before corn was given to men.

62 *the Tuscan books*: the books of the Etruscan soothsayers (see on 2. 121), the usual mentors of the Romans in religious matters, telling how to interpret and expiate portents like those described in the following lines.

78 Jupiter's temple was on the Capitoline Hill, of which the rock of Tarpeia was a part: see on 6. 48 f.

79 f. The seer of Cirrha (near Delphi) is Apollo: see on 6. 555, 7. 64. The maiden goddess is his sister Diana.

93 Blindness, a common condition in Egypt, was attributed to the anger of Isis. She is often represented carrying a *sistrum* or rattle.

96 *Ladas*: two Olympic runners of this name are known.

97 *Anticyra's cure*: i.e., hellebore, which was often prescribed for the treatment of madness. Two places of this name, one in Phocis, one in Thessaly, produced the drug.

98 Archigenes is the distinguished Syrian physician of the period: see 6. 236 and 14. 252.

111 *Catullus*: the playwright of 8. 186.

113 Stentor is the name of a brazen-voiced herald in Homer's *Iliad* Book 5). Mars similarly, in *Iliad* 5. 859, when wounded, roars like nine or ten thousand men.

119 Vagellius is the declaimer with the brains of a mule at 16. 23. Why he should have a statue is not clear.

121 f. At one level Juvenal means that the Cynics dispensed with this garment as being something more than nature required. At another he means that Cynicism was in many ways the 'near relation' of Stoicism, to quote D. R. Dudley *History of Cynicism* (1937) p. 187. Zeno, the founder of Stoicism, lived his life after the pattern of the Cynics (Diogenes Laertius 6. 104). Both

systems were rooted in the idea of living in accordance with nature, but the Stoics stopped a long way short of Cynic 'shamelessness'.

122 Epicurus (341–270 BC) was the founder of the philosophical school called after him, which he established in a garden bought for 80 minae at Athens, where his life and diet were of the simplest.

125 This Philip is some unknown physician.

150 ff. The statues of the gods were overlaid with gold-leaf. Castor and his twin-brother Pollux, the sons of Jupiter and Leda, were honoured with a temple in the Forum, for helping the Romans defeat the Latins at Lake Regillus, *c.*496 BC. The Thunderer is, of course, Jupiter himself.

155 f. The punishment of parricides: see on 8. 213 f.

157 C. Rutilius Gallicus, now long dead, as City Prefect (*praefectus Urbi*), had exercised criminal jurisdiction under Domitian from AD 89 until his death in AD 91 or 92: an interesting example of the timelessness of some of Juvenal's allusions to real people.

162 *swollen throat*: i.e. the goitre (Latin *guttur*, throat), an enlargement of the thyroid gland, once common in the Swiss Alps.

163 *Southern Egypt*: more precisely a district of Ethiopia on the Nile, called Meroë. 'Large pendulous breasts are common in negro women' (Courtney).

[166 'Clearly because this one natural feature is common to all.' An interpolation.]

167 ff. For the legends of battles between cranes flying south and the Pygmies of Ethiopia, see Homer, *Iliad* 3. 3 ff.

[183 'Any occasion, however small, is an excuse for anger.' Another interpolated comment.]

184 ff. Chrysippus (3rd century BC), the so-called second founder of the Stoic school of philosophy. Thales of Miletus (7th–6th century BC), one of the Seven Sages, was the founder of physical science and the first to postulate a physical, as opposed to a mythological, origin for the world. The great old man is Socrates (5th century BC), accused in his old age of corrupting the youth of Athens and condemned to drink hemlock.

[187b–189a 'Benign philosophy gradually takes off most of our vices and all our errors; she is the first to teach us what is right.' Bracketed by C.]

197 Rhadamanthus, Aeacus, and Minos are the judges of the Underworld, but who the 'fiendish Caedicius' is is not clear. The name is plebeian: see on 11. 112 and 16. 45. Perhaps the 'fluent Caedicius' of 16. 45 is considered to have expatiated on cruel punishments in his declamations (Courtney), or perhaps the name is meant to suggest the word *caedere*, meaning 'to flog or slaughter'.

199 ff. This story is told of Glaucus, a Spartan famed for his honesty, who received money in trust from a certain Milesian. When this man's son claimed the money, he denied all knowledge of it and asked the oracle of Apollo at Delphi to connive at his deception. He was punished, both for his dishonesty and for tempting the god, by the destruction of his entire family (Herodotus 6. 86).

213 ff. The wines of Alba in Latium were among the best in Italy. Faliscan wine from Falerii in Etruria would have been considerably inferior.

   [*Falisco* is the conjecture of Nisbet (ii) for *Falerno* of the manuscripts.]

[236, translated in the text, is bracketed by C.]

245 f. Condemned prisoners were executed in the Tullianum prison and their bodies were cast down the Gemonian Steps into the Forum or dragged with a hook (see on 1. 157, 10. 66 f.) for exposure to the people. For exile on islands cf. 1. 74, 3. 5, 6. 564.

249 Drusus is the emperor Claudius (3. 238), who was dull-witted and slow. Tiresias is the blind seer who plays such a prominent part in Greek mythology.

SATIRE 14

12 *bearded teachers*: i.e., teachers of philosophy and ethics, who affected beards.

15 *Rutilus*: a rich man, therefore not the same as the Rutilus of 11. 2.

19 For the Sirens see on 9. 149 f.

20 Antiphates and Polyphemus the Cyclops are ogres in Homer. The former was king of the Laestrygonians in Sicily, man-eating giants (*Odyssey* 10. 80): for the latter see 9. 64. A similar coupling occurs at 15. 18.

35 *the Titan*: Prometheus. See on 4. 133.

42 *a second Catiline*: see on 8. 231, 10. 287 f.

43 *Brutus*: M. Junius Brutus, the most famous of the assassins of Julius Caesar in 44 BC. See on 5. 36.

   Brutus' uncle is the great Stoic hero, M. Porcius Cato Uticensis. He committed suicide at Utica rather than survive the defeat of the Republican cause at Thapsus in 46 BC.

50 *the censor's anger*: see on 11. 90. Under the Empire the title was usually held by the emperor himself: cf. 2. 29 ff.

58 *cupping-glass*: doctors used to apply the mouth of a warmed cup to the skin of a patient in order to draw the blood to the surface.

59 ff. The comedies of Plautus have several scenes of this sort.

86 ff. Wealthy Romans like Cicero and Pliny the Younger had what to us seems an incredible number of country houses. Tiberius had twelve villas on Capri. Cf. Juvenal 1. 94.

   Caetronius is only known from this passage.

   Caieta: a town on the Latian coast, supposedly called for the nurse of Aeneas (Virgil, *Aeneid* 7. 2). Tibur (Tivoli) and Praeneste (Palestrina) are also in Latium to the East of Rome. Hadrian's villa at Tibur dates from this period. See on l. 90 below.

90 These temples were at Tibur and Praeneste respectively.

91 Posides was a eunuch freedman of Claudius. The baths he built at Baiae are mentioned by the elder Pliny. This is the sole reference to a house of his at Rome that allegedly dwarfed the temple of Jupiter on the Capitoline Hill.

98 There is a similarly contemptuous account of the Jewish dietary laws at 6. 159 f., cf. 3. 11 ff. Juvenal's predecessor Persius is equally supercilious regarding the Jews (5. 179 ff.): these attitudes were not confined to the satirists, however.

102 ff. The Jewish scriptures and religious observances were (probably wilfully) misinterpreted as tending towards the exclusion of gentiles from even the most ordinary courtesies and kindnesses of human life.

113 The golden apples of the Hesperides (5. 152) were guarded by the sleepless dragon Ladon, and the Golden Fleece at Colchis in Pontus by another.

127 f. i.e. he feels he must keep some for tomorrow.

134 Beggars often took their stand on bridges, where the flow of people became concentrated: cf. 4. 116 and 5. 8.

160 Titus Tatius was king of the Sabines, who, after his death, united with the Romans under Romulus to form one state.

162 Rome fought three wars with Carthage, 264–241, 218–201, 149–146 BC. The war with Pyrrhus, king of Epirus (see on 12. 107 f.) was from 280–275 BC. The Molossians were the most powerful people of Epirus, whose kings had extended their dominion over the whole country. They traced their descent back to Pyrrhus, son of Achilles, and Andromache, widow of Hector.

180 The Hernici, Vestini, and Marsi were some of the peoples Rome had to subdue and then win over in order to become mistress of Italy. All were synonymous with steadfast courage and hardy simplicity of life.

182 f. Man's original food was the acorn: cf. 6. 10. It was Triptolemus, prince of Eleusis, who was given the seeds of grain by Ceres, and who travelled the earth teaching men the principles of agriculture (Ovid, *Metamorphoses* 5. 642 ff.). In historical terms, bread came rather late in the development of Italian nutrition: cf. l. 171 above.

193 The first words of a law were rubricated, i.e. written in red. The vine-staff was both an indication of rank and an instrument of punishment: cf. 8. 247.

194 Laelius must be the commanding officer. The use of combs, mirrors, and the like by soldiers on active service was frowned on: see on 2. 99 f.

196 Mauretania and Britain were trouble-spots in the earliest years
     of Hadrian's reign. Britain here means more particularly Brig-
     antia, the area north of the Humber, which Hadrian visited in
     AD 122. This expedition was followed by the building of
     Hadrian's Wall and a continuous process of pacification. The
     passage implies no first-hand knowledge on Juvenal's part.
     'Brigantia is one of the few areas where hill-forts are notably
     rare' (S. Frere, *Britannia*, 1967, p. 150 n. 1).

197 f. i.e. so that by the time you retire you may be the senior
     centurion of a legion (*primipilus*) with charge of the standard,
     which was in the care of the first cohort.

202 Trades likely to be offensive, e.g. tanning, were banished to the
     Janiculan or right bank of the Tiber. Thus Martial speaks of
     'Transtiberine hide' (6. 93. 4).

204 f. Vespasian crushed his son Titus' objections to a tax on urine
     (it was used by fullers) by demonstrating that the money it
     raised had no smell (Suetonius, *Vespasian* 23).

[208–9 'This is what withered old nurses teach to boys as they are
     crawling and what every girl learns before her ABC.' Bracketed
     by C.]

214 Ajax the Great and his cousin Achilles belonged to the generation
     that fought at Troy. They performed deeds and enjoyed an
     acclaim in which their fathers, Telamon and Peleus had no
     share.

219 Oaths by Ceres and other divinities who presided over mystery
     religions were more binding than others. Touching both altar
     and image suggests an unusual degree of effrontery in a man not
     intending to keep his oath.

[229 The translation adopts *quippe et . . . conduplicare*, Amyx's
     conjecture, for the manuscripts' *et qui . . . conduplicari*. C.
     assumes that a line has fallen out after 229.]

239 *the Decii*: see on 8. 254.

240 Menoeceus killed himself when the seer Tiresias (13. 249)
     declared that his death would ensure the victory of Thebes over
     the seven Argive heroes who marched against it. Thebes was
     peopled by the descendants of the armed warriors who miracu-

lously sprang up when Cadmus slew the dragon and sowed its teeth (Ovid, *Metamorphoses* 3. 1 ff.). (For Juvenal's sceptical view of Greek history and legend cf. 10. 174.)

249 *the spindle*: see on 9. 135 f., and cf. 3. 27, 12. 63.

252 *Archigenes*: the physician of 6. 236 and 13. 98.

Mithridates' special compound: by which he made himself immune to poison. See on 6. 661, and cf. 10. 274.

257 For a picture of the praetor presiding over the games and dramatic entertainments he provided at times of public holiday, see 10. 36 ff.

260 Money was often deposited in temples for safe-keeping, but temple-robbing was not unknown: cf. 13. 147 ff. There was a guard on the Temple of Castor in the Forum, hence 'vigilant'. In the circumstances, the title 'Mars the Avenger' is somewhat ironical.

263 Flora's shows, 28 April–3 May, were the occasion of great licentiousness: cf. 6. 250. The Cerealia, 12–19 April; the games of Cybele, the Ludi Megalenses, 4–10 April: see on 6. 69, 11. 193. The entertainments were by this time mainly theatrical.

267 *a Corycian boat*: i.e. a boat plying between Rome and Corycia, a port of Cilicia, famous for saffron.

271 Jupiter was supposed to have been brought up in a cave on Mount Ida in Crete.

278 f. The Carpathian Sea, between Rhodes and Crete, took its name from the island of Carpathos. The Moroccan (or Gaetulian) waters were a source of purple-fish.

279 Hercules' adventures took him out of the Mediterranean and into the Atlantic Ocean. On his return he set up Hercules' Pillars at the entrance to the Mediterranean. Gibraltar, anciently called Calpe, was one.

284 f. This is Orestes (8. 215 ff.), comforted by his sister Electra in his dread of retribution for the murder of his mother Clytemnestra.

286 *slaughter an ox*: Ajax (l. 213 above) again. In his madness following the award of Achilles' arms to Ulysses (who came from Ithaca) he attacked a herd of cattle (sheep in Horace, *Satires*

2. 3. 197) believing them to be the Greek chieftains. See on 10. 85.

291 A satirical description of minted coins stamped with the emperor's portrait and titles.

299 The Tagus is the gold-bearing river of the Iberian peninsula (3. 54 f.); the Pactolus, the gold-bearing river of Lydia in Asia Minor, whose king was the fabulously wealthy Croesus.

302 Shipwrecked sailors, when reduced to begging, used to display a picture of the shipwreck, painted on a board or on a piece of wood salvaged from the wreck (Persius 1. 88).

305 *Licinus*: see on 1. 109.

309 Diogenes (4th century BC), the famous Cynic philosopher (see on 13. 122), is said to have gone to such excesses in his search for self-sufficiency that he eventually made his home in a large earthenware pot, often described as a tub.

312 When Alexander the Great (cf. 10. 168) visited Diogenes in his jar at Corinth and asked if there was anything he could do for him, the latter is supposed to have said 'Yes, stand out of the light!' Note how Juvenal transfers the conventional epithet 'great' from Alexander to Diogenes.

315 f. This line and a half are awkwardly repeated from the end of Satire 10.

319 *Epicurus*: see on 13. 123.

324 i.e. 400,000 sesterces, the property qualification for members of the equestrian order. For Otho's Law see on 3. 154, 159.

328 *Croesus*: proverbially wealthy king of Lydia. See on l. 299 above.

329 Narcissus was the powerful freedman of the emperor Claudius. For his part in the execution of Messalina, Claudius' empress, see on 10. 329, 341. Tacitus' version is that Narcissus hurried on the execution when he saw that Claudius' initial shock was likely to turn into pity (*Annals* 11. 37).

SATIRE 15

1 Volusius is otherwise unknown. The opening lines are practically a versified form of a passage of Cicero, *Tusculan Disputations* 5. 78.

5 f. The statue at Thebes in Upper Egypt was actually of Amenophis III, but was dubbed Memnon (son of the Dawn) when it was overturned by an earthquake and began to emit 'magical' sounds at daybreak. The phenomenon was actually caused by the vibrations set up by the sudden expansion of the loosened fabric at sunrise after the cold of the night. Thebes, originally the capital of Egypt, was sacked by Cornelius Gallus in 30/29 BC. Juvenal echoes its Homeric epithet 'hundred-gated'.

13 ff. Juvenal refers to the account of his adventures that Ulysses gave to Alcinous, king of the Phaeacians (see on 5. 151), which occupies Books 9–12 of the *Odyssey*.

17 Charybdis in Homer's account was a monster, who thrice daily swallowed the sea and spewed it up again (*Odyssey* 12. 101 ff.). In later writers it is a whirlpool in the straits between Italy and Sicily.

18 *Cyclopes and Laestrygonians*: see on 9. 65, 14. 20.

19 *Scylla*: like Charybdis a navigational hazard, probably a reef, in the same area. In Homer she is a monster of the rocks with six heads, triple rows of teeth and twelve feet, capable of snatching six seamen at once and devouring them (*Odyssey* 12. 85 ff.).

Cyanean rocks: strictly speaking these are the Symplegades, the clashing rocks, negotiated by Jason and his Argonauts at the entrance to the Hellespont. Where Homer and Juvenal supposed them to be is not entirely clear (*Odyssey* 12. 59 ff.).

20 Homer, *Odyssey* 10. 19 ff. relates how Aeolus, keeper of the winds, presented Ulysses with a bag, made from the hide of a full-grown ox, containing the forces of all the winds.

21 Elpenor was one of Ulysses' men, who were turned into swine by the enchantress Circe (*Odyssey* 10) but later restored to their own shape. Elpenor however was killed in a fall from the roof of Circe's palace (*Odyssey* 10. 552 ff.).

23 *Phaeacia*: see on 5. 151.

25 Phaeacia is identified with Corcyra (Corfu).

26 *the Ithacan*: Juvenal's usual allusive way of referring to Ulysses. See on 10. 257, 14. 286.

28 L. Aemilius Iuncus was consul for the last three months of AD 127. The word 'recently' (*nuper*) prohibits a more precise dating of the satire than sometime after 127.

   Coptus (Keft): in Upper Egypt on the west bank of the Nile, not far from Thebes.

30 *Pyrrha*: i.e. from the time of the Flood. See Index and cf. 1. 81 ff.

33 Ombi and Tentyra were respectively to the south and north of Coptus (l. 28 above). Ombi is Negadeh, Tentyra is Denderah.

36 The crocodile was sacred to the people of Ombi but hunted by the inhabitants of Tentyra.

46 This observation need not be taken to imply first-hand knowledge of Egypt: a persistent complaint in the first book was the number of foreigners resident in Rome. On Canopus and its licentiousness see 1. 26, 6. 83 f.

65 ff. Rocks were a favourite missile of the epic heroes: Ajax (Homer, *Iliad* 12. 380), Diomedes, son of Tydeus (*Iliad* 5. 302) and Turnus (see on 1. 162 ff.) in Virgil, *Aeneid* 12. 896.

85 Prometheus (see on 4. 133, 8. 133) stole and gave to men the fire Jupiter had withheld from them.

93 Vascones: the modern Basques (cf. the name Gascony), situated between the Ebro and the Pyrenees. Their chief town, Calagurris, underwent a long and bitter siege by Pompey and his generals for its adherence to Sertorius, the rebel Roman general, in the course of which the inhabitants were reduced to eating human flesh before it fell in 72 BC.

[97–8 'For the instance now presented of this kind of food ought to be pitied, as in the case of the people I have just mentioned.' An interpolation.]

107 Zeno (4th–3rd century BC) was the founder of the Stoic school of philosophy, which taught that virtue was the only good and that as all else, even death, was indifferent, suicide was preferable

to sin and suffering. In certain circumstances they were, however, prepared to countenance cannibalism, a fact of which Juvenal seems to be unaware.

[107b–108a 'For they do not think that all deeds should be done for the sake of survival.' An interpolation.]

109 Q. Caecilius Metellus Pius was sent by the Senate to Spain against Sertorius in 79. See on l. 93 above.

111 Tacitus records how half a century earlier Agricola as governor of Britain encouraged the British in their desire to learn eloquence, once they had overcome their hostility to Latin (*Agricola* 21. 1). Neighbouring Gaul, whose schools of rhetoric were famous under the Empire, would have been a likely supplier of teachers: see on 1. 44, 7. 148. Juvenal's admiration is palpably lacking in sincerity.

112 *Timbuctoo*: Juvenal actually says Thyle, which, from its unknown location, stood for 'the back of beyond'.

113 Zacynthus, more usually called Saguntum, a city of Hispania Tarraconensis, about 15 miles to the north of Valencia, was supposed to have been founded by the Ionian city of Zacynthus. Its siege by Hannibal in 219 BC was the immediate cause of the Second Punic War. There is no historical evidence for recourse to cannibalism in the siege, though it may have become part of the folklore: cf. Petronius, *Satyricon* 141.

116 The worship of Artemis (Diana) in the Tauric Chersonese (Crimea), whose priestess was Iphigenia (see on 12. 118), demanded the sacrifice of strangers. Lake Maeotis is the Sea of Azov to the north-east of the Crimea.

123 The idea here is that the river-god could by some outrageous action on the part of the Egyptians be shamed into doing his duty, i.e. rising at the due time and causing the floods that make the land fertile.

124 *Cimbrian hordes*: see on 8. 245.

125 *Sarmatians*: see on 2. 1.

Agathyrsi: they were a tribe of Transylvania, originally connected with the Sarmatians. Like the Britons, they were wild and painted.

127 f. This refers to the use of pots as a means of keeping primitive
rafts afloat.

134 Roman litigants availed themselves of an astonishing range of
histrionic tricks in order to elicit sympathy in court. These
included exhibitions of bogus grief, aged parents, weeping
children, torn and dishevelled hair, shabby dress, mourning
clothes etc. For misconduct of guardians towards their wards
and their trust-funds, see 1. 46 f., 10. 223 (Hirrus).

141 In the mystery religions, like the currently fashionable Eleusinian
mysteries in honour of Ceres (Hadrian was initiated about this
time), the master of ceremonies began by ordering the uninitiated
(*profani*) and the unworthy to remove themselves.

171 The philosopher Pythagoras of Samos (6th century BC) en-
couraged a vegetarian diet, but his prohibition of the bean,
because it caused flatulence (Cicero, *On Divination* 1. 62) and so
disturbed the soul, which was breath, coupled with his doctrine
of metempsychosis, the transmigration of souls after death,
gave rise to the ribald suggestion that this was from fear
of laying his teeth into one of his own kin: cf. Horace, *Satires*
2. 6. 63.

SATIRE 16

[After line 2 there is a lacuna. The sense of the missing line has
been indicated in brackets.]

 5 f. Young men entering the army frequently brought letters of
commendation from powerful friends to their commanding
officer. Fate, says Juvenal, has more influence than such a letter
addressed to Mars, the god of war himself, by his mistress
Venus or his mother Juno. The Aegean island of Samos was an
important cult-centre of Juno.

15 M. Furius Camillus (5th–4th century BC), saviour of Rome
during the wars with the Gauls and hailed as its second founder.
The far-reaching military reforms of his period included the
institution of a standing army paid out of the public funds.
There is nothing to support Juvenal's assertion that Camillus
introduced this rule forbidding soldiers to leave camp to attend

trials, but it was at this period that soldiers were first required to be under military rule at all times (Livy 4. 59. 11, 5. 2. 1).

23 For Vagellius cf. 13. 119.

26 f. Pylades is the archetypal faithful friend, the man who would go anywhere and dare anything to serve his beloved cousin Orestes, the son of Agamemnon.

the massive rampart: see on 5. 153 f.

38 The boundary-stone or Terminus, the divinity who presided over boundaries, was set up with prescribed religious ceremony and honoured with yearly sacrifice at the festival of the Terminalia on 23 February.

45 *fluent Caedicius*: the name recalls the plebeian M. Caedicius and his encounter with the God Aius Locutius ('Sayer and Speaker') in Livy 5. 32. 6. See on 11. 112, 13. 197.

Fuscus: there is an advocate of this name in Martial 7. 28. This Fuscus is not necessarily the same as that of 12. 45.

56 *wooed by his father*: a new and even more cynical twist to the constantly recurring theme of legacy-hunting, the more so as there is a good chance of the son's being killed on active service. The name Coranus (54) occurs in an unrelated anecdote of Horace's on the same subject (*Satires* 2. 5. 55 ff.).

INDEX OF NAMES

(The following list is selective. Allusions have been placed in brackets.)

BC, a pattern of simplicity and frugality; 2. 3; 8. 4, general references to him and his family.

CYBELE 2. 111; (3. 138); (6. 512); (9. 123); 14. 263, the great mother-goddess of Anatolia (modern Turkey); her worship came to Rome in 204 BC and it grew steadily under the empire. She was attended by eunuch priests.

CYCLOPES 15. 18, Polyphemus and his people (*Odyssey* 9).

CYNTHIA 6. 7, the beloved of Propertius, lived in the second half of the 1st century BC.

DAEDALUS (1. 54); 3. 25; (3. 80), the legendary aviator and architect.

DANAUS 6. 656, instructed his fifty daughters to kill their husbands, the sons of Aegyptus. All but one, Hypermnestra, obeyed, and were punished in the underworld by having a fill a leaky jar with water.

DECII 8. 254, 14. 239, in 340 BC P. Decius Mus, after invoking the gods, gave his life in battle. His son performed a similar act in 295.

DEMOCRITUS 10. 30, 33 (5th and early 4th century BC) was known as the laughing philosopher, probably on account of his treatise 'On Cheerfulness'. He was one of the founders of ancient atomism.

DEMOSTHENES 10. 114, the great Athenian orator of the 4th century BC.

DIANA 3. 321; 10. 292; (13. 80); 15. 8; (15. 116).

DIOGENES (14. 311), the cynic philosopher of the 4th century BC.

DIOMEDES 1. 53, (15. 66), one of the major Greek heroes of the Trojan cycle.

DOLABELLA 8. 105, possibly Cn. Domitius Dolabella, condemned in 78 BC for extortion in Cilicia; but other members of the family were guilty of the same crime.

DOMITIAN (2. 29); (4 *passim*), emperor AD 81–96.

EGERIA 3. 17, a water deity, worshipped with the Camenae (Muses) at the Porta Capena. She was said to have been Numa's consort and adviser.

EGNATIUS CELER (3. 115 f.), the Stoic, who was born in Beirut and educated in Tarsus. In Rome he gave evidence against his pupil and patron Barea Soranus.

ELECTRA 8. 218, daughter of Agamemnon, and sister of Orestes.

ELISSA 6. 435, Dido, queen of Carthage.

ELPENOR 15. 21, a member of Ulysses' crew.

ENDYMION 10. 318, a beautiful young man, beloved of the moon-goddess. He is represented as sleeping on Mt. Latmos.

EPICURUS 13. 122; 14. 319 (341–270 BC), his garden in Athens became the centre of his school. He preached a doctrine of atomistic physics and hedonist ethics, but his hedonism was of a cautious and negative kind.

EPONA 8. 157, goddess of muleteers, originally from Gaul.

MARIUS (8. 245); (10. 276 ff.), Gaius Marius, born *c.* 157 BC near Arpinum. He reorganized the Roman army, defeated the Teutones in 102 BC and the Cimbri in 101, and was consul for the sixth time in 100. After being ousted by Sulla, he was in danger of execution, but survived to hold a seventh consulate. He died in 86 BC.

MARS 1. 8; 2. 31, (128); 6. 59; 9. 101; 10. 83, 314; 11. 107; 13. 79, 113; 14. 261; 16. 5.

MARSYAS 9. 2, a satyr who claimed to be superior to Apollo in music. After defeating him in a contest, Apollo flayed him alive.

MATHO 1. 32; 7. 129; 11. 34, a rich and flashy lawyer who eventually went bankrupt.

MEDEA (6. 644), princess of Colchis at the eastern end of the Black Sea. She helped Jason obtain the golden fleece, and escaped with him. When he deserted her in Corinth, she murdered his betrothed and also her own children.

MELANIPPE 8. 229, daughter of Aeolus. After being raped by Poseidon she bore twins. What happened to her and them was dramatized by Euripides in two plays now lost. One was adapted by Ennius.

MELEAGER 5. 116, the heroic champion of Calydon in Aetolia. He slew the giant boar that was ravaging the country, but enraged his mother by killing her two brothers. She then took a piece of wood, which represented his life, and threw it on the fire.

MEMNON 15. 5, an Ethiopian, son of Aurora (the Dawn), who was killed by Achilles at Troy. His name was applied to a statue (actually that of Amenophis III), because it vibrated, producing a musical sound, at dawn.

MENTOR 8. 104, a famous Greek silversmith, referred to several times by Martial.

MESSALINA (6. 116); 10. 333; 14. 331, the dissolute wife of the emperor Claudius.

METELLUS (3. 139); 6. 265, L. Caecilius Metellus, who lost his sight in rescuing a statue of Minerva from the burning temple of Vesta in 241 BC. 15. 109, Q. Caecilius Metellus Pius, a supporter of Sulla, who was sent to fight against Sertorius, the rebel governor of Spain in the 70s BC.

MICIPSA 5. 89, king of Numidia in the last part of the 2nd century BC.

MILO 2. 26, T. Annius Milo, tribune 57 BC carried on gang warfare against Clodius, which culminated in the murder of Clodius in 52.

MILO OF CROTON (10. 10 f.), a famous strongman of the late 6th century BC. When he was trying to rend a tree, his hands became trapped, and he was eaten by wolves.

MINERVA 3. 139, 219; 10. 115; (12. 4); 13. 82, Italian goddess of crafts, identified with Athena.

THE WORLD'S CLASSICS

A Select List

SERGEI AKSAKOV: A Russian Gentleman
Translated by J. D. Duff
Edited by Edward Crankshaw

HANS ANDERSEN: Fairy Tales
Translated by L. W. Kingsland
Introduction by Naomi Lewis
Illustrated by Vilhelm Pedersen and Lorenz Frølich

ARTHUR J. ARBERRY (Transl.): The Koran

LUDOVICO ARIOSTO: Orlando Furioso
Translated by Guido Waldman

ARISTOTLE: The Nicomachean Ethics
Translated by David Ross

JANE AUSTEN: Emma
Edited by James Kinsley and David Lodge

Northanger Abbey, Lady Susan, The Watsons,
and Sanditon
Edited by John Davie

Persuasion
Edited by John Davie

ROBERT BAGE: Hermsprong
Edited by Peter Faulkner

WILLIAM BECKFORD: Vathek
Edited by Roger Lonsdale

KEITH BOSLEY (Transl.): The Kalevala

CHARLOTTE BRONTË: Jane Eyre
Edited by Margaret Smith

JOHN BUNYAN: The Pilgrim's Progress
Edited by N. H. Keeble

FRANCES HODGSON BURNETT: The Secret Garden
Edited by Dennis Butts

A complete list of Oxford Paperbacks, including The World's Classics, OPUS, Past Masters, Oxford Authors, Oxford Shakespeare, and Oxford Paperback Reference, is available in the UK from the Arts and Reference Publicity Department (RS), Oxford University Press, Walton Street, Oxford OX2 6DP.

In the USA, complete lists are available from the Paperbacks Marketing Manager, Oxford University Press, 200 Madison Avenue, New York, NY 10016.

Oxford Paperbacks are available from all good bookshops. In case of difficulty, customers in the UK can order direct from Oxford University Press Bookshop, Freepost, 116 High Street, Oxford, OX1 4BR, enclosing full payment. Please add 10 per cent of published price for postage and packing.